BLUE THREAT
WHY TO ERR IS INHUMAN

—— HOW TO WAGE AND WIN ——
THE BATTLE WITHIN

TONY KERN

PYGMY BOOKS
Smaller. Smarter.

Colorado Springs, Colorado

A Pygmy Book
PUBLISHED BY PYGMY BOOKS, LLC

Blue Threat: Why To Err is Inhuman
Copyright © 2009 by Tony Kern. All rights reserved.

Printed in the United States of America. No part of this book may be used or reproduced in any manner whatsoever without written permission except in the case of brief quotations embodied in critical articles and reviews. No part of this publication may be used, reproduced or distributed in any form or by any means, or stored in a data base or retrieval system, without the prior written permission of the publisher.

Pygmy Books takes environmental sustainability very seriously. We utilize print on demand publishing to conserve our natural resources, reduce overstocking, warehousing, and unnecessary waste while maintaining the highest standards of editorial review and quality. Additionally, we ship direct from printer to buyer to reduce the overall carbon footprint of our products.

This Pygmy Book is available at a discount for business, education, organizations, corporations and others interested in bulk purchasing.

For information please email:
Special Market Department, Pygmy Books, LLC,
pygmybooks@gmail.com

Cover & Book Design by Vanessa Saenz
Printed and bound by Thinline Communications

ISBN 978-0-9842063-0-8

Information contained in this book has been obtained by Pygmy Books, LLC ("Pygmy Books") from sources believed to be reliable. However, neither Pygmy Books nor its authors guarantee the accuracy or completeness of any information published herein and neither Pygmy Books nor its authors shall be responsible for any errors, omissions, or damages arising out of use of this information.

This work is published with the understanding that Pygmy Books and its authors are supplying information, but are not attempting to render engineering or other professional services. If such services are required, the assistance of an appropriate professional should be sought.

Also From Tony Kern
Redefining Airmanship
Flight Discipline
Darker Shades of Blue: The Rogue Pilot
Controlling Pilot Error: Culture, Environment and CRM
Controlling Pilot Error: Approach and Landing

Coming in 2010
Doppelgangers: The Dark Side of High Achievers

Praise for Tony Kern's Previous Books
Redefining Airmanship

"This is an enthralling book about risk management on the flight deck. Anyone who needs to minimise risk in other professional situations will also find it helpful. Good energetic writing, lots of fascinating stories, makes managing risk exciting."
 – Dr. J. F. M. Oldham

"I am pretty sure that I can get by being a lousy fly caster and poor wing shot and still enjoy a pretty good life . . . I know that being anything other than an excellent pilot is unacceptable. Tony Kern has given us all a model to work with that is both comprehensive and systematic. He has illustrated it with clear real-life examples making each of the component concepts vivid. This book is a real treasure. It is at once a clear description of the destination and it is the map and the compass that we can all employ along on the way."
 – John Brietlinger, Minneapolis, Minnesota

"How important is this book? It is as important for pilots to read and re-read as Wolfgang Langewiesche's 'Stick & Rudder' . . . there is no higher praise. Dr. Kern proposes herein a simple but profound model to help us understand airmanship and he proceeds to support, explicate and instantiate that model using clear and well-chosen case material. This is good stuff!"
 – Frank Van Haste, Trumball, Connecticut

"Tony Kern has written a detailed, yet compelling, story for airmanship in the 21st century. His research is thorough, his examples are vivid, and his personal experience ties them together. As a safety professional, I was amazed to see that almost all of his 'lessons learned' could be applied to ground operations, as well as flight. Wish I'd written the book!"
 – Commercial Pilot, O'Fallon, Illinois

Flight Discipline

"This is certainly a must read book for pilots, from students like myself, to those on the top of the aviation food chain. Mr. Kern provides the WHY pilots MUST follow procedures like using checklists to making good decisions on when and when not to fly or the need to be in strict compliance. His points are illustrated with numerous mishaps and close calls when pilots chose to break the rules. There is nothing more riveting than to 'stand on the shoulder of giants' and learn from countless mistakes from both the military and civilian arenas of aviation. This most certainly will make me a better informed pilot. Thanks Lt. Col. Kern"

– Richard Teves, Massachusetts

"Kern's Flight Discipline gives the reader an enormous education on professionalism in the cockpit in just under 400 pages. His book is one that should be on the required reading list for any serious pilot, especially those in crewed aircraft."

– Instructor pilot, Michigan

Darker Shades of Blue: The Rogue Pilot

"I am a commercial pilot and a physician. This book was introduced to me as a part of my recurring flight training. Ultimately, the themes made me redefine my medical practice as well. I have shared this book with dozens of people, pilots and non-pilots alike. Tony Kern has touched a fundamental theme by defining rogue behavior, including rogue behavior by individuals and by organizations. Fellow pilots understand the themes easily. Other people, including fellow physicians, have privately told me that they fundamentally changed their practice procedures as a result of reading this book. One non-pilot told me that I had "saved his life" by suggesting that he read this book. Contemplative people, involved in aviation or not, will do soul searching as a result of reading this book. Rogues will be angry (as could be expected from the basic tenants of rogue behavior). Almost all will recognize rogue tendencies in their own behavior and will confront a decision to make corrective actions or to continue. This is not a book with a lot of confusing technical jargon. I highly recommend that you read this book if you get a chance. I hope that demand will bring a new printing."

– Dr. Marvin Bowers, Tennessee

"Mr. Kern has succeeded in bringing to the forefront what I consider one of the greatest challenges to aviation: the rogue, undisciplined pilot. Rogues will continue to be a source of danger not only to themselves but their crews, passengers and people on the ground and this book should be required reading for everyone with a certificate (and even those who aren't pilots). Kudos to Mr. Kern for an eye-opening look at this threat."

– Seth Beckhardt, Port Orange, Florida

Contents

	Acknowledgements	viii
	Author's Preface	ix
	Introduction: Welcome To The Fight	1
Part One	The Problem Of Human Error	11
ONE	How Human Error Destroys Lives, Loves, Careers And Potential	13
TWO	A Call To Arms	30
THREE	Personal Alchemy: Turning Human Performance Lead Into Gold	41

Part Two	Making It Happen: Practical Error Control In Action	69
FOUR	The Myth Of Compliance	71
FIVE	The "Me" In Team	94
SIX	Proof Of Life: Error Control In Action	108
SEVEN	Common Enemies: Error Producing Conditions	122
EIGHT	Blind Spots: Hazardous Attitudes And Mental Bias	140

Part Three	Empowered Accountability: Implications And Applications For The Real World	161
NINE	A Few Matters Of Faith	163
TEN	Speaker For The Dead	179
ELEVEN	The Business Of Error Control	187
TWELVE	The Blue Threat Proverbs	214
	Appendix	236
	Glossary	240
	Selected Bibliography And Resources	243
	Index	251

"This is not a war story—and yet it is. Any tale in which the protagonists are so seriously threatened they may lose their lives demands an enemy capable of destruction.

The difference between what is told here and familiar war is that the designated adversary always remains inhuman, frequently marches in mystery, and rarely takes prisoners. Furthermore, armistice is inconceivable and so is complete victory for either side.

This war continues as you read these words and must prevail so long as man insists on striving for progress."

– Ernest K. Gann

Fate is the Hunter, Preface

Acknowledgements

"At times our own light goes out and is rekindled by a spark from another person. Each of us has cause to think with deep gratitude of those who have lighted the flame within us."
– Albert Schweitzer

Even though this book is primarily about personal accountability and individual effort, it would not have been possible without a robust team of believers in the project. I would like to thank the production team of Shari Kern, Vanessa Saenz and everyone at Pygmy Books for their tireless efforts on edits, reviews, and overall management of the publications process.

Regarding content, I would like to specifically thank Mr. Andrew O'Connor for expanding on the concept of the *Blue Threat Proverbs* as well as testing and refining the Blue Threat Reporting and Analysis Tool™. I would like to thank Mr. Ben Cook from the Australian Civil Aviation Safety Authority for his insights on refining the core message of empowered accountability. In addition, Pat Daily provided keen insights on *lean six sigma* and other quality processes and the clear link to personal error control. I would like to offer special thanks to Mark Cioffi and Gaylon Richter for providing their assistance on the interfaith chapter as well as Bill Scott and John Nance for helping refine the overall message of the book. First and last, I thank God for the ability to research, write and give back to a world that has given me so much. I pray that I can continue to do His will.

Author's Preface

"Ain't much learnin' that occurs in the second kick of a mule."
– Appalachian Folk Wisdom on Error Control

Thanks for picking up *Blue Threat*.

This book is my first literary venture outside of aviation and I hope the message of *empowered accountability* resonates with the expanded audience, because this is life changing information on how to learn the right lessons from our mistakes.

Before you begin, let me mention a few notes on my writing style for those who are first time readers. I write mostly in the first person narrative, not because I am a definitive authority on any given subject, but simply because I communicate best in this manner. I write like I talk, in straightforward layman's terms to the best of my limited vocabulary. I also share many personal experiences and ask a lot of questions I do not answer. This is also by design. I believe that for a book to be engaging, it should be a *dialogue*, not a monologue.

Speaking of dialogue, the following interview provides a short framework of the subject matter in this book for those who only have a few minutes to make a decision on whether to buy it, read it or set it back down. All the subjects mentioned in this short interview are contained and developed thoroughly inside these covers.

Uncommon Sense: **An Interview with Dr. Tony Kern**

Q: Let's start with the basics. What is the *Blue Threat*?

A: The Blue Threat is the internal threat – the things we do to ourselves and each other that end up sabotaging our goals and missions. The term comes from the business and military threat assessment models where the red threat is what the competition and the situation can throw at you, and the blue threat is the damaging things we are capable of doing to ourselves that derail projects, programs, profit and potential.

Q: Aren't making mistakes just a part of being human?

A: To some degree, maybe. But just saying "to err is human" is a cop out for avoidable and correctable mistakes and gives up far too much ground. For too long, we have accepted human error as an inescapable part of our lives or tried to "manage" it after it occurs. It has resulted in unnecessary compromise of our life's mission and goals. Recent research provides a body of knowledge that is capable of changing our performance, and our lives, for the better. This is life altering knowledge. Applying it successfully demands a rigorous approach that results in known competencies and predictable performance. But it is well worth it.

Q: Don't you think that "declaring war" on human error in 2002 was a little over the top?

A: Not at all. Every year, on average, human error results in more unnecessary death and suffering than all of the wars in the world combined. But getting beyond safety statistics, industries suffer billions of dollars in lost revenue as a direct result of *preventable* human error, which results in job losses for thousands. And these numbers don't factor in the lost opportunities for progress and improvement. No, declaring a war on error was not over the top, it was long overdue.

Q: OK. How do you go about battling the Blue Threat?

A: The key to victory over the randomness and variability of human error is first to realize that error is only random in a group setting. When you get down to a sample size of one – you – error is both predicable and preventable. After that it is just a matter of learning some new information and applying a set of tools. Of course, first you need to accept the fact that you are making avoidable errors and desire to change.

Q: Certainly something this critical must be taught in technical training or somewhere else inside most occupations, isn't it?

A: Oddly not, and I think I know a couple of reasons why. First, we have long assumed – incorrectly – that when we train someone to do something right, we are simultaneously training them not to do it wrong. This fundamental premise of our education and training programs is grossly in error and responsible for hundreds of thousands of lost lives and billions in lost revenue every year. The skill set for error prevention is unique and currently not taught anywhere except the few places where it was researched and developed over the past few years.

The second reason I believe we don't yet teach personal error control is because the world has gone brain dead on the issues of *personal responsibility* and *accountability*. These aren't politically correct terms in some circles.

Listen, no one wakes up in the morning wanting to screw up – or thinking that they are going to. If we can provide them with the knowledge and tools to recognize and prevent their personal mistakes, most people who care about their performance will do so of their own accord.

Q: How long does it take someone to get a handle on the Blue Threat?

A: Some results are almost immediate; others will be refined over the course of a lifetime. It is important to realize from the start that error control is far less about training than it is about *understanding*. Self-awareness is a personal mastery skill that encompasses many complex variables, ranging from an accurate assessment of one's skill and knowledge to the physiological readiness to perceive, interpret, evaluate, plan and act in a tightly-coupled, error-intolerant environment. These skills are within our grasp, but they are not intuitive. They must be learned. Error control is not common sense as many would have us believe. It is uncommon sense, yet well within our reach if we just take readily available information and apply it.

This is the reason the Blue Threat program was designed and developed. If I could leave you with one thing, it would be this: Personal error control is a *discipline* – a way of life. And once you've mastered it, you will be amazed at the results and wonder why you waited so long to do something this simple and powerful.

INTRODUCTION

Welcome to the Fight

"Keep away from people who try to belittle your ambitions. Small people do that."
– Mark Twain

This book is about human performance – yours. It is also about how we sometimes fall off the track while on the path to well intended goals through seemingly trivial errors and missed opportunities. It is about how we sometimes fall hard – and get back up, only to fall again, and again – not understanding why. It is about how to avoid these pitfalls and reach your full potential as an individual, and therefore improve your team, organization or system. This is both a "how come" and a "how to" book. If the knowledge and tools inside these covers are applied with sincerity and rigor it can change your life. It has mine.

What is the Blue Threat Approach?

There is a very real and lethal threat within each of us – our own propensity for error. For reasons that will be explained in the pages that follow, this internal threat is referred to as the *blue threat*, the tendency to subvert our own plans and desires through human error. The blue threat approach advocates and instructs *empowered accountability*, a personal performance improvement approach that ripples downstream (yes, I said *downstream*) into your team, organization and system.

If words like *responsibility* and *accountability* offend you as insensitive or politically incorrect – stop reading, this book will only frustrate you and won't help you or your organization until and unless you can get past it. If however, you are tired of waiting for a guru to bring a magic bullet, and ready to make the most of your own gifts – this is right up your alley. If you believe in the power of the individual and that the human is not the weakest link in most systems – read on and welcome to the fight.

> "If words like *responsibility* and *accountability* offend you as insensitive or politically incorrect – stop reading...."

What this Book is Not

Two paragraphs into this book, you are already forming some impressions. Perhaps you are even feeling a bit of *Deja Moo* – the feeling you've heard all this bulls**t before. So let's define a bit of what this book *is not* to allay any fears. This book and the empowered accountability approach it advocates is not a course, although we offer many courses to teach the key blue threat elements at deeper levels. It is not a tool kit or checklist to be applied, although both are options provided within it. It is not personal motivation training, wellness, risk management, leadership, or how to make more of your team – although we will touch tangentially on all of those areas.

The blue threat approach to personal performance is a *discipline*, a body of knowledge and new way of viewing and interacting with the world around you. Once you learn to see the world through the lens of your individual behaviors and uniqueness (for better and worse) you achieve a level of self awareness and self assurance unreachable to those without your newly acquired skills. The time it takes you to develop this point of view will come back to you tenfold and more. You will make a new friend and mentor – the one that looks back at you in the mirror each day.

This book is not a cure-all for human failings. Ten hours of reading will not undo 30 years of life experience or 30,000 years of evolution, but it may give you an edge. And that is all many of us need – an edge to leverage into an opportunity – an opportunity to shape a better future. One thing this book will definitely provide you is a place to start.

In addition, I hope that this book will also help some readers to gain traction against personal performance demons against which you have been heretofore impotent. It might be something as innocuous as procrastination – or as serious as an anger management or substance abuse challenge. Whatever the challenge, if you are looking to tackle it head on, the words of French Field Marshall Ferdinand Foch during the First World War speak to one vital prerequisite – "the will to conquer is the first condition of victory."

Choices

The fact that you have picked up this book and made it this far indicates your interest in personal improvement (or insomnia), so let's take the next step with regards to personal accountability. You have a choice to make. If you choose to reject this empowerment approach, we ask only that you make it a conscious choice – and here is the choice clearly spelled out.

If you choose to decline the offered improvement, you are agreeing to endure the pain of regret should your future avoidable errors lead to unwanted consequences or tragedy.

That choice is yours and yours alone – as are all choices and options inside these covers. Remember, this book is about **you**. The reason I want to force this early decision, is that in today's fast paced society, far too many choices get made for us by our own indecision.

Here is another way of looking at it. If you are not mindful of the dangers posed by avoidable errors and lost opportunities, you can reach a point where you have made unintentional but vitally important choices without thinking, without reflection, without planning and with no way to reset the chess board. You can end up not having the career you thought you would, the family you had, or living the life you meant to.

> "If you choose to decline the offered improvement, you are agreeing to endure the pain of regret should your future avoidable errors lead to unwanted consequences or tragedy."

It might be the one you deserve, but not the one you intended.

Or, you have the opportunity to choose a different approach to the rest of your life.

Life is not something that happens to you, you are something that shapes the present and future of your personal and professional life. You intentionally and mindfully create your future by

- Systematically structuring and learning from experience
- Mindfully living in the present
- Deflecting violation- and error-producing conditions, and
- Seeing and seizing new opportunities in real time

Thereby creating the future you both intend and deserve.

Let me state up front that empowered accountability skills require conscious effort on your part. Fear not. They are relatively easy and can be learned and systemically applied by average people with a serious intent. The clock is ticking and the choice is yours. Pass or play – once again, it's your call.

The Limits of Current Error Control Approaches

One of the classic pitfalls for any writer is to try and write too big a book – to fail to limit the scope and target a specific audience. In one aspect – limiting the target audience – I openly confess to this failing here. If you are human – this book will help you if you allow it to. It is written for individuals who want to achieve more, but also for leaders and members of teams, programs, projects, large organizations and systems. It is for the CEO and the mail clerk – the coach and his players – the minister and her congregation – the husband and the wife. However, in a second sense, this book is tightly woven and limited in scope.

> "When faced with the unique characteristics and circumstances of each individual, traditional training and academic theories falter – and falter badly."

Abraham Lincoln reportedly once said that "if he had more time he would have written a shorter letter." This is a shorter letter. Those who have read my previous books will find many similar stylistic traits, such as the use of the case study to explain complex points. But this book has been written – and rewritten over a five year span, allowing refinements and distillation of a grand landscape of interdisciplinary material to be crystallized into what I sincerely hope is a succinct and very readable book for those without any background in behavioral science or human improvement related topics.

The reasons this material crosses such a wide band will be made clear in the pages that follow, but in a nutshell – this book proposes to dramatically reduce avoidable human error at all levels by empowering individuals to become better predictors and executors of their performance based on heightened self- and situation awareness. Additionally, the material provides a skill set to manage real time conditions in your favor to not only avoid error, but to see and seize new opportunities. And since human error is the bane of performance at all levels in nearly every setting – the lessons here apply broadly.

> "The more we dissect and study human performance, the more we understand the parts but the less we understand the whole."

Although there are literally scores of books on human error control from the team, organizational and system approach, the effort has focused largely on studies of large groups – and therein lays the problem – and opportunity to do something different based on providing individuals with the understanding and skills necessary to perceive and react in real time.

When faced with the unique characteristics and circumstances of each individual, traditional training and academic theories falter – and falter badly. In large studies, even those who target people like you (for example, "doctors think this way," or "CEOs tend to handle stress like this"), your uniqueness is intentionally blunted by statistics to make the findings more generalizable to a larger population. When these systemic approaches fail to identify individual error – the white flag of "to err is human" is raised.

But what if it were possible to study every individual in their own unique environment? "Preposterous!" – shout cloaked academics from the ivory towers – "This is highly scientific and specialized work. There are not enough Ph.D.s or grant money to go around." More on this fallacy later.

Teaching People to Teach Themselves

Former Chief of the U.S. Forest Service, Jack Ward Thomas, referring to the complexity of natural ecosystems, once said "They are not only more complex than we think, they are more complex than we *can* think." So it is with people.

The more we dissect and study human performance, the more we understand the parts but the less we understand the whole. The social scientists have added greatly to the sum of our knowledge, but in doing so have made it more difficult for the individual to merge all of this new information into a gestalt of performance in the real world. There is a real need to put it back together.

I believe – better said – I *know* – that it is far easier and certainly more reliable, relevant and beneficial, to teach you some rudimentary behavioral research and self awareness skills, than it will be to get any Ph.D. to understand you as an individual. There are many logical reasons for this, including:

- You care more about the subject of your analysis than any research team ever will.
- Your data come from a very real and very relevant world.
- You will be less tempted to manipulate the data to get a .95 confidence interval in support of your hypothesis to get published in a peer reviewed journal so you can get the next research grant. (If the previous sentence makes no sense to you, consider yourself lucky and thank your high school guidance counselor for pointing you in the right direction.)
- Your uniqueness will not be blunted by others in this study.
- Finally, and most importantly, you will be provided with self-discovered truths based on who you are, where you are, and who you live and work with. These facts provide evidence based results at the level of you – the only place it really matters.

I can already hear some readers closing the book and putting it back on the shelf. Don't be in such a hurry. Having been through this process myself, I full recognize that at first blush, systematic self discovery might seem a bit strange or a bridge too far. That is why the blue threat discipline is laid out in tasty, bite-sized morsels that allow you to stop eating when you are satisfied and pick up the next meal when you are ready. This entire approach is crafted for you in the following pages and simply designed to allow you to grow where you are, with the resources at hand. Not a small promise. But this type of analysis and heightened self awareness leads to powerful insight, and blasts through the smog of day to day life to enable us to see performance-robbing pieces of the puzzle coming together in time to take appropriate action.

A U.S. Navy pilot once wrote "In aviation you very rarely get your head bitten off by a tiger – you usually get nibbled to death by ducks." What he meant was that most error caused accidents or incidents are the endgame of a series of inter-related events, interpretations, decisions, warnings or actions that are allowed to progress without recognition or intervention. The final trigger decision, action (or inaction) may be relatively innocuous, but sufficient in itself to totally remove a margin of safety previously eroded by other events. So it is in life, where we allow the detritus of poor performance to pile up, unaware that the next straw may well be the back breaker.

Shape and Overview of the Book

With the notable exception of the *Blue Threat Proverbs* in Chapter 12, this book is intentionally organized to be read linearly. In order to keep the narrative flowing and enjoyable for those seeking to simply understand blue threat concepts at a macro level, I have sought to avoid too much "in the weeds" explanations and definitions except where the details are essential. For those who desire deeper explanations and references, the book is referenced and expanded with footnotes throughout. Additionally, there is a supplemental *Blue Threat Field Book* and software support that provides a great deal more of the "how to" detail for those who are ready to begin improving today and who want all of the resources available from the start.

It is important from the very start to comprehend that human error is a complex – but understandable – phenomena. It becomes far less complex when we make the time and effort to view it through the lens of the individual – in this case ourselves. Error becomes manageable and eventually controllable – when we learn to come down from the 25,000 foot reconnaissance viewpoint we normally view our performance from to get a close look, where distinguishable features of our personal performance landscape become much clearer.

This book is organized in three distinct parts.

In Part One, the problem of human error is examined. Chapter 1 details how human error destroys lives. Chapter 2 is a call to arms to take control over preventable errors and to seize the levels of performance that are rightfully ours. Chapter 3 explains why our "good enough" lives really aren't, and how we can learn to see and practice improved performance in our everyday activities.

Part Two is the "How to" section where the required theoretical and practical elements of human error control are provided. In Chapter 4 we look at the "myth of compliance" and learn why current *compliance through enforcement* approaches are doomed to eventual failure. Chapter 5 looks at the role of the individual inside teams, and challenges some long held beliefs about how good teams operate. Chapter 6 introduces the I CAN™ (Identify, Categorize, Analyze, and Neutralize) process for personal error tracking and developing individualized countermeasures. Chapter 7 outlines the essence of identifiable error producing conditions and how they can be used to see and avoid trouble in advance. Chapter 8 continues the theme of early detection through an analysis of hazardous attitudes and mental bias, both of which can derail our normally sound decision making.

Part Three analyzes implications for various aspects of our lives including personal, spiritual, and professional. Chapter 9 delves into the spiritual issues interacting with error control from an interfaith perspective. Chapter 10 is titled *Speaker for the Dead* and looks at what those who have made their last mistake might want us to know. The appropriately named Chapter 11 looks at the economic costs of human error on 21st century business and government and provides a list of immediate opportunities for application of the empowered accountability approach across a wide variety of industries and professions. The book concludes with the *Blue Threat Proverbs* in Chapter 12, a list of 30 insights for immediate action.

In general, each chapter typically includes a discussion of key error control insights supported by case studies and scenarios, tools and references to make the points on how and why people as individuals hold the key to many of the toughest issues we face.

Human Error: Problem or Mystery?

While re-reading my dog-eared copy of Steven Pinker's *How the Mind Works*, I ran across an interesting insight that applies to this project. Linguist Norman Chomsky maintains that human ignorance can be roughly subdivided into two simple categories – *problems* and *mysteries*. Problems may not yet have a solution, but are generally frame-able and discussable as something that may be solved at some future point. In Pinker's words, we may not have a full grasp of it, but we have insights.

Mysteries, on the other hand, are more magical. Mysteries continue to be beyond our grasp to shape a meaningful discussion about what any solution or explanation might look like. In truth, it is likely that given the right set of data and time to work through it; we could turn all mysteries into solvable problems. The difficulty with doing so is always managing the moment when a previously supernatural, unknowable, magical thing comes into the realm of the real and manageable.

Human error is at just such a "cusp" moment for individuals and organizations who are tired of the Reaper's toll.

One reason is that the scientists are doing their jobs, and new insights on human motivation, performance and error are being rolled out at an ever increasing rate. Recently, I read a complete set of fully referenced articles on the scientific explanation for romantic love – yet I must confess it remains a mystery to me, but perhaps only because I could not understand the chemistry or technical jargon – a likely product of my mis-spent youth.

A second, and perhaps more important reason for this amazing opportunity to confront human error head on, is that human beings who have now been born and raised in the information age, are far more comfortable perceiving, acting and reacting within the torrents of data that flow by us nearly every moment of every day than members of my Baby Boomer generation.

> "This combination of new knowledge and better adapted human vessels sets the stage for a dramatic change in how we manage human performance."

This combination of new knowledge and better adapted human vessels sets the stage for a dramatic change in how we manage human performance. It will require the courage to dive deep into the nature and causes of general, specific and individual human error patterns and tendencies – as well as the ability to stay adaptable and flexible in the heat of battle. But the solution to human error is closer than it has ever been in the history of the human race.

In short, human error is no longer a mystery – but is still one hell of a problem. Relatively speaking, that's a very good thing.

Part One

The Problem of Human Error

*"You are not here merely to make a living.
You are here in order to enable the world to live more amply,
with greater vision, with a finer spirit of hope and achievement.
You are here to enrich the world,
and you impoverish yourself if you forget the errand."*

– Woodrow Wilson

ONE

How Human Error Destroys Lives, Loves, Careers and Potential

"From the error of a moment, comes the sorrow of a lifetime."
– Chinese proverb

A Thief and Murderer: Nothing Less

Human error is the thief of human happiness and the slayer of dreams, careers, potential, and all too frequently – life itself. Viewing it as anything less hostile is to willfully expose your throat to the knife.

Harsh words – intentionally so.

For thousands of years, mankind has hidden behind Cicero's famous quote "to err is human." The cost is too great to continue on this apathetic and complacent path. So we are going to change the dialogue. To *improve* is human, to *grow* is human, to *learn* is human. But to persevere in avoidable error at great risk to our lives, family, friends and career – that is <u>in</u>human. It's time for some new poetry on this subject.

The global cost of human error, which is highlighted in multiple ways throughout this book, is almost incomprehensible, and very few will look at these costs without agreeing that something more should be done to prevent it. When viewed from a personal perspective inside our routine daily lives, the danger posed by our own errors appears remote. Like criminals who live among us in the shadows, error producing conditions lie in wait, hidden, almost invisible. We ignore the threat because most error is petty theft, annoying, occasionally resulting in minor loss of productivity, but certainly not life threatening.

Unintentional and avoidable errors end lives, poison relationships, squanders wealth, feeds addictions, and ruins careers. It has ever been so. Error is a persistent and progressive thief, who will continue to steal from you and your potential as a human being on an ever greater scale until you make a conscious decision to stop being a passive victim.

> "Unintentional and avoidable errors end lives, poison relationships, squanders wealth, feeds addictions, and ruins careers."

Most of us don't recognize our own potential for error as a serious threat to ourselves or others. This is an often costly or lethal mistake, because errors that result in trivial outcomes of little consequence on one occasion can suddenly and without warning result in a life changing or career ending result on another.

It is important to recognize from the very start of our performance improvement journey that our decisions and actions are only one set of many variables that result in a positive or negative outcome. Sometimes our actions are the catalyst for success or failure. Other times external factors or the situation itself gets the final vote. That is why *outcome* based assessment – judging an action or decision by its end result is a fool's errand when it comes to error control.

People are lulled into a false sense of security because a tragic outcome has not yet occurred. Our personal lives seem to support this *laissez faire* approach, at least so far. After all, how many of you reading this book right now have ever died due to an error? Me neither, but I've been close.

Let's put human error lesson #1 on the table right now:

Things that have never happened before, happen all the time.[1]

In the blink of an eye, the same petty thief you have grown accustomed to as a minor annoyance on the street corner becomes your worst nightmare. In hindsight, it becomes all too clear – you could have and should have seen it

---

1   Attributed to Professor Kathleen Sutcliffe, University of Michigan Ross School of Business, 2006

coming. The signs were there, the hazard was present, but you could not and would not believe it could happen to you. Those that have been though this life changing phenomena sing a common refrain – "I had no idea this simple problem could turn so ugly so fast. This had been going on for years without serious consequence." These individuals have fallen victim to a phenomenon known as the *normalization of deviance*, a dangerous dumbing down of our risk perception, and a subject we will discuss in depth later.

> "... *outcome* based assessment – judging an action or decision by its end result is a fool's errand when it comes to error control."

The first purpose of this book is to raise the alarm, to point out how prevalent and destabilizing human error is in our daily lives, as well as how quickly small errors can lead to tragedy. Human error lesson #2:

> *Anything less than a conscious commitment to understanding and reducing personal error is an unconscious commitment to accepting their continuing presence and all future consequences.*

Please reread the previous paragraph. Unnecessary and avoidable human error is likely the most dangerous threat to your health, family, professional development and life that you face in your day to day life – at home, in your car, at work or at play. To the unprepared, error strikes like a thief in the night, manifests itself without warning, and changes lives forever.

To more fully comprehend this point that lives can and do turn tragic in the blink of an eye, consider the following story, taken from the front page of the Fredericksburg, Virginia *The Free Lance Star* in April 2005.[2]

Case Study: Drivers' Duel Ends in Death

By ROB DAVIS

Race's survivor pays a price, too

Drivers had cut off Clifford Robinson at that merge before. On this day, June 2, 2004, Robinson later told police he wasn't going to back down, not after 30 years in the Marine Corps. Sitting at a stoplight on Gordon Road in Spotsylvania County, the 67-year-old retired Marine warrant officer saw, in his peripheral vision, a red Ford Mustang pull up on his left.

---

[2] Reprinted with permission. Fredericksburg *The Free Lance Star* April 14, 2005. p. 1

Christy Antonuccio, a petite 31-year-old mother of three and a president's-list student at Germanna Community College, was driving. Her 4-year-old son, Justin, was directly behind her in the back seat. When the light at Harrison Road turned green, Robinson hit the gas. So did Antonuccio. In front of them, two lanes funneled into one. Their cars were side by side, their speeds growing as they raced downhill toward a curve.

The Mustang began to pull ahead. Robinson, in a 2003 Mercedes SUV, knew he couldn't beat the sports car's power. If he didn't stop, they both would crash. Robinson backed down. He braked. The battle for position had lasted only a few seconds, playing out over less than a quarter-mile stretch of road.

Antonuccio didn't touch her brakes, according to an accident reconstruction. She lost control as her car moved into the right lane, ran off Gordon Road and spun into one tree, then a second. Authorities estimated she was going 76 mph when she crashed. The impact bent her car in the middle like an L and knocked down a tree. It pushed the driver's seat into the passenger's side. The car was so mangled that rescue workers would need nearly 90 minutes to get the victims out.

> "To the unprepared, error strikes like a thief in the night, manifests itself without warning, and changes lives forever."

Robinson saw the crash and turned around. By the time he arrived, a neighbor was already removing pieces of the shattered tree from atop the car. The neighbor, Kenneth Phillips, saw the 4-year-old in the back seat. He heard the boy take one breath. Then he didn't hear anything more.

Justin Antonuccio, whose father thought of him as a miniature version of Christy, was dead. Less than two hours later, his mother was dead, too. Robinson did not tell police about the frustration he'd felt at being cut off before. He did not tell police their cars had been neck and neck seconds before Antonuccio crashed. After a state trooper dismissed one person from the scene, Robinson left. Authorities didn't remember seeing him there, and attributed the accident solely to excessive speed.

A day later, after a brief about the crash was published in *The Free Lance-Star*, a newspaper reporter received an anonymous tip. The caller gave a description and tag information for a Mercedes SUV. Spotsylvania deputies traced the information to Robinson. When deputies visited his home and spoke to him about the accident, he cried.

The story of the crash and Robinson's subsequent arrest on charges of reckless driving and leaving an accident scene without talking to police unfolded during testimony yesterday in Spotsylvania Circuit Court. Families on both sides of the aisle cried. Judge William H. Ledbetter Jr. lamented how tragic the case was. He didn't blame Robinson for the crash. The two cars never touched. Bad judgment simply converged at a merge in the road. If she had crashed a mile away, Ledbetter said, Robinson would have been just a witness.

But for a few seconds, neither driver was thinking properly, the judge said.

Ledbetter found Robinson guilty on both counts, and sentenced him to 21/2 years behind bars, with all but six months suspended. Robinson will serve 90 days, with good behavior. He also was fined $2,000.

"Foolish decisions at the snap of a finger," Ledbetter said, as he issued his verdict. "So sad. So unfortunate."

This case study is ideal to introduce the need for a reevaluation of our approach to human error. Two apparently rational adults at different points of highly successful lives meet at a stoplight. In the blink of an eye, both lose control of their decision making and flood their bodies with powerful and mind altering chemicals[3] and the result of this tragic combination of events snuffs the life out of a completely innocent victim and devastates two families.

> "... error haunts our families and societal existence in many unseen ways."

Like all avoidable tragedies, one wishes to be able to turn back the clock, and provide the tools to recognize, understand and manage the moment in time when things began to spiral out of control. We call this moment of truth a "trigger event." Trigger event recognition and control is a vitally important component of

---

3 Collectively referred to as catecholamines; adrenaline, epinephrine, norepinephrine and cortisol hijack our higher thinking capacity. We refer to this crisis mode as "fight or flight" and will discuss the physiology of these events in a later chapter.

the blue threat performance approach. In his excellent book, *Preventing Chaos in a Crisis*, Patrick Lagadec describes the problem of lack of recognition or preparation for an unexpected event as it unfolds.

> ... the event can in some ways be considered an abrupt and brutal audit: at a moment's notice, everything that was left unprepared becomes a complex problem, and every weakness comes rushing to the front.[4]

Of course this insight comes too late for the Robinson or Antonuccio families – but it's not too late for you and me if we choose to prepare ourselves.

The Long Reach of Human Error

Beyond cases of sudden loss of judgment (SLOJ) like the one above, error haunts our families and societal existence in many unseen ways. For example, the alcoholic or drug addict who honestly seeks to reform but consistently falls back into negative habit patterns and behaviors. Or those with anger management issues that often end up destroying their own lives as well as injuring those near them, once again – sincerely desiring to change, yet curiously unable to see trouble coming at them before they lose control. Or even the habitual overeater, who simply can't control their urges in spite of a desire to do so and the knowledge of the risk they pose to their long term health.

These are all real problems caused, enabled or exacerbated by predictable and preventable human error.

I can already hear your thoughts. *Aren't there programs available for all of these challenges?* Of course, and they are all based on dozens of studies of large groups of alcoholics, drug addicts, domestic abusers, overeaters, etc.. This research results in valuable programs, such as Alcoholics Anonymous that work for many, but not for all. One of the consistently heard cries from the wilderness of those who fall short of their goals is that "those programs just don't work for me in my circumstances." The typical reply to these well meaning folks is to tell them they don't have the willpower, desire or discipline – or that they are in denial and won't seek help.

What if we could give these people *traction* instead of criticism? What if we could provide the tools to assist each man or woman who truly desires change to avoid the pitfalls that bedevil their most fervent desires to im-

---

4 *Preventing Chaos in a Crisis*, Lagadec, Patrick. p. 54

prove or recover? What if we could develop the means for individuals to take account of their own unique challenges and circumstances within these greater struggles? Wouldn't that be worth a hard look?

Other examples of avoidable error's long reach include communications and attitudinal problems that drive wedges between coworkers or husband and wife; or the overbearing parent who wants to develop a better relationship with his children, but can't stop his life-long habit of criticizing. The list of examples of where simple human error and our inability to take personal control of it haunt our lives extends well beyond this short list.

But what does this discussion of overeaters and substance abusers have to do with the rest of us – the so called "well adjusted?"

Errors come in many forms and impact our performance at many levels. For some, error control will keep them from physical harm to themselves or others. For others who are already on the high end of the performance scale, it will make you more effective, efficient, and precise. In short, the empowered accountability approach will give you a competitive advantage, and in today's turbulent economic times, that may indeed be a survival skill.

The Good News and Great Debate

There is good news. Like any known criminal, the majority of the human error threat can be identified, tracked, countered and rendered harmless. The knowledge and tools exist.

If this is true, the question that must be asked is, "Why have we not done so?" The answer is dangerously simple. We are complacent. "It hasn't happened to me yet" becomes engrained as an attitude of personal invulnerability – "It won't happen in the future." See *human error lesson #1* on page 11. On a larger scale, something more insidious is going on.

What I am about to say next will undoubtedly upset some people who are in the human performance business. I only ask that they read the remainder of this chapter before they throw the book in the fire.

Some very smart and extremely well meaning people have given up on personal accountability and individual error control because of a few reasons.

- It does not lend itself well to academic study
- There is not a lot of money in it
- It is politically incorrect

Let's very briefly look at each of these obstacles.

Academic Issues

First, academic studies of human error almost exclusively demand large enough numbers of participants to reach statistical significance. This is intended to create generalizable and replicable findings based on groups, usually a good thing. But almost by definition, when you get the numbers large enough for statistical significance, individual variance is muted. What is good for the Ph.D. is bad for any individual who does not fit the profile of the typical member of the group. That is a problem for me – I'm a weird guy who doesn't match up well with most standard profiles. My guess is that many readers feel the same.

Of course, if we studied a single individual long enough, we could get a large enough sample of behaviors, decisions and errors to reach a statistical significant sample – *but who cares about the performance of a single Jane Doe?* (Jane might. Now there is an idea worth considering.)

Even more to the point, what respectable academic journal would publish a peer-reviewed article on such a topic or what government agency would fund a grant for a study on "Jane Doe's Personal Error Patterns and Performance Improvement Opportunities?" That article would likely only have one reader, but she would be very interested. What if we could teach everyone to research and write their own plan?

> "The profit motive, along with western civilization's bizarre cult of trying to find techno-solutions for every human failing, is part of the reason why we have resisted trying to fix people."

The bottom line here is that academics live by the "publish or perish" principle and build their careers through getting grants for future research. It's that simple. It's not that they couldn't study an individual if they wanted to, there is just nothing in it for them, so no one has. Nor are they likely to do so in the future.

But the skill set to do it for ourselves is available to anyone who desires it. Ph.D.'s don't advertise this often, but in truth, once you cut through the unnecessary technical jargon, behavioral analysis is not beyond the capability of the average human being.

Accountability Doesn't Sell

While we are on the topic of money, it is important to recognize human error management is a growth industry where many companies make billions of dollars on automation and technologies to prevent or manage human error. The profit motive, along with western civilization's bizarre cult of trying to find techno-solutions for every human failing, is part of the reason why we have resisted trying to fix people. To speak more precisely to this point, here is an example taken from *Commander's Intent* (www.convergentperformance.com/gwoe/blog/).

Hurricane Survivors and Train Wrecks

(Posted Monday, September 15, 2008)

This past week has seen tragedy strike Americans on two coasts; one the result of a natural disaster, Hurricane Ike; and the other man made, the head on collision between a Los Angeles Metrolink commuter train and a freight train near Simi Valley, California. Interestingly, the grim reaper's toll is nearly the same for both. As we sort through the rubble in a search for lessons, a few items stand out. In one particularly interesting story, one brave but foolish soul found his 15 minutes of fame by being the only person in Surfside Beach, Texas who defied authorities and refused to evacuate before the oncoming hurricane. Sixty-seven year old Ray Wilkinson, a retired carpenter, refused the mandatory evacuation order from police and drank the night away as the winds and rain howled. Authorities found him Saturday morning after the storm – safe and stone drunk. When interviewed after the event, he stated "I consider myself to be stupid." No argument there.

Further west, there was little or no warning for the victims of the worst train crash in the U.S. since 1993. Early words from the investigation hint definitively at human error as the primary cause, with two possible threads emerging in the early investigation. The first is that recorded audio tapes from the Metrolink train seem to indicate that the required crew coordination calls between the engineer and conductor did not take place on the two signals prior to the crash. If this is indeed what occurred, it is a simple case of noncompliance with regulations and procedures. Another lead said that two teenagers reported receiving a text message from the engineer just moments before the crash, possibly indicating the engineer was not paying full attention to the task at hand. Both are errors of personal origin and both can be trained (no pun intended) out of existence. But it is unlikely that we will do so. I fully expect we will once again hide behind the oft heard refrain that "to err is human." In this case – as in many similar cases where the outcome of an avoidable mistake results in an immeasurable toll on innocent victims – to err is inhuman.

Already there are cries for technology to save the day and prevent this type of error from ever occurring again. If the past is prologue, whomever markets the "Positive Train Control" system, which supposedly stops a train if a signal is disobeyed by the humans, is about to get a new contract. But technology is **never** the complete answer, and I seriously doubt it will be here. Don't get me wrong, I am all for gadgets that makes things safer, but my experience tells me that if you make something foolproof today – tomorrow someone will give birth to a more sophisticated fool. And while this is a good way to keep the wheels of the "safety-industrial complex" turning, there is a simpler and far more effective measure we can and should be taking. More on that in a moment.

> "It is difficult to convince a society who would rather manage their wellness by taking pills than by exercising, to see the value of putting in the time to learn a new discipline of thought and awareness."

So my point in bringing these two tragedies together is simply this; I'm not sure that Mr. Wilkinson, currently Surfside Beach's most famous resident, isn't the key to understanding the human dynamic in both of these events. While I don't advocate his Jack Daniels approach to problem solving, he at least recognizes his own human limitations and has found a way to deal with them. As the NTSB and government officials work out the details of the Metrolink disaster, perhaps someone will realize our current collective limitations in understanding the nature of error and advocate getting serious about training to control these events.

The science is available and the means are here for such error control programs to become a part of every employees' training. But that is not the typical American response to large scale disasters. Why make people learn when we can build a machine so we don't have to think? If the past is a guide, the response to this tragedy will be to (1) blame the dead engineer, (2) sue the hell out of Metrolink, and (3) put some new technology in place to prevent this specific event from occurring again at this specific location, and (4) claim the problem is fixed … until the next time.

But we can do better. Error control will never be engineered out of existence with technology. Human error is a force of nature, and just like the hurricane it can be studied, its movements tracked and predicted. To be certain, there are places where technology can help, but at the end of the day error is an individual phenomena that can be measured, understood and predicted. In the words of the brilliant Gordon Graham,[5] "Predictable is preventable."

The forgotten key to error control is personal responsibility and accountability. As simple as it sounds, we can teach people to make fewer errors. This cannot be done in the traditional sense of training against someone's last mistake, but rather through a systemic approach to comprehending how and why we get unintended consequences from our well intended decisions and actions. It is no longer enough to train people to do things right – they must learn why they do things wrong, and these are two very different skill sets.

> "Here's a little insight from the front lines of error control. When I make a mistake, it is usually my fault. Not society's, not some systemic hobgoblin. It's not my boss' fault or my wife's or my mom's – its mine."

I've always found it interesting that the same companies and organizations that spend millions on technologies to prevent human error are extremely reluctant to spend serious resources on what they call "soft skills." More on why this is a critical business mistake will be forthcoming in the appropriately named "Chapter 11." Beyond economic reasons for inaction, there appear to be considerable societal obstacles to human error control.

Political Incorrectness

Personal accountability and *responsibility* are not easy sells for another reason that has far less to do with money and more to do with societal norms and personal motivation. It is difficult to convince a society who would rather manage their wellness by taking pills than by exercising, to see the value of putting in the time to learn a new discipline of thought and awareness. We

---

5   Gordon Graham is a 33 year veteran of California Law Enforcement. His education as a Risk Manager and experience as a practicing Attorney, coupled with his extensive background in law enforcement, have allowed him to rapidly become recognized as a leading professional speaker in both private and public sector organizations with multiple areas of expertise. He can be reached at www.gordongraham.com

will discuss this "level of effort issue" in a section on the *Normalization of Excellence* in a future chapter. Then there is the whole issue of anyone in our modern society having to take accountability for their actions.

Here's a little insight from the front lines of error control. When I make a mistake, it is usually my fault. Not society's, not some systemic hobgoblin. It's not my boss' fault or my wife's or my mom's – its mine. Typically my personal errors result from bad habit patterns, over-competitiveness, time pressure or fatigue – things under my control or influence. That is not to say that there are not external influences that often lead me down the path to error – there are. But that does nothing to relieve me of the task of performing to the best of my ability within those error producing situations and systems. Even when there are external factors that put me in a position where I am more likely to make errors – the awareness of those factors and a skill set to account for them is mine for the asking if I will put the effort into developing them.

The softer, easier way is to blame something less personal – and many in our society choose the path of least resistance. This approach has led to the development of two models to explain human failing. Here is my take on social science models. Most models are useful – all are flawed. This holds true with both the *disease model* and *systems model* of human performance, which we will introduce below and discuss in depth later in this book. They can help us see the challenge of error from different perspectives, but they are not all encompassing. But before we get to them, we need to have a short discussion on something called *locus of control*.

Locus of control refers to any individual's perceived level of control over their circumstances. People with a high *internal* locus of control believe, for the most part, that they have control over the circumstances in their lives. Individuals with a high *external* locus of control perceive that external forces primarily control their destinies. Of course in real life, both internal and external forces are in play in all of our lives and their daily outcomes. However, in recent years, it seems to be trendier to take an external locus of control perspective – and blame outside influences for our problems. Now let's return to our discussion of two examples.

The Disease Model

The disease model is frequently used in describing addictions and effectively used in addiction recovery programs. It postulates that our problems and addictions are not our fault but rather an illness that is either genetic or otherwise caused by external factors. Not surprisingly, not everyone

> "It seems to be OK if we continue in our error prone ways, injure ourselves or others, and continue to put our careers and families at risk – but it's not OK to offend anyone. In many circles, *accountability* seems to be a four letter word."

agrees. According to some critics of the disease model, labeling people as *addicts* keeps them from developing self-control and stigmatizes them. These critics also argue that the disease approach has not discovered any biological mechanisms to identify addictive behavior and therefore does not fit the definition of disease. Please understand that I do not take sides in this argument – as that is well outside my sphere of expertise or understanding. I point out only that if we do not take responsibility for *anything* – if we refuse to believe our knowledge, thoughts and actions matter – we are doomed to living our lives as a leaf in the wind.

The System Model

The *system model* is largely used in industrial safety and quality programs and begins with the premise that "to err is human" and errors should be expected to continue to occur. Safety is provided by "defenses in depth." That is great as far as it goes. Most recent advocates of this model go out of their way to articulate it as the antithesis of the "person model" where individuals who make errors are publicly humiliated, strung up by their thumbs and whipped with a wet noodle. System model advocates go on to say that most errors are the result of the systems in which people live and work, and therefore the fixes ought to be systemic – not personal. This pretty much lets everyone off the hook. Once again, this model is useful and explains a great many issues that are systemic. But not all problems are system problems. Many problems are people problems – with personal solutions.

It seems to be OK if we continue in our error prone ways, injure ourselves or others, and continue to put our careers and families at risk – but it's not OK to offend anyone. In many circles, *accountability* seems to be a four letter word. Go figure.

Why Do We Need a New Way of Looking at Human Error?

Like I said earlier – these models are all useful but flawed. Both the disease and system models add a great deal to our understanding and allow us another point of view. Both are somewhat successful and easily accepted in most settings. They lend themselves well to academic study. Companies are willing to pay for them to help control their error problems and perhaps best of all, they are politically correct since no one is really at fault as an individual.

There are a couple of problems. The first problem with both models is that neither of them account for the huge capacity of the individual in addressing the challenge of errors made that lead to negative and even destructive behaviors. This is an oversight of the largest magnitude and an opportunity for a new approach.

The second problem is that neither model really address the unique but controllable issues that cause most of our error problems. Neither the disease or the system model has any way of knowing that, for example, I (as a unique individual) have a nasty habit of trying to do 90 minutes of work every hour. The system doesn't force me to; it's not some kind of genetic time distortion disease – it's me and a habit I developed long ago while simultaneously working full time and pursuing a full time doctorate. It causes me to err – often. Neither the system model nor the disease approach can predict the errors of someone who is fatigued and distracted by a sick child they were up caring for all night. But a personal awareness and error control approach can effectively deal with both of these situations.

> "Perhaps it is time we begin to inform those in high risk industries about their own propensity for error … they do, after all, pose the most serious threat to the high risk systems they work in."
> – Professor James Reason

The final reason a new approach is needed is that while most of us do not suffer badly from our errors, we live and work in systems that are not fully developed to help us reduce error. But we all suffer from error induced consequences from time to time – and we are all at risk of having the next one have a serious consequence, or even catastrophic outcome.

Professor James Reason, arguably the smartest man on the planet on the topic of human error and a strong supporter of the system model, puts it plainly in his book *Human Error*, "Perhaps it is time we begin to inform those in high risk industries about their own propensity for error … they do, after all, pose the most serious threat to the high risk systems they work in." Whether it is in a high risk industry or our day to day lives – the good professor hit the nail on the head.

Yet while it is important that we develop a working knowledge of certain error causes and controls, this book is not about classification systems or a deep academic rendering of known causes of errors. Not only is that beyond the scope of what the author is capable of, but also blurs the playing field with the smog of academic jargon and pointless precision. The "new way" of looking at human error is to provide you a map and a compass – both of which will require some up front instruction and explanation – and convince you to start down the path of improvement. Toward that end, it is the task of this book to both educate and motivate – inform and inspire.

The Truth is in You

Over the past three decades (1980–present) vast amounts of new information have come out on the subject of human error causes and countermeasures. Some clues to error reduction and management are found in the so-called "psychology of achievement" books, more answers are found in neuroscience and behavioral and cognitive psychology. Additional insights come from the mouths of world class athletes, chess players and musicians who perform error free under incredible pressures as if it did not exist. One only need to look within the ranks of world class performers across multiple spectrums to find that personal error awareness and reduction are as foundational and practiced as their technical skills or sound nutrition.

> "One only need to look within the ranks of world class performers across multiple spectrums to find that personal error awareness and reduction are as foundational and practiced as their technical skills or sound nutrition."

On the organizational level, the rationale for accepting human error at current levels is more complex, with a wide variety of resource and attitudinal issues coming into play. Often large organizations become enthralled with the latest management fad or the myopic approach of high-end academics, failing to see obvious solutions available in the potential of their own people. In both cases however, a lack of understanding and the acceptance of human error as unavoidable, fuel the apathy and feeling of helplessness that paralyzes progress against this eternal foe.

Therefore, the second purpose for this book is to empower individuals and organizations to take the fight to this enemy through a combination of new knowledge and understanding, heightened awareness and vigilance. By providing specific strategies, tactics and weapons, we will proactively counter the blue threat at its source.

Human Error: An Opiate for Unfulfilled Potential and Poor Performance

Human error has been called the "central aspect of the human condition," something we have become so comfortable with that we have become blind, deaf and mute regarding it. This is at once tragic and ironic. Tragic – because unnecessary error hurts not only the individual involved, but often also others around them to include their family, friends, and innocent bystanders. Ironic – because we have – and have always had – the power to correct the vast majority of life altering and injury causing errors. Unfortunately, we have not had the knowledge or skills to systematically attack this dangerous foe at the personal level.

Human beings and their behaviors are extremely complex. There is a very real need for a crystallized and actionable description of key components of error reduction to enable the individual or organizational manager to shift the odds in their favor.

Error has become a governmental and societal opiate for explaining away serious performance and safety issues. But where the government, industry and society have failed – the individual remains empowered. The science is there, the means and methods available – all that is lacking is the transfer of knowledge and the individual will to proceed. It is the goal of this book to address both of those gaps.

> "Error has become a governmental and societal opiate for explaining away serious performance and safety issues. But where the government, industry and society have failed – the individual remains empowered."

Now let us turn for a moment to the vital issue of *motivation*. Why would the average man or woman, comfortably living a normal life, take on the burden of learning something new? We have stated the risk that error poses, but admitted to ourselves that through familiarity with the thief, our fear of the unknown error biting us hard is really not that scary. Maybe it should be, but perhaps not enough to prompt a personal change agenda. So let's pose the question another way. Five years from now, who will you be?

Kobe Yamada, the CEO of Compendium, Inc. says it this way, "The future is sending back good wishes and waiting with open arms." Are we willing to do what it takes to accept its embrace?

The Law of Grow or Die

Every living thing is in the process of growing or dying. Nothing stays the same. These simple truths underlie the entire purpose of this book – personal and professional growth – done by you, for you, viewed through the lens of your own uniqueness, first as an individual, then as a function of your own circumstances and environment. The bad news is that the law of grow or die is ignored by most adults. The good news is that it doesn't have to be.

In nature – and we are a part of nature – there are three stages of physical energy – dynamic, static, and entropic. Dynamic energy is growing; entropic energy is decaying and stasis is the infinitely small moment when the growth or decay reverses its course. The point here is that if we are not growing – we are decaying.

Uninterrupted, our body begins its natural downward spiral sometime in our mid-twenties. Mentally, the decline begins shortly after thirty. But we have a choice. We can choose to reverse the natural decline and grow. But how?

One of the first issues is to decide what it means for an adult to *grow*? There are many dimensions of our lives in which we can grow: professional, family, spiritual, emotional, learning, relationships, romance, financial ... just to name a few. The one constant in all of these elements – for good or for ill – is *you*. Interestingly, people tend to make the same types of errors across the boundaries of their lives – so getting a handle on this agent of decay is a wonderful first step towards growth in all areas of your life. By stopping the mistakes, we position ourselves in that temporary moment of stasis – and poised to grow through deeper self awareness and enhanced personal insight.

Five years from now ... one year from now ... one month from now, you will not be the same person. Your family will not be the same family. Your marriage will not be the same marriage. Your organization will not be the same organization. You will be better or you will be worse, but you will not be the same. This is your one and only life, so let's get off the porch and live large.

In our next chapter, we will look at a slightly more aggressive model, one with a definite bias towards *internal* locus of control.

TWO

A Call to Arms

Si vis pacem para bellum.
"If you wish for peace, prepare for war."

I'm sick of hearing about failure, crisis and tragedy caused by human error. I'm even more upset that we don't appear to be doing much about it.

Too many people are dying unnecessarily. Too many careers are being ruined unnecessarily. Too many businesses are failing unnecessarily. Too many families are suffering unnecessarily. Too many people are not reaching their potential; all due to our cavalier attitude towards human error. It's time to get serious.

Occasionally when I speak to new audiences, I get feedback that some felt my language and bearing were "a bit too military." OK, I'm busted. This book is not about me, but if I am going to ask you to join me in battle, I feel obligated to share a few words on my qualifications for the fight. Like everyone else, I am a product of my environment, education and training and I make no apologies for it. My life as a drone for Uncle Sam included duty as a military officer, B-1B bomber pilot, joint warfare planner and former Director and Professor of Military History at the United States Air Force Academy.

I am both honored and humbled that my nation saw fit to invest millions of dollars in training and formal education on this prior juvenile delinquent. In addition to helping me pay for three graduate degrees, I was given the opportunity to learn about many of the nuances of armed conflict: threat assessment, operational art, grand strategy, small unit tactics, economy of force, decisive points, centers of gravity, fog and friction of war, and weaponeering. I have read – better said, *devoured* tens of thousands of pages of Xenophon, Cicero, Clausewitz, Jomini, Napoleon, Sun Tzu, du Picq, von Leeb, De Saxe, Frederick, Gorshkov, Mahan, Zhukov, Douhet, Arnold, Patton, Rommel, Boyd and more.

For that opportunity, I am – and will always be – profoundly grateful. So when I was looking for a new way to get leverage on the problem of avoidable human error, it was natural for me to approach the challenge though the lens of my expertise. Contrary to the opinions of many, *military science* is not an oxymoron. It is the study of the strategy, tactics, techniques, psychology, practice and other phenomena which constitute war and armed conflict. It strives to be a scientific system that if properly employed, will greatly enhance the practitioner's ability to prevail in a conflict with any adversary. To this end, it is unconcerned whether that adversary is an opposing military force, unconventional warfare guerrillas or other adversary. Nor is human error the first non-military application of this approach.

"Contrary to the opinions of many, *military science* is not an oxymoron."

Over the years we have seen the *War on Poverty*, the *War on Drugs*, and other pseudo-military applications of the term. Most of these efforts are more rhetorical than actually following a true war planning process, but they set a precedent none the less.

In order to assess a warfighter's approach to the rather vague notion of "human error," two questions were posed:

1. If we were experiencing the same casualties and economic losses currently inflicted by human error at the hands of a human adversary, how would we respond?
2. If a comprehensive war planning process were applied to human error, what strategy and tactics would be designed to defeat it?

The answers to these two simple questions were immediately illuminating, deeply insightful and profoundly actionable. In 2004, convinced that this approach would provide leverage and improve performance in multiple settings, we launched the *Global War on Error*,® which evolved into the blue threat empowered accountability approach outlined in this book.

Waging a Global War on Error® (GWOE)

History's most successful generals have seldom been the ones who invent a new weapon, formation or tactic. Rather, the victories have usually gone to those who can take the weapons and tactics of others and integrate them in a new way to bring force to bear at critical points known as *centers of gravity*.[1]

The GWOE effort began in earnest in late 2004. While working with the U.S. Marines Corps aviation program – who were coming off a pretty gruesome safety year – a senior Marine asked me a simple question. *"Tony, why do highly skilled, highly intelligent and highly trained pilots continue to make dumb mistakes that kill them?"* This simple question would lead to five years of exhaustive research and development by a team of experts resulting in the world's first systematic personal error control program. Within one year of prototype testing, the results were so positive and promising the Deputy Commandant of the Marine Corps for Aviation mandated the full *Global War on Error* program for every Marine aviator. Within 24 months, the U.S. Coast Guard aviation program joined the effort and the race was on to flesh this new approach out for the rest of the world.

> *"Why do highly skilled, highly intelligent and highly trained pilots continue to make dumb mistakes that kill them?"*

But to understand how this research came to a different conclusion than previous error management studies let's go back to the war planning model for a minute, where we will ironically see why this new approach is so effective for everyday people who know nothing about military doctrine.

War planners are tied to the principles of military science that have been proven out over thousands of years in the crucible of armed conflict. When confronted with the challenge of defeating human error – we asked a simple question. *If this were a human adversary, how and where would we attack it to have the maximum impact?* From there, we simply applied the standard planning processes beginning with *threat assessment*.

---

1 A *Center of Gravity* is a point of maximum leverage against an enemy's strongpoint. These might include such things as their fielded forces, infrastructure, supplies, mobility or will to continue the fight.

Threat Assessment

The initial threat assessment proved stunning in terms of sheer magnitude. Hundreds of thousands die unnecessarily each year in America alone as a <u>direct result</u> of human error. In healthcare settings alone, it is estimated that nearly 100,000 patients die per year due to iatrogenic (doctor/nurse induced) causes. On our highways every year, tens of thousands more drive fully functional cars into trees, bridges and each other resulting in completely avoidable deaths. Accidents are the leading cause of death for people under the age of 45.[2]

> "... errors and their consequences are not predestined elements of fate."

In business, billions of dollars are lost each year as a direct result of human error, and not just from accidents, injuries, lawsuits or increased insurance premiums. As evidence mounts on the causes of the recent global economic meltdown, it is becoming readily apparent that human error played a major role. Miscalculations and unchecked egos were principal components of the fiscal collapse of many organizations. Add to this the number of senior executives and fast rising managers who derail themselves through completely avoidable human error. The list continues with error induced product defects, inefficiencies, supply chain delays, and poor customer service and it becomes obvious that human error puts the very engine of our profitability and economy at great risk.

But if all these facts are known, why are we still making such little progress?

Experts cite the randomness and wide variability of human error as the reason for these disappointing results. Some small successes are reported, but globally, human error is culpable in nearly 80% of mission failures with outcomes that include degraded productivity and recovery costs from preventable errors, accidents and incidents.

Contrary to popular opinion, errors and their consequences are not predestined elements of fate. They are the product of internal and external conditions that can be seen and controlled in advance by people operating in real time environments armed with the right body of knowledge, tools and techniques. In the global industrial setting, the wild card of human error has

---

[2] 2008 statistics. http://www.disastercenter.com/cdc/

cost hundreds of thousands of lives and billions of dollars in North America alone. Traditional error control approaches have been only marginally effective against this insidious threat.

If these losses had been intentionally inflected by a human adversary, there would be an enormous public and political outcry resulting in immediate mobilization of forces against the foe. One need only look as far as 9/11/01 to see the validity here. Of course the reason we have not responded aggressively to the challenge of human error as opposed to *Al Qaida* or some other terrorist threat is that we have grown accustomed to the presence of this enemy – it walks with us daily, so we do not recognize human error as what it is – the favorite scythe of the Grim Reaper.

> "… we have grown accustomed to the presence of this enemy – it walks with us daily, so we do not recognize human error as what it is – the favorite scythe of the Grim Reaper."

One of the basic tenets of war planning is that preparation depends upon defending against an enemy's *capability*, not their intent. *Intent* is easily hidden through deception, distraction or circumstance. Capability, on the other hand, can be determined by analysis. Forget for a moment that we are not talking about a thinking human enemy, although it often appears to be such. The capability of error to harm is beyond question, and therefore deserves additional respect as an active and lethal adversary. Let's look at this threat in greater depth using a new model, in hopes that it may allow us to plan and take action against this deadly foe in earnest.

Red Threat – Blue Threat

This initial step – the analysis of the enemy threat – is the first order of business professional war planners and business strategists take in preparing to apply firepower against an adversary. This is a methodical and disciplined process, and evaluates an enemy's troop strength, logistical support, known weapons and tactics, training, mobility, leadership and strength of will, among other multiple factors. The evaluation and synthesis of these factors related to external threats to success are collectively known as the *red threat*.

Following the completion of this external analysis, thorough strategists conduct the same analysis on their own capabilities to identify weaknesses, trends and other information that might be used against them *or result in self defeating behaviors*. These factors include lack of logistical support, disciplined execution, planning, knowledge in key areas, and failed teamwork all which could result in human error counterproductive to the mission. Collectively this group of factors is known as the *blue threat*.

A little known insight on the western way of war is that the American military typically loses far more soldiers to human error and mishaps than to enemy actions, although this number is changing somewhat due to the nature of the recent wars in Iraq and Afghanistan. For example, in the two decades between 1975 and 1995, Department of Defense accidents accounted for over $50 billion in reported losses, more than 2,000 aircraft destroyed and more than 15,000 deaths.[3]

> "A little known insight on the western way of war is that the American military typically loses far more soldiers to human error and mishaps than to enemy actions...."

In industry and our personal lives – where the red threat is far less of a factor than in military operations – the numbers are much, much worse. The full extent of the human error epidemic on our personal, professional and organization lives is incalculable.

The synergy of several scientific disciplines provides a path forward against this foe. The applied disciplines include neuroscience, behavioral, cognitive and sports psychology, military science and complexity theory. Make no mistake, the science to dramatically reduce personal error and seize more opportunities is there, but the willpower and organization may not be. In fact, many of the best and brightest minds in the world on this subject appear to have thrown in the towel.

White Flags of Surrender

The most basic problem we face is that the battlefield upon which we must wage this struggle is strewn with millennia of status quo defeatism, centuries of apathy, and decades of techno-hubris – the belief that we can technically engineer our way out of human error. To some degree, many have already capitulated to the idea that "to err is human" and current losses are simply "the cost of doing business" until we can design the human out of the system altogether. That is certainly not the approach taken here. I believe that the human being is the strongest part of the safety and performance equation, although a lot of engineers and technology salesmen would tell you differ-

---

4   Diehl, Alan. *Silent Knights: Blowing the Whistle on Military Accidents and their Cover-ups*. Brasseys, Inc. 2002. Washington DC. p. 47

ently. Don't believe them. While technology, technical training and organizational influence (culture) are all important, you – as an individual mind operating in real time – are more so.

Not all believe this to be true. The following statements are all taken from current writings or talks given by highly respected professionals:

- "People will always make mistakes, that's a given."
- "Trying to stop human error is a fools' errand."
- "It's easier to change situations than people."
- "People make mistakes because of the design of the systems they operate in."
- "Focusing on individual error is a blame and shame game."
- "To err is human … it is easier to *manage* error than to prevent it."
- "Human error mishaps are just the cost of doing business."
- "We are forced to work with the crooked timber of human fallibility."
- "Serious human factors experts moved beyond the individual error approach 20 years ago."
- "The weakest link in the cockpit is wearing a headset."

Wow – I'm glad these folks didn't coach my little league team or I'd have given up on excellence in 5th grade. I will address each of these human error fallacies and half truths in due course, for now it is enough to say that while these "experts" may well know more about the pure subject matter than I do, they are not the ones to lead a serious and close in battle against this foe. That, my friends, is a personal matter.

"… the battlefield upon which we must wage this struggle is strewn with millennia of status quo defeatism, centuries of apathy, and decades of techno-hubris – the belief that we can technically engineer our way out of human error."

In summary, our threat analysis revealed a far more complex and lethal adversary than we expected, as well as many vulnerabilities in our defenses. The next step is to determine where and how to counterattack.

Identifying and Defining the Enemy

War planners look for leverage points – locations in time and space where the least force can provide the most impact. This location has been called by many names; Achilles heel, point of least resistance, and the "quick kill zone." Serious war planners know these vital intersections as *centers of gravity*, spots around which other things happen and depend. The vast majority of human errors can be alleviated or avoided altogether with a combination of two factors – *knowledge* and *intent*. If error were truly a sentient being, it would seek to keep you dumb and apathetic on the subject matter that this book addresses. We are not going to let that happen.

A Short History Lesson: 216 BC

On the 2nd of August, 216 BC, the two largest armies in the civilized world stood face to face on an open plain near the mouth of what is now the Ofanto River on Italy's east coast – and the fate of the civilized world hung in the balance.

The Romans held the better ground and had nearly double the troop strength of their adversary. Nearly 80,000 armed men – over 55,000 in the heavily-armed and legendary Roman Legions were arrayed in three bristling lines of attack. Opposing the Roman juggernaut was a far weaker adversary in an inferior tactical position. With the river on one side and the ocean to the rear, an estimated 49,000 Carthaginian forces – mostly mercenaries who did not even speak a common language – prepared for what appeared to be a certain crushing defeat from the Roman sledgehammer.

But Hannibal knew his adversary was commanded by a hot head named Varro, and though a series of maneuvers designed to embarrass the Roman commander, he drew the entire Roman center into an unwise advance.

Less than four hours later – in spite of superior troop strength and advantage of favorable terrain – nearly 60,000 Roman soldiers lay dead or dying on the ground near the village of Cannae – victims of poor decisions born of the common human errors of ego and anger. Perhaps even more important than the errors committed, was the fact that the Carthaginian commander – Hannibal Barca – predicted, induced and leveraged these errors to defeat a far superior force on unfavorable terrain. Therein lies the lessons for us today.

In 216 BC, Hannibal was one of the few commanders in the world that understood the intricacies of human error and how to leverage them to his advantage. Today, that information is available to all who desire it. Over the past two decades, human error research has expanded exponentially. Error causes and effects have been studied and codified to the point of being actionable for behavioral change for all of us – both as individuals and as organizational team players and leaders. Human error is no longer the shadowy, ill-defined foe it once was, yet few have utilized the new discoveries to attack error as a system – an oversight we intend to change inside these covers.

> "... the human being is the strongest part of the safety and performance equation, although a lot of engineers and technology salesmen would tell you differently. Don't believe them."

In the next few chapters, we will undertake a fundamental and aggressive approach to combating the life-taking and resource-draining enemy we lump into the category of "human error." Like Hannibal in his day, the enemy we face is formidable and the terrain not advantageous, but we also understand our enemy, have a sound strategy and a solid plan of attack. No matter what role you play in your organization, or even if you are not a part of any organization – you are a foot soldier in this war.

One final observation and question from the battle of Cannae. Hannibal was able to use Varro's predictable ego as a weapon to achieve his objectives. The real question for our purpose, *is it possible for each of us to do the same in the battle we wage within ourselves?*

Into the Fight With an Army of One

For the past four decades, the cure for the disease of human error has been approached indirectly (if at all) in most of the industrialized world through a variety of efforts that can be broadly lumped into the following five categories:

1. Blame and punish the individual

2. Emphasize leadership (then blame and punish the leader for failures that occur under his or her command)

3. Teamwork strategies to capture or contain errors through better communication

4. Systemic approaches that put multiple layers of protection in place to avoid or respond to errors, and most recently,

5. Cultural approaches that focus on social factors such as trust and fairness to create a so called "just culture"

To some extent all approaches have been effective in the short run, many are still very useful, but even in combination have only been marginally effective in addressing the challenge of human error. Experts cite the randomness and wide variability of human error present even in relatively small groups, as the reason for these meager results. These are compelling arguments made by bright and well meaning people. Every year, millions of dollars are expended to provide education and training on these subjects – and every year we look at the statistics and continue to see less than desirable results. Some small successes are reported, but on the whole, human error remains culpable for nearly 80% of failures in high risk, high reward industries.

Human performance experts continue to struggle to find a broad spectrum antibiotic to cure the human error disease. If we extend this metaphor another step, we can shed some light on why it is not working. Human error is not an infection that can be fought with a broad spectrum antibiotic – it is more like a virus that the immune system must handle from within. Although the antibiotics can help fight other infections, when you're fighting a mutating virus, every battle is eventually an inside job, won or lost at the individual level. As we continue to search for a more effective remedy against human error – the sample size – or "N" – must eventually equal 1.

> "Human error is not an infection that can be fought with a broad spectrum antibiotic – it is more like a virus that the immune system must handle from within."

Uncommon Sense

Over the past few years, I have reviewed a series of personal, business, military and industrial failures from a variety of settings where highly experienced and well trained individuals and teams made the most fundamental of errors with often tragic – and always embarrassing – results. These events were things like aircrews shutting down the wrong engines or inadvertently landing gear up; ships running into each other or aground in broad daylight and known waters, and project teams forgetting the most fundamental communications factors resulting in snatching corporate defeat from the jaws of victory.

In each case, the reason these highly skilled and highly trained professionals did not realize what was going on with their situation, team or equipment is because they first lost awareness of what was going on with *themselves*. Interestingly, and not surprisingly, the organizational response in each case was to create more procedures and training to deal with the tactical operational scenario that caused the failures. While this is an appropriate step in error proofing that specific sequence of events, it does little to address the greater danger of lost **self awareness** – a far more common occurrence than we like to admit, and nearly always a precursor to lost situation awareness (SA).

Self awareness encompasses many complex variables, ranging from an accurate assessment of one's skill and knowledge to the physiological readiness to perceive, interpret, evaluate, plan and act in a tightly coupled, real time environment. Self awareness is not "common sense" as many would have us believe. It is complex stuff – but it is also learnable stuff. To truly cut to the heart of human error, we must pull back the veil with regards to our current and dynamic state of readiness, and engage with the situation to accurately assess ourselves in a real time manner. Developing this "uncommon sense" is the reason the *Global War on Error* was launched. The strategic battle continues to heighten awareness of these key issues across industrial settings and around the globe. But the tactical battle is waged within each of us.

> "… the reason these highly skilled and highly trained professionals did not realize what was going on with their situation, team or equipment is because they first lost awareness of what was going on with themselves."

So as we prepare to take on this most lethal of human enemies, we need to approach the battlefield with a beginner's mindset and a healthy respect for our adversary. Although most of us have lived with our errors for a lifetime without serious damage, make no mistake, errors big and small are already robbing us of time, energy and performance.

In the next chapter, we will look at multiple aspects of our being to evaluate and enhance levels of performance we never dreamed were within our reach.

THREE

Personal Alchemy: Turning Human Performance Lead into Gold

"I long to accomplish a great and noble task; but it is my chief duty to accomplish small tasks as if they were great and noble."
– Helen Keller

Wouldn't it be great to have one of those fusion powered cars that ran on garbage? In the 1985 hit *Back to the Future,* Doc Brown shows up at the end of the film with a "Mr. Fusion" garbage recycling unit on top of his tricked out DeLorean time machine. He arrives from the future to warn Marty McFly and his girlfriend about the risk posed to the world by their as yet unborn children (and set up the sequel, of course). The idea of recycling supposedly worthless materials into useful ones is not new. In fact, in his writings over the past two decades, architect William McDonough[1] has argued for a culture of sustainable design based on the guiding principle of "waste equals food." If we could all view our jobs in this way, he says, we could radically improve our world and transform everything from architectural design to manufacturing.

---

1 William McDonough's book, *Cradle to Cradle* (written with his colleague, Michael Braungart) is a manifesto calling for the transformation of human industry through ecologically intelligent design.

What if these same principles applied to human performance? What if the worst things about us could be transformed into "food" for improvement? If we could pull off this trick, what rapid advancements might be possible in our own lives?

The term *alchemy* comes from both Greek and Latin and can be liberally translated as *first separate and then join together;* or more directly from the Latin, *dissolve and coagulate.* In medieval times, alchemists attempted to discover how to take base metals such as lead and turn them into silver and gold though metallurgical and chemical processes. This is a reasonable metaphor for the way in which we will wage our personal battle against human error, but where the alchemists of old failed to find the way to achieve their objective, modern science has illuminated a path for our success. Let's begin with attacking the myth that human performance is too complex for mere mortals to understand.

> "What if the worst things about us could be transformed into *food* for improvement?"

Mihaly Csikszenmihalyi, (whom we will refer to as "Professor C" for obvious reasons) Senior Fulbright Fellow and former Chair of the Department of Psychology at the University of Chicago, has made a career out of studying optimal performance. In his book, *Flow: The Psychology of Optimal Experience,* he explains how certain individuals are able to make huge, non-linear leaps in their performance. We will lean heavily on Professor C in this chapter, beginning with his thoughts on human complexity.

> Complexity is the result of two broad psychological processes: *differentiation* and *integration*. Differentiation implies a movement towards uniqueness ... integration refers to its opposite: a union with other people, ideas and entities ... Complexity is often thought to have a negative meaning, synonymous with difficulty or confusion. That may be true, but only if we equate it with differentiation alone. Complexity also involves a second dimension – the integration of autonomous parts ... A complex self is one that succeeds in combining these opposite tendencies.[2]

So our first insight is that our complexity is an advantage, not an obstacle. Before we can turn anything into the gold of high performance, we first need to find the lead of personal error and missed opportunity. In step one we need to indentify and separate out our error prone activities (find the lead

---

[2] Csikszenmihalyi, Mihaly. Flow: *The Psychology of Optimal Experience*. p. 41

through differentiation) and then reintegrate heightened awareness and countermeasures into our daily performance (create the gold through integration).

In this chapter we begin to define the means for each of us to evaluate our performance with a much finer discrimination than previously possible. Armed with this new awareness, we can escape the crushing grip of mediocrity by finding areas that need improvement and applying new levels of awareness for self directed improvement. But this process offers far more than escaping mediocrity. Once free of the shackles of our own avoidable errors, a whole new horizon of performance beckons.

> "So our first insight is that our complexity is an advantage, not an obstacle."

Professor C refers to this state of excellence as *flow*, a state of performance where "thoughts, intentions, feelings and all the senses are focused on the same goal (and) experience is in harmony." I know this sounds a bit New Age, but I assure you that it is not. I am from Colorado Springs not from Boulder (an inside Colorado joke). The knowledge we will provide and the process we will outline in the next few chapters will give you all you need to prove it to yourself. The information provided allows you to *apply* these concepts – not just think about them.

By examining our current behavior to identify error patterns, discovering improvement opportunities and then reintegrating a new set of knowledge and skills, you will learn how to achieve personal mastery over your unique errors. For some, this simple process may seem difficult to accept, especially for those who have been exposed to dozens of so-called *human factors* or *personal improvement* programs in the past.

Do not underestimate the power of *you* armed with a science-based and evidence-based process to remove self-imposed obstacles to performance and unleash your full potential. This approach has already been life and career changing for many, and it can be for you. Here are a few reasons why it works.

First, the key to successful change is to get you to view yourself as a unique individual. From this point of view, it becomes a challenge of understanding what drives your performance – both positive and negative. Typically this is the exclusive realm of the behavioral scientist. However, it is far easier to teach you some rudimentary behavioral science skills than it will ever be to get a competent behavioral scientist to study you as an individual. In the past, those who wished to embark on a self improvement program attended some kind of workshop or hit the bookstore or the library and started reading. You might find some excellent insights and studies on human error from either of these approaches – in fact there are hundreds of them in professional literature – but what you will not find on the shelves of any library is a study on **you**. Life provides us all the free performance lessons we need to create that study, and it may be the best possible use of your time if you are seriously interested in improving. The problem is most of us don't know how to structure or evaluate our experiences and daily behaviors as learning experiences.

> "Do not underestimate the power of you armed with a science-based and evidence-based process to remove self-imposed obstacles to performance and unleash your full potential."

Even if we are fortunate enough to already possess this gift of reflective and accurate self assessment, we probably have no process for rigorously collecting and analyzing our performance to see if the changes we are making are having the desired result. Nor do we have a systemic process for creating specific performance interventions or testing and refining them for maximum impact.

Finally, the blue threat empowered accountability process is both uplifting and refining. In the final section of this book, you will find one example in the *Blue Threat Proverbs* – a series of insights collected over a decade of research into human error control.

Blue Threat Proverb 17 states that **self improvement defies gravity** and reads as follows:

> There comes a point in every improvement effort where we begin to see the results of our efforts. From that point forward, what was once an uphill climb – laborious effort for no apparent gain – becomes worth the time and effort, and eventually effortless and nearly automatic behavior. Indy race car driver Danica Patrick explains, "I really had this obsession to keep getting better. I got hooked on the improvement, and the gains that can be made, and the satisfaction that comes from it." This crucial point – the apex of the improvement effort where gains become apparent – is where permanent change becomes a serious reality. Manage this correctly, and you will achieve the "normalization of excellence" where further improvement fuels itself.

The process outlined in the next few chapters is well within the grasp of anyone with a sincere desire to improve. We will guide you every step of the way.

One Missing Piece of the Puzzle: Perseverance

This is where you get to make another choice. This book will provide you the tools you need to begin this life changing process, except one – the personal will to begin and stay with the process long enough to see results. When looking for the best examples of perseverance, one cannot help but run into the name Cal Ripken, the legendary Iron Man of the Baltimore Orioles. Most baseball fans remember his last game, nationally televised with great fanfare. But to understand the simple elegance of this world class athlete, we need to go back to the first game.

*"... what you will not find on the shelves of any library is a study on **you**. Life provides us all the free performance lessons we need to create that study, and it may be the best possible use of your time if you are seriously interested in improving."*

Small Victories Lead to Big Improvements[3]

Chewing sunflower seeds and sitting on the bench, for the first time in his life, was not quite what Cal Ripken, Jr. had in mind when he achieved his goal of being called up to the majors. Day after day he weighed his dismal odds of breaking into the lineup as he watched more experienced and talented major league players. He knew that even though his father was a major league coach, his name alone would not give him an advantage. If anything, he would have to prove himself even more than the others. He had a strong will and work ethic but realized the improbability of achieving greatness in one giant step. To minimize his errors and maximize his chances of success, he challenged himself to two simple objectives: play well and play every day. The objectives were simple and not mutually exclusive. If he didn't play well on each pitch, he would *not* play every day. He pursued his objectives with passion, integrity, clarity, and resilience when the inevitable mistakes did occur. The small victories that he allowed himself to win every day along with his determination and perseverance advanced his career steadily forward. Remaining in the lineup and showing up for work every day earned him the nickname "The Iron Man." He played 2,131 consecutive games. With

---

[3] This short analysis courtesy of Convergent Performance's Take2 For You™ program

his characteristic self-effacing style, he admitted that he didn't possess extraordinary talent, a bionic body, or a burning desire for the spotlight. What he did was show up and honor the game of baseball by playing as well as he could and as often as he could – every day. By focusing on two simple objectives, he eliminated the overwhelming mental chaos and personal pressures that so often lead to confusion and errors.

Henry Ward Beecher succinctly stated, "The difference between perseverance and obstinacy is that one comes from a strong *will*, and the other from a strong *won't*." As you review this new approach to personal accountability and error control, *will you* or *won't you* have the staying power to see the change you desire?

> "… while education and training programs teach us how to do many things *right*, they do not adequately instruct us on how *not to do them wrong*."

The real challenge in implementing this empowered accountability program will come for most individuals within the first few days of implementation, when apathy creeps back in, and you will begin to revert to old habits of behavior. This is a negative performance pattern in and of itself and can be addressed inside your improvement effort. In the pages that follow, you will learn the I CAN™ process (Identify, Categorize, Analyze, and Neutralize) to identify and track it. Expect complacency and pushback, plan for it, counter it and continue the process. Your old habit patterns want to hold onto you. They are powerful and persuasive; however, if you can reach the point where "gains become apparent" the rest is easy – and incredibly satisfying.

In summarizing our basic path, Sir Edmund Hillary, the first European to scale Mount Everest, said it best. "It is not the mountain we conquer, but ourselves."[4]

Why do we need to conquer ourselves? Most of us are doing fine already. Or are we?

Why "Good Enough" Really Isn't

To understand why "good enough" really isn't good enough, we need to challenge a couple of deeply held perceptions. The first is that our formal

---

4   Found at http://thinkexist.com/quotation/it_is_not_the_mountain_we_conquer_but_ourselves/10675.html

education and technical training provides us with all we need to achieve success in life. It does not, not by a long shot. There are two reasons for this. The first is that while education and training programs teach us how to do many things *right*, they do not adequately instruct us on how *not to do them wrong*. Although this sounds like an apparent oxymoron, it is not. The second reason that our formal education and technical training falls short of guaranteed success, is that once we achieve a comfortable level in life – we often have little incentive to improve. Almost by definition and design, this often results in apathy and complacency, a phenomenon that actually gets *worse* with greater experience. More on the myth of *experience = wisdom* later.

A Shaky Alliance

Most of us live and work in a world where safety, security and some guaranteed measure of success is primarily provided by others. Even those of us who fly airplanes, fight fires or work in other so-called high risk industries are surrounded by devices, processes, and procedures that have been developed and refined over decades to keep us safe and secure while we go about working and playing in our day to day lives. The world seems stable, so our situational awareness grows dull, and we lose our respect for things that can bite. We trust that the world will stay tame – as it always has for us up to this point. This is a shaky alliance at best, but one we grow increasingly reliant upon as we gradually lose our edge. When it goes bad, it goes bad quickly, ends badly and usually leaves a lost career, broken family or humbling epitaph.

> "The world seems stable, so our situational awareness grows dull, and we lose our respect for things that can bite."

For those of us who work and play in lower risk environments, the problem is even worse. We become so far removed from the mental possibility of having to perform at our best – we can't comprehend that danger lurks nearby. We text as we drive, ignore dark corners of the parking lots, and allow our skills and awareness to atrophy as if every tomorrow is guaranteed.

No tomorrow is guaranteed.

Over the past few years, I have reviewed more than a few tragic endings where good men and women were overwhelmed by conditions they should have been able to handle. Out of respect for their memories, I will not go into further detail here. It is sufficient to say, that they had the training and technology to handle the situations they were put in, but when the world turned on them, they did not respond with their best – or what should have been their best based on their training and experience – and they died ingloriously. In many cases, they also took others with them.

To put a somewhat finer grained analysis to this line of thinking, I believe many of us have lost the distinction between *accuracy* (good enough to get by) and *precision* (as good as I can be in this situation). Or perhaps better said, we have lost sight that precision is important in life – or worth the effort. Or maybe, in a world where competition is devalued and every kid in Little League gets a trophy – we never understood the importance or value of staying at the top of our game in the first place.

In truth, striving for precision is seldom critical to either safety or success. *Good enough* is usually good enough. But not always, and the time of reckoning is not of our choosing. The world is not bound by any law to stay stable or safe for us or those we protect. Rogue waves – once thought to be a myth of drunken sailors – exist everywhere in our world. There are times when the alliance will be broken and we will be given **one chance** to respond with our best judgment and our most refined skills.

> "*Good enough* is usually good enough. But not always, and the time of reckoning is not of our choosing."

On the back side of this challenge – we will be judged.

The Performance Evolution Ladder

To help in combating this professional malaise, I developed the *Performance Evolution Ladder*™ (Figure 3.1), a tool to assist individuals and organizations to establish and sustain forward momentum in their improvement efforts. Let's begin with the assumption that the reader is a fully qualified *something* – husband, wife, executive, doctor, lawyer, or whatever. By definition, you have already climbed the ladder past *safety* to *effectiveness*. You are *good enough* to earn a paycheck and to do it safely 999 times out of 1000. It's that .001 that is of concern. In this region, good enough to earn a paycheck may not be good enough to survive.

One way of looking at this challenge is to equate our personal and professional levels of competence and readiness to a marksman shooting at a target (Figure 3.2). If the minimum standards for our profession (marriage, hobby, etc.) require a score of 85, the marksman who shot the pattern on the left of Figure 3.2 is fully qualified with a score of 88. He is accurate enough and therefore good enough. In my old days in the Air Force, we used to have a saying that "if the minimum wasn't good enough, it wouldn't be the minimum." Right? Wrong. Sometimes, "dead wrong."

There are many situations where simply being *fully qualified* (to a minimum standard) is not good enough. Moving back to aviation for an example, let's assume an emergency landing at an unknown field with low fuel, equipment malfunctions, high winds and low cloud ceilings. This is the proverbial situation where you get a single opportunity to perform at your best. Here the need to be both *accurate* and *precise* (right side of Figure 3.2) is required merely to survive the event.

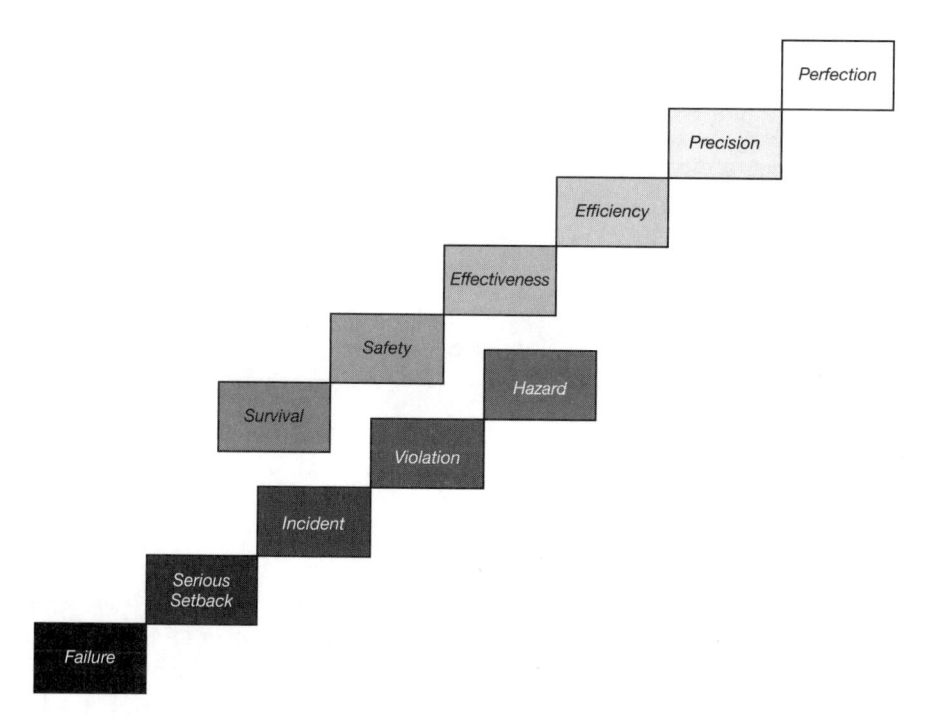

Figure 3.1
The Performance Evolution Ladder[5]

The problem is that many of us who are good enough to get by are not training ourselves to be precise and when we need it, we find that we cannot

---

5   Copyright Tony Kern, 2006

perform at this level. This should come as no surprise and is how so many of our colleagues – our equals – have ended up in actual or metaphorical graveyards with the stain of "human error" attached to their lost lives, lost careers, or lost families. Simply stated, they had not practiced to hit the bullseye because there was no incentive or perceived need to – and when the ultimate challenge came, they were unable to call up the capacity to meet it – and they failed at the task with draconian consequences. What is needed is not only accuracy, but the evolving quest for higher levels of precision that will continually improve that accuracy and simultaneously, your readiness for that once in a lifetime challenge.

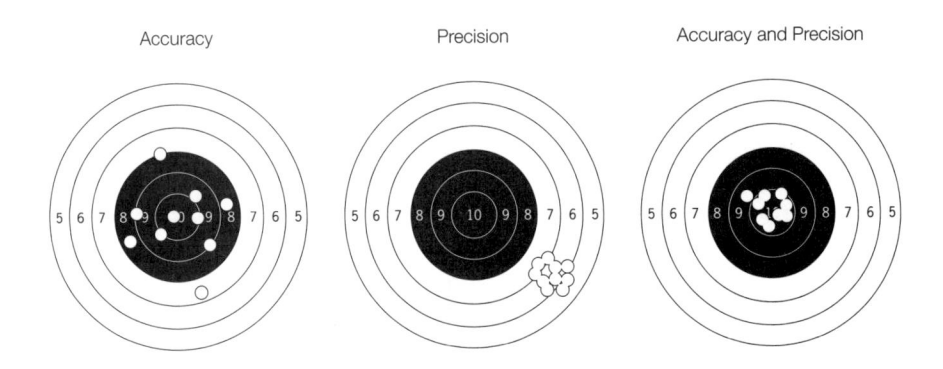

Figure 3.2
The Relationship Between Accuracy and Precision[6]

Aim Small, Miss Small

Wyatt Earp, the famous western lawman from Tombstone, Arizona was once asked about his ability to win gunfights against younger and faster opponents. He replied, "fast is fine, but accuracy is final."[7] My father taught me a similar concept while teaching me to hunt and shoot a rifle. "Aim small, miss small."

The same situation can occur in any aspect of our lives. A family or personal challenge can require the same level of precise modes of thought and action as any vocational trial. But most aspects of our lives do not have score-able targets, or any other way for us to tell if we are merely "good enough" or ap-

---

6   Chapanis, A. Theory and method for analyzing errors in man-machine systems. *Annals of the New York Academy of Science*, 1951, 51, 1179-1203.

7   History Channel, *Famous Lawmen of the West*

proaching our best. In these cases, we must make our own targets, first by picturing what perfection might look like in areas where it is currently undefined, and next by finding levels of refinement against which to measure ourselves.

As we take a look at each level of the *Performance Evolution Ladder*, I encourage you to conduct an open and honest assessment of where you are – and where you need to be – both personally and professionally. You will come to understand that there are many subtle variations in performance, and if you can learn to recognize them, it will open the door to deeper personal insight and levels of achievement. You may also uncover hidden burdens that keep you tied to mediocrity and discover that even *perfection* – at least in small doses – is not out of your reach.

> "… good enough to earn a paycheck may not be good enough to survive."

There is far more to performance than success or failure, winning or losing. These are the *outcomes* of performance, albeit ones we would like to influence in a more positive direction. In order to do so, we will return to our discussion of alchemy, by first breaking performance into small discrete pieces, and then reassembling them into an improved comprehensive whole. This is the beginning of our discussion on how *empowered accountability* really works.

The Road to Hell

The Performance Evolution Ladder has two "staircases." The bottom staircase goes to the basement, or what I commonly call "the road to hell." Please keep in mind as we discuss these elements that the purpose of the discussion is to get you to reflect on your performance more *specifically*, to see and evaluate your day to day activities in greater detail for the purpose of improving.

At the very bottom of the staircase, we see *failure* which refers to some of the darkest outcomes in our lives such as fatal accidents, a divorce, being arrested, fired for cause from a job, or a major health failure. Organizationally, this is the level of fatal mishaps, systemic corruption and business failure.

Just above that, we see *serious setback*. This level might include close calls, broken friendships, and other near misses in our lives. In organizations these might include systems failures that result in injuries, failed programs and projects that significantly impact the bottom line.

Third up from the bottom, we see *incident*. These are events such as unnecessary arguments, traffic tickets, and other minor events that don't go as we intended due to something we did or did not do. In organizations, this level includes safety and security incidents that don't quite reach the level of disastrous outcomes.

Violations are the first level on the performance ladder where there is no overt negative outcome. Violations are any intentional or unintentional failure to comply with official guidance. At the personal level, it includes some of our most frequent crimes such as rolling through stop signs and exceeding speed limits, as well as more serious organizational ethical issues such as "borrowing" supplies from the workplace, or doing prohibited activities at work.

At first, the term *hazard* doesn't seem like a performance level at all, but rather a description of unsafe elements in our world. For our purposes, *hazards* are performance robbing conditions, trends and other elements in our lives that do not rise to the level of a *violation*, but are still ever present latent conditions that rob, inhibit excellence and might bite hard when combined with other environmental factors. On a personal level, this might be inadequate knowledge or training to conduct a specific task, or something more physiological such as fatigue, distraction, or pre-occupation that robs our focus and attention. Organizationally, it includes such elements as substandard training, inadequate supervision or poor quality assurance.

No matter what level of performance we routinely operate at, we remain vulnerable to temptations and let our standards slip, and even those who practice precision on a daily basis operate with known hazards and occasional violations. The trick is not to dwell on the bottom half of the performance ladder, because those who do are operating too close to the edge and will sooner or later feel the pain.

The Stairway to Heaven

The top of the performance ladder is referred to as the "stairway to heaven" for many good reasons, not the least of which is that it provides the means for many to achieve their God given potential and claim the level of success that is within their grasp. As we will see, this upper end of the performance staircase has two distinct performance zones. The first is where most successful people operate every day, surviving and safe, and good enough to earn a living or do whatever it is that they do on a daily basis reasonably well. But it is at the top three steps on the ladder where high achievers find the traction they need to optimize their lives and break away from the pack.

Survival seems like a pretty modest place to begin a hierarchy of success, yet we all live in a world full of capacity to take our last breath from us without much notice in a wide variety of ways. It – along with its big brother *safety* are also unique among all the other levels on the performance ladder because they are the only levels *that move*.

In most circumstances, static layers of readiness will provide for survival and safety, but not always. There are times when the world turns mean without warning, and the requirements for safety and survival change suddenly, a phenomenon we discussed earlier when we explained why good enough really isn't.

Safety is one of those "mom and apple pie" phrases that has lost its potency in our society. It is often equated with words like *timid* and *cautious*. That is unfortunate and misleading, because safety represents our ability to sustain an effort. Without a sustainable effort, great things will never be accomplished by individuals or organizations. For that reason alone, safety needs to be considered in all aspects of our lives. But the flip side of the coin is also true. Overly cautious approaches are not appropriate in all settings. This is one of the reasons why slogans such as "Safety is Paramount" or "Safety is our Goal" are unrealistic. There are two main points here. The first is that we must consider both risk and reward in each of our decisions. The second is that if you are aiming for safety, you are aiming way too low to expect it. To sustain safety, we have to seek a higher level of performance.

> "... we all live in a world full of capacity to take our last breath from us without much notice in a wide variety of ways."

Effectiveness is the level at which we earn our paychecks, practice our hobbies, and in general, satisfactorily conduct our day to day lives. In our professional lives, it usually means we have accomplished some level of training and achieved some sort of formal certification or evaluation of our readiness. Unfortunately, for many, perhaps even most of us – this is where we think we have made it, and we stop improving. And when we stop improving we start decaying. From this point, errors creep in and unchecked will eventually lead to frustration, poor performance and even obsolescence. In our personal lives, it is much the same, except for the formal certification. We become husbands or wives, parents, little league coaches, or elders in our churches. We soldier on, meeting minimum requirements, never realizing there is so much more within our reach. Ironically, it is at the *effectiveness* level – where we think we have made it in the world – that most of us begin to die as learners.

Efficiency is the first stop on the ladder for those who choose to go beyond the minimum requirements. Efficiency simply means a never ending quest to find better ways of doing things with less energy, resources, etc. It is the elimination of wasted effort, time or money. In many companies and organizations, this effort towards efficiency is called *Lean Six Sigma* – a fancy name for a program that provides tools and techniques seeking to eliminate waste and inefficiencies in organizational process.

There are a few in the world that are always trying to refine their performance to the level of constant and replicable *precision*. Often, these individuals have a competitive reason or other job related need to seek this refined level of performance. Olympic athletes in the skill sports (shooters, divers, gymnasts, skaters, etc.) must combine athletic capability with precision to be competitive. Other vocations such as vascular surgeons, microchip makers and genetic engineers, all have various levels of precision as a requirement of their jobs. But, the true master is the individual that seeks precision because it is the next step for them in their personal improvement efforts.

> "Ironically, it is at the *effectiveness* level – where we think we have made it in the world – that most of us begin to die as learners."

In my previous life as a B-1B bomber pilot, I flew with two individuals that exemplified this type of behavior – Craig Wolfenbarger and Tim Bailey. These two guys were the type of pilot who was <u>always</u> correcting towards perfection. Their tolerances were smaller than mine, they saw smaller deviations than the average guy, they were not satisfied with five knots fast or 50 feet off of an assigned altitude. Their radio calls were by the book, every time. They ran their checklists flawlessly. They aimed small and they missed small. It wasn't that I couldn't fly as well as they did, it was just that I *didn't*.

Tim and Wolf had a picture of *perfection* in their minds. They knew what it looked like and they actively sought it. Not obsessively or compulsively – but routinely. It was in the observation of these two men, that the seeds were sown for one of the most misunderstood and powerful self improvement concepts I have discovered in my lifetime – the simple idea that *perfect is possible*.

To test this concept in the real world, I spent some time in what might seem at first to be a rather trivial and bizarre exercise, which I posted during the effort reprinted below.

Small Doses of Perfection
(posted at *Commander's Intent* weblog 29 October, 2008)

I've been talking with a lot people lately about a hot button word – ***perfection***.

Toyota's vaunted quality system claims to seek it, some religions claim it is unattainable, and most of us don't think about it much. In a time stressed world faced with declining resources, "good enough" seems to be a common – if seldom stated – mantra. Who's got time to think about *perfection*?

Fortunately, thinking about improvement is my job, or I probably wouldn't have time either. As one who spends considerable time and money researching and applying new human performance concepts, I know that there is no such thing as the *status quo*. You are either getting better at something – or you are getting worse. And since I don't like to begin anything with a presumption of ineptitude (especially when thinking about my own performance) – I start most days with the attitude that I am good, need to be better, want to be great and should strive for perfection. But how?

"... if you are aiming for safety, you are aiming way too low to expect it."

As I began to seriously engage with the subject, it became clear that the two biggest obstacles to seeking perfection are 1) the inability to picture what it looks like, and 2) the commonly held fallacy that perfection is unattainable. It turns out that neither of these obstacles are insurmountable.

I've started a bit of a strange exercise lately to work on these challenges. To test the idea that "thinking perfect" might improve my performance, I took one of the most mundane activities I do every day – the ten minute drive to and from work – and began a quest to do it *perfectly*. Not just flawlessly – which means error free, but perfectly – which means ... what?

So here was the first challenge – what would a perfect drive to work look like? This seemingly simple question proved not to be so simple.

On Day 1, my view of the perfect drive was pretty straight forward – don't hit the curb when backing out of the driveway, stop at all the stop signs, follow the speed limit, stay in my lane, arrive on time.

By Day 3, I had added a few items: conserve fuel, avoid following too close, time the two traffic lights to minimize delays.

By Day 5, some rather interesting new opportunities began to present themselves. In addition to driving more safely and efficiently, I began to look for opportunities to practice proactive courtesy, spread good will, wave, smile, help someone else start their day a little better. I was beginning to view perfection from a systems angle.

By Day 7, I was looking at parking strategies to minimize the chance of a dinged door and to allow others to get in and out of our parking lot more easily. I had started scouting alternative routes for traffic congestion and bad weather days.

You can see where this is going. My insights on perfection have grown from the little world of my F-250 cab to a part of the larger system, where my random acts of driving and parking courtesy might have some type of ripple effect beyond my previously misperceived sphere of impact or influence. I'm better, and just maybe, the micro-world around me is too.

From my initial starting point on Day 1, I could not see the same performance landscape as I did on Day 3. Likewise on Days 5 and 7, a new horizon of performance revealed itself. The insight was that – at least in my little test – perfection reveals itself in small bits. As one piece of improved performance was achieved, the next beckons. My emerging vision of perfection – much like our physical vision – improves the closer you get to the object of your efforts. What was started as a silly test of a concept, has become effortless efficiency.

There have been other ancillary benefits to this little experiment. Upon arrival at my destination – be that work or home – *I am thinking about how to do things better* and this mindset carries across the home-work threshold. In previous days, I would reflect or project on the worries of the day and often arrive distracted or occasionally even morose. No longer. An odd but nice side effect.

"It wasn't that I couldn't fly as well as they did, it was just that I *didn't*."

If this whole exercise sounds weird – it is because it is weird. *But the point here is that in a resource strapped world, I have found a way to grow without spending a dollar or adding a minute to my schedule.* And along the way I have gained an insight or two through a self discovered truth – the only kind that really works for a skeptic like me.

I've taken to task the twin demons of *complacency* and perceived *competence* – and beaten them back a bit, at least in this small corner of my life arena. It appears that perfection is certainly approachable and perhaps even attainable in small pieces – two minutes today, three tomorrow.

At the completion of this effort, not only did I achieve these intangible results, but had improved the gas efficiency of my vehicle (which I used only for this purpose during the evaluation) by 18%. Simple steps, big results.

Three Performance Zones

So, in summarizing the performance evolution ladder, we see three distinct zones of performance, illustrated in Figure 3.3. The first – and worst – is the *Personal and Organizational Failure Zone*. Here we tread perilously close to the edge of failure and fight daily battles for survival in our professional and personal lives. Life seems to be one near miss after another and it seems just a matter of time before the hammer drops.

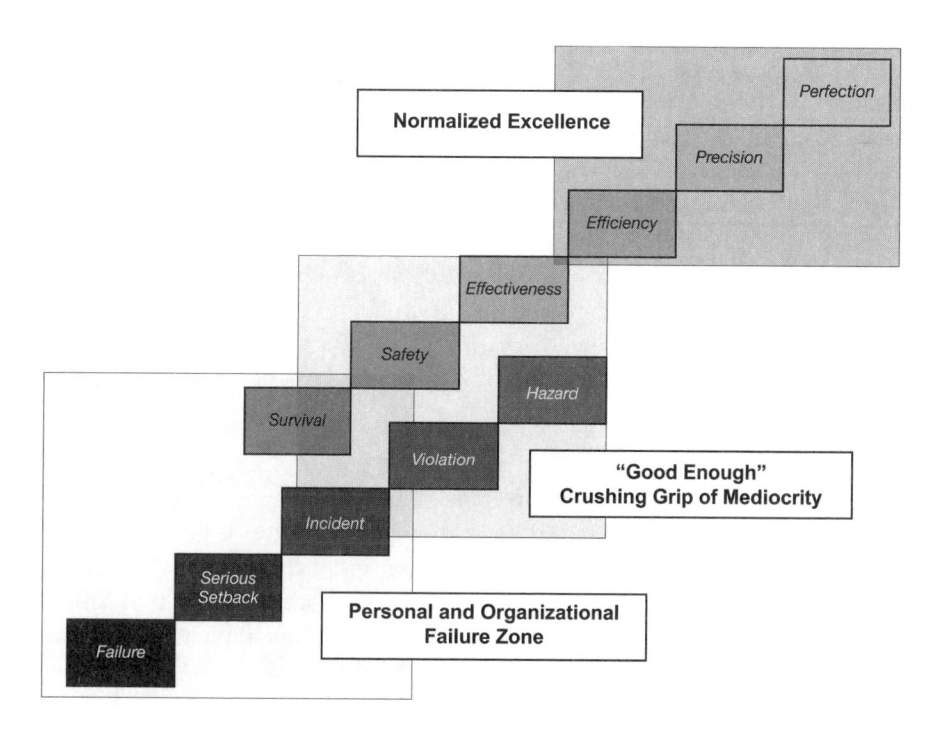

Figure 3.3
Personal and Organizational Performance Zones

One step up, we find ourselves in the middle of the proverbial bell shaped curve with masses of working drones like ourselves, good enough to get by but firmly stuck in the *Crushing Grip of Mediocrity*. Here we may feel safe and secure, but we coexist with some performance robbing and potentially dangerous bedfellows.

For the few who have figured it out, *Normalized Excellence* is the key to both continuous improvement and personal fulfillment. This is the true high performance zone where we aim small, miss small and flirt with occasional perfection. We are aware that by practicing precision and seeking perfection, we are also improving our readiness for the day when the world turns mean and we need to be near perfect just to survive.

Now that we have dissected these performance levels into their individual parts, let's attempt the alchemists' magic of reassembling them into something precious. Descriptions are helpful, but specifics are required to help us determine our starting point. When using the performance ladder, one of the first questions we need to ask is "how can we tell where we are operating at in our day to day activities?" The most simple – and therefore most useful – manner is to look at how you currently make and perceive mistakes in your life. In Figure 3.4, we see a set of observations by a hypothetical individual (in this case a professional pilot) who has evolved from the *Personal and Organizational Failure* zone to *Normalized Excellence*. Initially, he viewed his actions as mistakes only if they had a negative and unconcealable outcome, such as a damaged car or hard landing that was automatically recorded by the aircraft's instrumentation.

"Do you view noncompliance without consequence as a mistake – or a "no harm-no foul" routine activity?"

The reason that concealment is an issue here, is that many who find themselves trapped in this zone, find ways to externalize responsibility for bad outcomes, routinely blaming others or the world for their troubles. The first step towards empowered accountability is the cold slap of reality that comes when you stop making excuses and realize that you personally were responsible for a bad outcome.

In the central zone of the performance ladder we see a significant change in how we view mistakes. We no longer need a negative outcome, but are mature enough to realize that noncompliance or unintended actions rise to the level of concern. In this case, we see that our pilot has grown to realize that speeding through a residential area or violating a regulatory requirement[8] is a mistake that needs recognition and correction.

This stop on the ladder provides an immediate self-assessment opportunity for each reader. Do you view noncompliance without consequence as a mistake – or a "no harm-no foul" routine activity? If you fall into the second group, you may be closer to the failure zone than you realize, and need to read the next chapter thoughtfully.

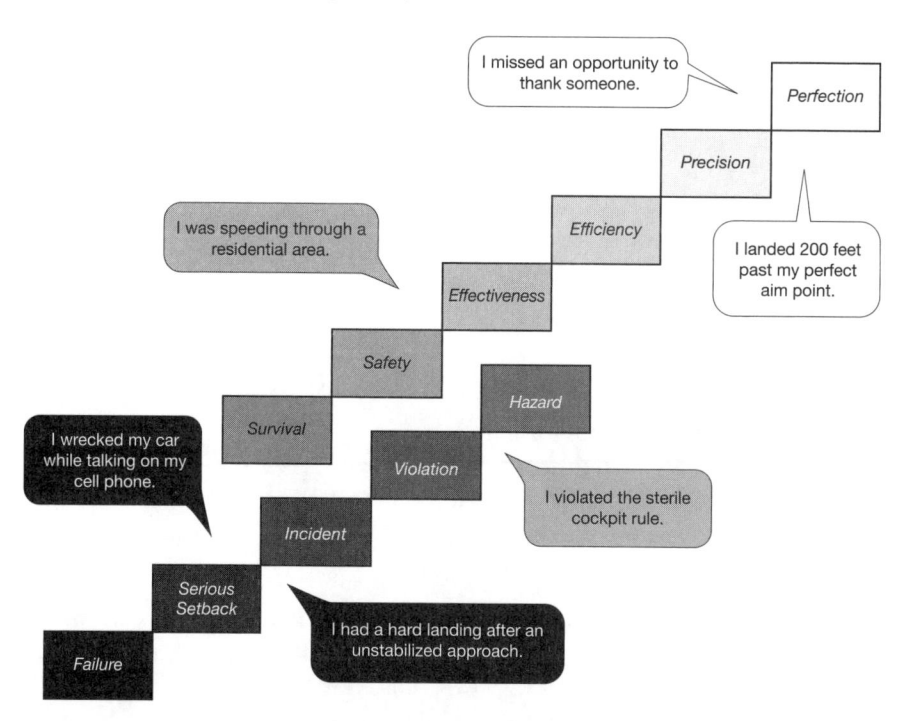

Figure 3.4
Different Types of Mistakes – Different Levels of Consequence
Where are you on the ladder?

In the zone of *Normalized Excellence*, something very interesting and powerful takes place. Our intrepid and fast improving pilot *now recognizes and*

---

8   *Sterile cockpit* is a term used to describe a critical period of time and activity in a flight where no non-mission essential discussion or activity is allowed. This is an FAA regulation that is required during critical phases of flight and ground operations, but is frequently violated, even by professional flight crews.

perceives minor deviations from perfection and missed opportunities as errors that need attention. Once this level of connoisseurship is achieved, continuous learning and improvement becomes a daily byproduct. In addition, this is the level where we begin to fully appreciate the benefits of the empowered accountability approach in our lives. We get better, life gets easier, and we feed on the improvements we are making to fuel our next advance.

The Parallel Escalator[9]

Now that you have the concept of self-defined levels of performance in your mind, picture the *Performance Evolution Ladder* as floors in a hotel, with a slow moving parallel escalator – moving <u>down</u> next to it. We are on that escalator, and unless we keep climbing we will be dragged down to the next level. If we fall off the escalator entirely, we may fall quickly. The world and its demands are ever changing and constant, always challenging us in some way or another. Without an improvement process in place, we will eventually find ourselves operating at lower levels, and eventually obsolete.

The battle is *complacency* and *apathy* versus *action* and *improvement*, and it is a battle we all fight each day whether we recognize it or not. If you don't recognize you are in the fight, you are losing it.

> "The battle is *complacency* and *apathy* versus *action* and *improvement*, and it is a battle we all fight each day whether we recognize it or not. If you don't recognize you are in the fight, you are losing it."

There is an old parable about two wolf brothers who fight inside each of us. One fights to protect existing hunting grounds, arguing that at least they know what is there, and although they may not be able to grow, they can survive. The other wolf argues to expand the hunting grounds, to find more food and grow stronger. The one who wins is the one we feed. Choose to feed the wolf who wants to grow. When you choose not to grow, eventually you lose both the courage and the strength to challenge the unknown. Surrendering to the status quo can be the final defeat.

So how can we avoid this fate and ensure we stay on a positive vector? Ironically, the answer resides in one of the rarest, vital and underappreciated resources in our world today – *negative feedback*. Don't misunderstand this term. There are lots of people who disapprove of our actions and are not

---

9   Thanks to my friend and colleague Andrew O'Connor, of ABC Australia for this concept

shy about verbalizing it, but very few of these yap dogs are either willing or capable of supplying *constructive criticism,* the essential variant of negative feedback that will help us improve.

How Do We Keep Climbing? The Criticality of Negative Feedback

When it comes to personal improvement, people are self regulating systems, for better or worse. A *self regulating system* is an engineering term defined as a "complex system that regulates its own performance."[10] Certainly there are some physiological and legal sideboards that define what we can and can't do as human vessels in a gross sense. For example, after a certain number of hours awake, we will sleep whether we want to or not. Likewise, if we violate the law often enough or in a serious enough fashion, it is highly likely someone with a badge will provide some formal controls on our actions. Subsequently, we can reflect on our performance for hours – and sometimes years – from the inside of the Graybar Hotel dressed in a fashionable orange jumpsuit.

For the most part, however, once we reach adulthood we are left alone to work our will on the world and vice versa. Inside these wide borders of acceptable behavior, most of us wander about on the *effectiveness* level of the performance ladder without much motivation or means to achieve forward momentum. There is a very simple reason why.

One of the core principles of self regulating systems is that they all require negative feedback to function properly. The performance problem we all face as human beings should now be coming into a sharper focus. In a world where political correctness reigns supreme and people have become so conflict averse that an honest employee appraisal is nearly illegal, where are we to get the essential constructive criticism required for us to learn and grow as a self regulating system? The answer is obvious and immediately actionable. We must provide it to ourselves.

In Figure 3.5, we see diagrams of self regulating systems representing three feedback conditions. In each illustration, the highest level of performance is represented by the star in the middle of the scale at the bottom; any movement left or right of that spot represents declining performance. In each of our three cases, the black ball begins at this high performance state and begins to move – or deviate.

On the left, we see a situation where an individual receives *no feedback* and therefore is unaware that they have drifted away from a more desirable state

---

10   Dictionary of Sustainable Management.

of performance. Since no one says his/her effort is not good enough, this individual is free to drift about inside the lines of acceptable behavior, invisibly chained to various degrees of mediocrity and the status quo. But it could be worse.

In the center, we see an individual that receives *only positive feedback*, perhaps from a boss or colleague whose only management style is that of a cheerleader. "Keep up the good work!" they say. "You are all doing a great job!" Even when you aren't. Or perhaps we follow the guidance of self-help gurus who tell us to continuously recite positive affirmations like "I deserve to be successful," or "I am gifted." In the absence of a reality check, positive feedback can actually propel you further and faster from a high performance state. But at least we feel better about ourselves, so we've got that going for us.

| No Feedback | Positive Feedback | Negative Feedback |

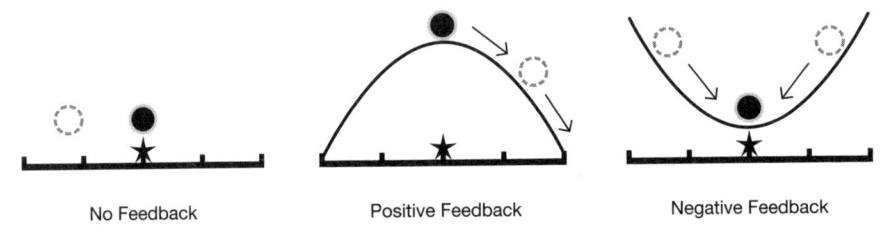

Figure 3.5
Neutral, Positive and Negative Feedback in Self Regulating Systems

Negative feedback systems, illustrated by the diagram on the right, provide clear and actionable information when deviations occur, thus providing both motivation and direction back to the desired state of performance. Much like a pilot who follows his instruments to safely land on a very narrow ribbon of concrete through dense cloud cover, being able to see and correct personal and professional course deviations in real time is vital to reaching our goals. Not only are these vital cues mostly absent in our daily lives, our "happy face" culture of conflict aversion makes it nearly impossible to expect them from others even if we ask. It's simply too impolite.

Now that we (1) see the essential nature of negative feedback and (2) realize the only reliable source is from ourselves, we are ready to move on to the final critical point. The key to a lifetime of continuous improvement is to *routinely and progressively redefine the negative feedback we provide to our-*

selves towards higher levels of performance. We do this by redefining what constitutes an "error." Let's take a look at a simple example from our home life to see how this might work.

Suppose we want to be a better spouse or partner to our significant other. We might begin by responding to the *external* negative feedback we are probably already getting. In my case, this is as simple as putting the TV remote back where it belongs and tossing my dirty clothes in the hamper; both of which I have oddly resisted doing for the past 22 years. Once a conscious choice is made to correct these conditions, we apply error control measures (identified later in this book) to bring the deviations into alignment with our desired state. But when the external feedback stops, what then?

After conquering this hilltop, we simply ask ourselves what might make us even *better*. Perhaps we decide that the next step is to actually listen to what our partner is talking about in an active and attentive manner. Once we have made this commitment (secretly to ourselves), we observe ourselves and when we fail to perform at this level, we *view it as an error* and work our corrective processes again. This performance evolution can be repeated with ever greater refinements in any area of our lives. All the lessons are free and the process is relatively simple. So let's look at a short list of how we can change our perceptions of what constitutes an error to provide the progressive constructive criticism we need to grow.

Error Refinement Categories

Starting at the bottom of the performance ladder and proceeding upward, we see the gradual redefinition of error, all designed to provide fuel to improve the self regulating system that is you. As you progress towards normalized excellence, you will see a shift from Type 1, 2, 3 and 4 errors to Type 5 and 6. This is one of several ways we will measure our forward progress.

Type 1 Error: Your action (or inaction) resulted in a negative outcome that impacted you personally.

> *Example:* You rolled through a stop sign, got busted and received a $75 ticket.

Type 2 Error: Your action (or inaction) resulted in a negative outcome that impacted someone else.

> *Example:* You failed to pass on a customer's message to a coworker and the customer called back angry at them for not responding.

Type 3 Error: Close call. There was no negative outcome, but something bad <u>could</u> have happened to you or someone else had the situation been slightly different.

Example. While driving on a slippery road, you momentarily lost control but regained it before any damage occurred.

Type 4 Error: You violated existing guidance, but nothing happened as a result.

Example. You drove 55 mph through a 35 mph residential area but were not caught.

Type 5 Error: You missed an opportunity to help yourself or someone else to benefit from a situation.

Example. You failed to recognize and publicly thank a coworker who helped on a project.

Type 6 Error: You performed well with a successful outcome but not as well as you could have.

Example. Against all odds, your project team successfully landed the new multi-million dollar contract, but you realize there were a few things you could have done better.

Of course, in order to make any of this work, we must be willing to identify, and if need be, create our own measures of higher performance through self-defined models of excellence.

Picturing Perfect

There are many reasons why modeling excellence makes perfect sense for an individual or an organization. Here are just a few.

A model of self-directed excellence allows for self-directed learning in programs that often lean too heavily on instructors or computers to deliver content. It also perpetuates legitimate self-assessment in individuals against a self-defined set of standards.

Models allow high achievers to go beyond what is often the standard benchmark (where many times we simply try to insure *minimum* organizational standards are met). The British educational philosopher C.S. Lewis points out that high achievers often raise the standards of an entire organization through the simple yet powerful force of their daily example.

Models accommodate individual states of readiness, learning styles and cultural differences. Because models encourage self-assessment and self-directed learning, individuals will naturally select modes of learning that are conducive to their own level of preparation and learning style.

An Organizational Perspective

People are only as courageous and committed as they are convinced. The concept of performance evolution and idealization of expertise brings together three of the most important management revolutions in the past 30 years. Edward Demming's *Total Quality Management* movement told us that all levels of an organization are instrumental for high efficiency, as well as employee and customer satisfaction. Tom Peters' *In Search of Excellence* pointed out the need for leadership – including self leadership – to powerfully deliver a shared vision of excellence. More recently, Peter Senge's, *The Fifth Discipline* taught us that in order to create a true learning organization, we need to engage individuals in pursuits of personal mastery, utilize systems thinking, and insure everyone is aware of the interrelationships of change caused by their own personal improvement efforts and actions. Models of excellence like the *Performance Evolution Ladder* illustrate the values of self-directed improvement to every level of an organization by communicating a common notion of excellence, and visually represent the interrelationships between levels of performance for individuals, teams and entire organizations.

Who Has the Time?

Of course most everyone would like to improve, but in today's fast paced world, there are not many ticks of the clock not already accounted for or claimed by someone else. One of the most important lessons and best kept secrets of serious self improvement is that it *gives time back*. Through greater efficiency, focus and fewer mistakes, you will make more of each hour. Not immediately, but eventually, and in abundance.

In tactical military planning, most problems of maneuver can be reduced to discussions of *time* and *space*, massing force at a precise point and moment of your greatest strength and the enemy's most vulnerable weakness. Professionals call this the *decisive point* and if it can be achieved, victory is nearly assured even with a smaller force against a larger one. In the *War on Error*, we have to change this equation just a bit.

Instead of using the variables of *time* and *space*, we will use *time* and *effort*. Because the human error enemy will always be near, we have to fight a war of attrition over time instead of a war of annihilation at a single decisive point. A war of attrition is a conflict where you inflict constant casualties on the enemy until they no longer are a viable force. In point of fact, it is precisely the kind of war waged *by error against us*, slowly bleeding our potential until we lose our dreams, and sometimes our will to pursue them at all.

This story captures the essence and critical importance of understanding the concepts of *time* and *effort*. It has been published many times and I was not able to ascertain the name of the original author, but the message is clear.

The Daffodil Garden[11]

Several times my daughter had telephoned to say, "Mother, you must come see the daffodils before they are over." I wanted to go, but it was a two-hour drive from Laguna to Lake Arrowhead. "I will come next Tuesday," I promised, a little reluctantly, on her third call. Next Tuesday dawned cold and rainy. Still, I had promised, and so I drove there. When I finally walked into Carolyn's house and hugged and greeted my grandchildren, I said, "Forget the daffodils, Carolyn! The road is invisible in the clouds and fog, and there is nothing in the world except you and these children that I want to see bad enough to drive another inch!" My daughter smiled calmly and said, "We drive in this all the time, Mother." "Well, you won't get me back on the road until it clears, and then I'm heading for home!" I assured her.

"I was hoping you'd take me over to the garage to pick up my car." "How far will we have to drive?" "Just a few blocks," Carolyn said. "I'll drive. I'm used to this." After several minutes, I had to ask, "Where are we going? This isn't the way to the garage!" "We're going to my garage the long way," Carolyn smiled, "by way of the daffodils." "Carolyn," I said sternly, "please turn around." "It's all right, Mother, I promise. You will never forgive yourself if you miss this experience." After about twenty minutes, we turned onto a small gravel road and I saw a small church. On the far side of the church, I saw a hand-lettered sign that read, "Daffodil Garden." We got out of the car and each took a child's hand, and I followed Carolyn down the path. Then, we turned a corner of the path, and I looked up and gasped. Before me lay the most glorious sight. It looked as though someone had taken a great vat of gold and poured it down over the mountain peak and slopes. The flowers were planted in majestic, swirling patterns – great ribbons and swaths of deep orange, white,

---

10 Author unknown, found at http://www.bankofideas.com.au/Stories/fables.html

lemon, yellow, salmon pink, saffron, and butter yellow. Each different-colored variety was planted as a group so that it swirled and flowed like its own river with its own unique hue. There were five acres of flowers. "But who has done this?" I asked Carolyn.

"It's just one woman," Carolyn answered. "She lives on the property. That's her home." Carolyn pointed to a well kept A-frame house that looked small and modest in the midst of all that glory. We walked up to the house. On the patio, we saw a poster. "Answers to the Questions I Know You are Asking" was the headline. The first answer was a simple one, "50,000 bulbs," it read. The second answer was, "One at a time, by one woman. Two hands, two feet, and very little brain." The third answer was, "Began in 1958." There it was, *The Daffodil Principle*. For me, that moment was a life-changing experience.

I thought of this woman whom I had never met, who, more than forty years before, had begun – one bulb at a time – to bring her vision of beauty and joy to an obscure mountain top. Still, just planting one bulb at a time, year after year, had changed the world. This unknown woman had forever changed the world in which she lived. She had created something of ineffable (indescribable) magnificence, beauty, and inspiration.

The principle her daffodil garden taught is one of the greatest principles of celebration. That is, learning to move toward our goals and desires one step at a time – often just one baby-step at a time – and learning to love the doing, learning to use the accumulation of time. When we multiply tiny pieces of time with small increments of daily effort, we too will find we can accomplish magnificent things. We can change the world.

"It makes me sad in a way," I admitted to Carolyn. "What might I have accomplished if I had thought of a wonderful goal thirty-five or forty years ago and had worked away at it 'one bulb at a time' through all those years. Just think what I might have been able to achieve!"

My daughter summed up the message of the day in her usual direct way. "Start tomorrow," she said.

In our next chapter, we will investigate one of the most basic elements of performance; one we often take for granted but seldom achieve.

Part Two

Making It Happen: Practical Error Control in Action

"Nothing splendid has ever been achieved except by those who dared believe that something inside them was superior to circumstances."

– Bruce Barton

FOUR

The Myth of Compliance

"No Rules – Just Right"
Motto of the Outback Steakhouse

Let's face facts – compliance through enforcement doesn't work. At least not by itself or as a primary strategy to get people to follow rules. It certainly helps to have someone looking for violators, but there are strong social forces at play in this high stakes game that make enforcement-only programs doomed to fail. I think it begins with a general lack of self control, a virtue which is seldom talked about and rarely encouraged.

I'm not sure when it started, but there is a strong undercurrent of "wink and nod" pseudo-compliance going on in our world. This line of thinking follows two threads. The first one goes something like this – *"Yes, we have rules, but they are overly restrictive and no one really follows them, especially not the best of us."* The second thread is simply a denial of the problem, as in *"We don't have a noncompliance issue here because we haven't had any negative outcomes as a result."*

I refer to these as the *illusion* and *delusion* of compliance, so let me set the record straight on two points. First, noncompliance is rampant in our world – in our everyday lives (exceeding the speed limit) to our business activities (using the work computer for personal purposes[1]) to the most hazardous professional activities, such as with the professional first responders in this tragic story below.[2]

> Four firefighters were training on their newly purchased 95-foot midmount truck. The firefighters were standing in the bucket which was raised to the roof of an 8-story dormitory building at a local college. The bucket became stuck on the concrete parapet wall at the top of the building. During attempts to free the bucket, the top edge of the parapet wall gave way and the aerial ladder sprung back from the top of the building, and then it began to whip violently back and forth. Two of the four firefighters standing in the bucket were ejected from the platform by the motion and fell approximately 83 feet to the ground where they died from "blunt force injuries."

The NIOSH report concluded:

- Ensure firefighters are fully familiar with new equipment before training under "high risk scenarios."
- Ensure fall protection is used whenever firefighters and other personnel are working in elevated aerial platforms.
- Follow standard operating procedures for training, including the designation of a safety officer.

Put simply, if they had followed their own rules, they would be alive today. Perhaps the fact that this was "just a training exercise" or "equipment familiarization" mission dulled the normally sharp risk awareness of these first responders.

The second main point is that in spite of the cultural icon of the rogue rule breaker as *hip*, intentional acts of noncompliance are usually not the act of a cool *Top Gun* type who has moved beyond the need for rules. They are far more often the act of a child starved for attention or ego gratification.

It's not always as simple as that either. Even *intentional and willful* noncompliance has a wide variety of internal and external drivers that may or may not be recognizable or completely under the control of the individual or the organization.

---

1 An employee with a major retail store told me that on "Black Friday" – the day after Thanksgiving in 2008 – over 60% of their online sales came from computer email addresses that appeared to be sent from the buyers' work email

2 Found at http://www.cdc.gov/niosh/fire/reports/face200906.html and http://www.tylerpaper.com/apps/pbcs.dll/article?AID=/20090717/NEWS01/907170335

It is not enough to say we need to change the way we think and act. In order for us to break out of a mindset that is routinely accepted and culturally driven, we have to break it down to show both *why* and *how* a cultural revival of compliance is possible and necessary. Let's begin with a look at why even in western countries founded on the rule of law, normal people don't follow the rules.

What can be more simple than following the rules? Even the word gurus at Webster's think it's pretty straight forward.

non·com·pli·ance *n. Failure or refusal to comply*

Compliance is more complex than we think, and the oft used phrase "simple compliance" is a true oxymoron. Part of the problem is that in spite of the apparent simplicity of the concept, many in our 21st century society have never had much use for "the rules" – and for perfectly logical reasons.

The Ethics of Compliance

What if from an early age, you were taught that rule breaking – lying and cheating for example – was a competitive advantage? What if high achieving children learned early on that rules were often unfair and unjust? What if our value system made rule breaking a part of daily life? What then?

In his book *Winners Never Cheat*, Jon Huntsman argues that we need to take the issue of "shared values" much more seriously today than in any time in our history. He says this is especially true as we bridge the chasm between the classroom and the boardroom. "Values provide us with ethical water wings whose deployment are as critical in today's wave tossed corporate boardrooms as they were in yesterday's classroom."[3]

> "What if from an early age, you were taught that rule breaking – lying and cheating for example – was a competitive advantage?"

We know from an early analysis of the causes of the financial meltdown in 2008–2009 that we lack a set of shared values in the boardroom of some of the world's largest companies (as well as the government agencies who supposedly supervise their activities). Can we look to the next generation for improvement?

---

3   Huntsman, Jon. *Winners Never Cheat: Even in Difficult Times.* p. 37

When the Josephson Institute of Ethics released its *2008 Report Card on the Ethics of American Youth*,[4] the evidence was clear that some of our basic beliefs about rule breaking are <u>way</u> off the mark. The survey of nearly 30,000 high school students nationwide found that 64 percent had cheated on a test in the past year (up from 60 percent two years earlier) and 38 percent had cheated more than once. So what? Lots of kids cheat in school. What does that have to do with rule breaking by adults at home or in the workplace? Let's look a bit deeper at some issues with clear implications for future workplace behaviors.

- Nearly half (42 percent) said that they sometimes lie to save money.
- More than one in three boys (35 percent) and one-fourth of the girls (26 percent) – a total of 30 percent overall – admitted stealing from a store within the past year.
- Twenty-three percent said they stole something from a parent or other relative and 20 percent confessed they stole something from a friend.
- Nearly six out of ten agreed that "In the real world, successful people do what they have to do to win, even if others consider it cheating."

The data from the Josephson Institute have shown a progressive decline in ethical behavior and beliefs in American teens over the past decade. Many of the early respondents from the 1990s are the backbone of <u>today's</u> workforce. Did these beliefs somehow vanish when they entered adulthood? It is doubtful.

Colleen Carroll Campbell, an author, columnist and former presidential speechwriter who researches and writes on ethical issues in America, hits on what may be the most critical issue of all in the Josephson Institute survey data.

Despite their dishonesty, the students had a high view of their own ethics. More than nine in 10 said they were "satisfied with my own ethics and character," and nearly eight in 10 affirmed that, "When it comes to doing what is right, I am better than most people I know."

---

4 Following a benchmark survey in 1992, Josephson Institute has conducted a national survey of the ethics of American youth every two years. Data is gathered through a national sample of public and private high schools. Surveys conducted in 2008 had 29,760 respondents.

Now that is downright scary.

Campbell believes the cause of this self-centeredness may impact entire generations of current and future adults.

> It's significant that young Americans vulnerable to narcissism were raised in the heyday of the self-esteem movement, when well-meaning baby boomer parents, teachers and media gurus incessantly urged them to "love yourself first," "let nothing come between you and your dreams" and believe that "you're the best." Rather than stoking healthy self-confidence, such messages may have dampened work ethic while fueling unrealistic expectations and inflated egos. Neither is much use in the real world, where believing in yourself cannot guarantee success and putting your own immediate desires ahead of all other concerns can be a recipe for disaster in work, love and life.[5]

If noncompliance has roots anchored in self-centeredness, perhaps this aspect of our lives is an *error control center of gravity*, at least for a few of us. If so, we have a target, a place to start.

Corrosive Narcissism

Psychologists Jean Twenge and W. Keith Campbell, the authors of *The Narcissism Epidemic: Living in the Age of Entitlement,* believe we live in an age of "corrosive narcissism" where indulgent vanity feeds a wide variety of our social ills, not the least of which is rampant noncompliance and rule breaking. Narcissism[6] describes the trait of excessive selfishness and self absorption which can lead to a mindset where anything that is done in self interest is deemed acceptable. While it is well beyond the scope of this book to delve into the social ills that underpin these unhealthy trends, forewarned is fore-

"Nearly six out of ten agreed that *In the real world, successful people do what they have to do to win, even if others consider it cheating.*"

---

5 "Challenging America's me-first culture," by Colleen Carol Campbell, found at www.stltoday.com/stltoday/news/columnists.nsf/colleencarrollcampbell/story/A384AD3DCB07FEB2862575AE00810E3E?OpenDocument

6 The term is derived from the Greek myth of *Narcissus*, a handsome Greek youth who rejected the desperate advances of the nymph *Echo*. As punishment, he was doomed to fall in love with his own reflection in a pool of water. Unable to consummate his love, *Narcissus* pined away and changed into a flower that bears his name.

armed. By enhancing our personal and organizational awareness of these attitudes, we no longer see noncompliance as someone else's problem; it is **everyone's** problem.

If everyone is breaking the rules, one initially wonders if perhaps the rules are wrong or perhaps they aren't so important after all. But if everyone is breaking the rules because of *what is in it for them*, compliance becomes more critical than ever to protect ourselves from each other's "me first" ambition and desires. Or said in a less narcissistic way, *to protect others from us*.

Let's stop to ask a couple of important questions. *Could a simple focus on willful compliance be a key to overcoming the epidemic of self-centeredness in our homes and workplace? If we could foster a logical and willful change of heart about routine compliance, could we begin to turn the ethical decline around?* And if the answer to either one of these questions is *"yes,"* then isn't it worth a hard look at a new approach to make this effort?

"Could a simple focus on willful compliance be a key to overcoming the epidemic of self-centeredness in our homes and workplace?"

But how? If our problems are rooted in our very upbringing, this is going to be quite an uphill battle. *Blue Threat Proverb* number 12 states, *Where instinct and intuition fail, intellect must venture.* So let's begin by explaining the basics with the "Rule of Law 101" – why compliance matters.

Why Compliance Matters

Willful compliance brings order from anarchy. When guidance is well thought out and fair, written clearly, explained thoroughly, commonly understood and voluntarily complied with, it streamlines our world into an orderly and predictable efficiency.

Additionally, we must understand that when it comes to basic safety, even a single act of noncompliance can negate multiple layers of protection and thousands of man hours of research, engineering, testing and training. We will use the Figure 4.1 *How individual noncompliance nullifies systemic protection*, to explain this concept.

In most systems and in our daily lives we interoperate with other people and automation, some we see and others we do not. Let's use the example of operating a piece of company equipment. Perhaps it is a computer, a truck, an earthmover, or an aircraft. Regardless of the equipment we operate, we sit at the center of a system designed, engineered, tested and refined by dozens of people over thousands of man hours.

At the outer ring, the government or other regulatory authority apply broad guidance for design, manufacture and use to provide for the public safety and fairness.

Inside these general guidelines, the manufacturer creates the device and provides written guidance in the form of technical manuals or users guides detailing the operating limitations and procedures for using the tool safely and effectively.

At the organizational or company level, we are given more specific guidance on how to safely and effectively operate the tool in the job environment. This is usually where the first true training takes place to provide us with standard operating procedures (SOPs), which are mandatory rules everyone is supposed to follow.

> "The individual chooses to disregard the protections provided for them, and *in a single act of noncompliance, negates the protection of the entire system.*"

Inside these protective layers of "how to" common sense, most organizations have a safety officer or department, who refines this guidance to provide additional protection. In the home and family environment, this is usually one of the parents who establish age appropriate guidelines and rules for the children, which are very similar to corporate SOPs. These safety procedures and training are usually based upon experience, common sense, and relevant data from previous accidents and incidents. The SOPs usually relate specifically to the local workplace environment, job demands and workforce.

At the center of the safety system lies the individual – you and I – theoretically protected from harm and mission failure by all of the work listed in the paragraphs above. But here something odd happens, over and over again across industries, at work and at home. The individual chooses to disregard the protections provided for them, and *in a single act of noncompliance, negates the protection of the entire system.* This decision is represented by the line taking the individual outside of the boxes, where they are truly on their own in providing for safe mission accomplishment.

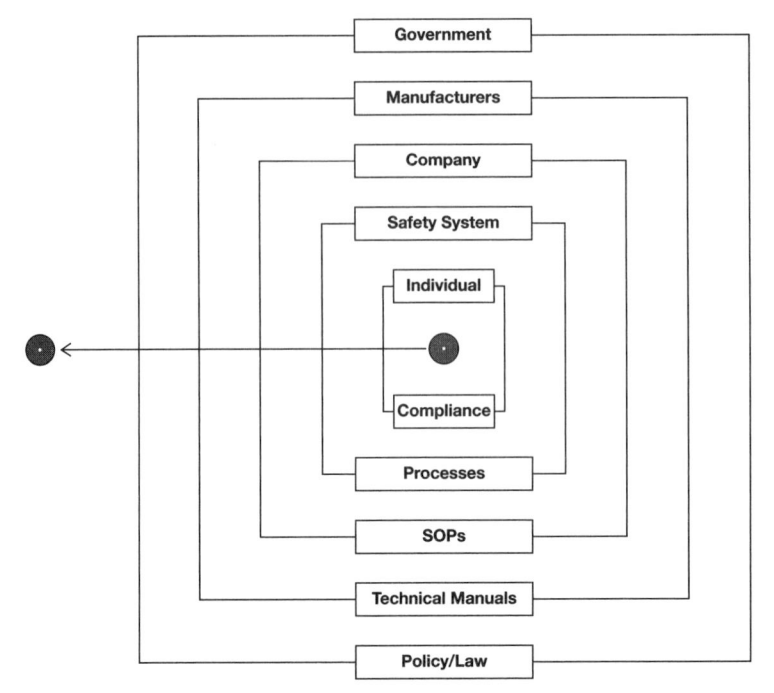

Figure 4.1

How Individual Noncompliance Nullifies Systemic Protection[7]

The Legal Perspective

Speaking of being on your own, I'd like to relate a discussion I had with an attorney from the U.S. Department of Justice a few years back when I was the National Aviation Officer for the U.S. Forest Service, in charge of all the aerial assets for wildland firefighting. Over time, I had become aware of the fact that many of the firefighting pilots were pushing the limits in several procedural areas. No one was purposely reckless, and all of the deviations I was aware of were done in the sacred name of the mission, in this case protecting people and property from the ravages of wildland fires. But I was still concerned about what would happen to these men and women, if during the course of some well intended procedural deviation, an injury or fatality should occur to someone other than themselves.

---

7 Created by Dave Ryan and Bob Agostino, two of the sharpest operational safety minds in the world today.

I asked the attorney, "To what extent will the government represent and protect an individual who is trying to do the right thing but is knowingly outside policy when an accident or incident occurs?"

After clarifying what I meant by "knowingly outside policy" (pushing past technical or operational limits, exceeding aircraft or duty limitations, etc.) the attorney's response was clear and to the point.

"You can tell your people that the U.S. Department of Justice will likely represent them to the extent they did their duty to represent the government. If they were willfully noncompliant and someone got hurt or died as a result, they should not expect the U.S. to defend them, but they should expect the government to potentially *prosecute them for their unlawful acts* (emphasis added)."[8]

I have had similar discussions with legal experts over the years and the answer remains consistent. *If you are outside the lines, you are out there by yourself, even if what you are doing is unofficially condoned or even expected behavior in your organization.* When the lawyers get involved, the best you can expect is for the organization to act in its own self interest. Hopefully, this insight will help us all act in our own self interest by getting back inside the legal and physical protective walls of compliance. Forewarned is forearmed.

> "When the lawyers get involved, the best you can expect is for the organization to act in its own self interest."

Now let's turn our attention to a few of the reasons why people with normally sound judgment stray across the lines of compliance.

Violation Producing Conditions

Violation producing conditions, or VPCs, are situational factors that often lead to noncompliance with technical limits, policy or procedures. In one short, undisciplined step, a single individual can nullify all margins of safety for themselves and those around them while putting the mission at risk. True professionals know how to get the job done inside the lines, and rarely require deviations from technical limits, policy or procedure for mission essential purposes. However, there are several conditions that can lead indi-

---

8   Private discussion notes from conversation with DOJ attorney, June 2001, Washington DC.

viduals to breakdowns of discipline. By increasing our awareness of VPCs, we can protect ourselves and others against a *sudden loss of judgment* (SLOJ) when faced with real time compliance decisions.

Mission Expectation

The perception that the rules must be bent to get the job done.

One of the most difficult challenges for individuals in any field is controlling the delicate balance between *risk* and *mission accomplishment*. Whether we have to make a decision to launch the Space Shuttle or simply trying to make a good judgment call after we have had a couple of beers before we try to make the drive home, we have to sort out the risk-benefit equation. There are a few basic principles to assist us.

- We must recognize that getting the job done is important – it is likely the reason we are doing what we are doing in the first place. However, when we reach a point in our pursuit of the objective where we have to violate the law, policies or procedures to accomplish it, we are in a very dangerous place that often results in loss of three objectives – good judgment, safety <u>and</u> mission accomplishment.
- The first red flag we should notice is the temptation to deviate from approved procedures.
- Should we fall victim to this temptation in the sacred name of the mission, we often see the next step towards a violation occur; *procedural drift* – the redefining of policies or procedures to meet our current need. This often takes the form of pseudo-compliance with the *intent*, but not the letter, of the original policy. Eventually, this VPC will manifest itself in full blown willful noncompliance through the normalization of deviance, if it is not brought under control.

Ego & Power

The belief that the violator has the skill and stature to do the job better outside the boundaries.

This VPC is particularly dangerous because it lives inside most high achievers. Somewhere in our lives, most of us will admit that we have moments where we think we are smarter than the people who wrote the rules. This may or may not be true, but it is a dangerously irrelevant question when it comes to compliance.

Here are a few red flags from one executive coach[9] to warn us when our egos start to get in the way of our common sense.

- You find yourself being defensive about an idea or plan and taking it personally when someone disagrees with your ideas.
- You routinely make a point of showcasing your brilliance, as in "those rules don't apply here because…."
- You view a colleague as a rival and are willing to bend the rules to "one up" them.
- You disagree with someone simply because you did not come up with the idea first.
- You prematurely criticize policies or procedures that get in the way of your goals without considering their value.

Keep in mind that as individual human beings we are limited, and when we continually compare ourselves to others in an attempt at ego gratification, we often end up looking foolish, undignified and unprofessional by our willful noncompliance.

Unlikely Detection

The perception that the violation is unlikely to be detected by anyone in authority.

It has been said that true character only comes to light when no one is watching. Yet, there is little doubt that the ability to "get away with it because no one will ever know" is tempting to even the most disciplined among us. The fallacy of the "no one will know" argument is that the most important person in the equation – **you** – will always know you took a shortcut. Therein lies the problem.

Here are a couple of things to think about:

- If we use *detection* as a decision criterion, we **already** know we are doing something wrong, or at least unacceptable in the eyes of others.

---

9   Maynard Brusman, "Executive Coaching For Leaders Driven by a Big Ego – Four Telltale Signs Your Ego is in Control" found at http://ezinearticles.com/?Executive-Coaching-For-Leaders-Driven-by-a-Big-Ego---Four-Telltale-Signs-Your-Ego-is-in-Control&id=1235275

- If we proceed with an action we know others disapprove of, we are at risk of developing an attraction to the 'forbidden fruit" of noncompliance – the feeling that we are somehow superior to the "rule bound" others. This is extremely dangerous ground.

In the long run, the world has a way of catching up with those of us who think we can evade detection. Either we cut corners until something very bad happens, or we simply fail to reach our potential due to sloppy habits of personal discipline. What happens in Vegas – never really stays there.

Poor Planning

Lack of adequate planning time or depth resulting in "free styling" during execution.

Thorough planning is one of the most recognizable traits of high achievers in all environments. Planning is seldom fun or glamorous. It occurs behind the scenes. There are many reasons people give for not planning: not enough time, don't really need it, won't work for me, it's too constraining, my work is too unpredictable, I'm a creative type, etc. According to many performance experts,[10] these reasons are merely excuses and rationalizations.

The real reason people don't plan is usually one of the following:

- They don't understand the value. People get into a worst practice because they don't know any better. Planning improves performance – period.

- Immediate gratification. People that want to get their payoff now will find it difficult to escape their practice of poor planning. Planning pays off later – procrastination does so now.

- They don't know how. Planning is a skill that is learned; there are good ways to do it, and there are bad ways to do it. Learn how to do it right and make it a permanent life skill.

- They haven't eliminated obstacles to effective planning. Other conflicts may be blocking or undoing the effectiveness of your planning efforts.

---

10 For an excellent overview of poor planning as a "worst practice" log onto *Time Thoughts* at www.timethoughts.com

The best way to escape the practice of poor planning is to make the time, learn how to plan effectively and to do it consistently until it becomes a habit.

Leadership Gap

Leaders who personally practice or are known to condone procedural noncompliance.

Leadership must be ethical at all levels of an organization – but it seldom is. Any organization, including families, that have a leader who practices noncompliance will eventually foster a sub-culture of noncompliance. This evildoer does not necessarily have to be the top dog, but can be anyone in a position of authority who is known by subordinates, friends, family members, peers or supervisors to be less than fully compliant in their day to day activities.

Here are a few things to consider about ethical leadership's role in compliance:

- You cannot be one thing and demand another from your people. The old adage of "do what I say and not what I do" never works for long.
- It is important for leaders at all levels to communicate how they successfully deal with the temptations to deviate in their own daily affairs.
- The recent rash of ethical failures in global business has demonstrated that crime doesn't pay (unless you qualify for a government bailout) and eventually an organization that is noncompliant at the top is prone to failure.

Compliance is more than supervision and quality assurance – it is leading by example.

Poor Role Models

Violations and compromise of standards can often be traced to a single individual who "gets away with it" and therefore encourages others to copy their example.

Role modeling is the strongest form of informal leadership. Yet, it cuts both ways. In 21st century western society, we often find ourselves admiring those who brand themselves as rule busting mavericks. Following those who try to make a name for themselves by flaunting the law, policy or procedural norms is a fool's errand. We get nowhere fast. The only thing dumber than being a groupie for a rule breaker is to lead others into the same trap by being the poor role model they choose to follow.

Here are a couple of guidelines for staying aware of this tendency:

- Be aware of the tendency to follow charismatic noncompliers. They seem to be everywhere these days. Remember, charisma often cloaks incompetence.
- Be aware of your actions in private and in public and act as if someone you care about and who admires you might be watching at all times.
- Identify your problem areas and work on them in public. Go out of your way to recognize an error you have made in front of someone else.
- Be an inspiration. Whether you're a parent, pilot, doctor, teacher, coach, athlete, artist, or anything else, do what you do best – and do it well each time. People you have never met and never will meet are watching you perform. It is up to you to meet their expectations and show them the right way through example.

If you are a bad role model, eventually it will hurt those around you. Turn your life around, and you will be turning around more than one life.[11]

Unique Event

Highly out of the ordinary situations have been shown to significantly increase the likelihood of noncompliance and error in all arenas of human performance.

Nothing tests the strength of an individual's or organization's will to do the right thing like a truly unique event. The temptation to deviate seems to be directly proportional to the weirdness of the situation. For example, many pilots with years of sound judgment have fallen victim to the "air show syndrome" where the opportunity to show off their skills presents itself to someone in the cockpit or on the ground. Their inability to stay disciplined is usually found in the first paragraph of the accident report. Here are a few cautionary thoughts about unique events.

- When confronted by a unique event, recognize it as such and give it the respect it deserves. High risk/low frequency events have been shown to raise the probability of error dramatically.
- On the other end of the spectrum, unless something is truly an *emergency*, don't conveniently label it as such to bypass normal procedures and cautions.

---

11 www.wikihow.com/Be-A-Good-Role-Model

Almost by definition, unique events negate our experience base and intuition. Stay both self-aware and situationally-aware. Approach unique events and circumstances with a beginner's mindset – in control, flexible and ready to roll with the next change and learn from the experience.

Violation Producing Conditions Countermeasures

There are some very specific steps that we can take to get a handle on VPCs before they hijack our decision making. While these countermeasures are primarily designed for organizational use, individuals are wise to read and heed their advice as well.

Clarify Mission Expectations

Emphasize that getting the assigned task done is important, but must be done within existing guidelines or appropriate waiver authority unless emergency conditions exist. The job gets done, but perhaps not right now, or not without help.

Taking a moment to clarify your expectations, especially in a time-compressed or unique situation can prevent a VPC from hijacking someone's usually sound judgment. Be sure to ask all parties involved to ensure they understand your intent and priorities. Emphasize that the mission is important, but must be done within the confines of sound judgment.

Don't Send Mixed Signals

Stand firm on compliance, with others and yourself.

Too many *normalization of deviance* sequences start with individuals who wink at noncompliance if the end result of the violation is successful. Compliance is a bit like a math problem, in order to get the right answer, you need to go back to the point of the error. Take the time to fairly but firmly correct all acts of noncompliance and make sure you are not sending mixed signals.

Create a Fair and Just Culture

Treat all personnel the same when it comes to disciplinary issues related to noncompliance. Honest mistakes, if corrected, lead to a learning organization. Intentional violations – by anyone – cannot be condoned.

If there is a perception that you and your organization do not treat everyone fairly, contempt can creep in insidiously and allow the VPCs to flourish and destroy even the best of compliance cultures. Part of creating a fair and just culture includes treating all personnel or family members the same when it comes to disciplinary issues related to noncompliance. Making exceptions based on personal favorites or in any way that doesn't pass the "sniff test" sets you on a very slippery slope. Think carefully and consciously about how you respond to errors and noncompliance. Keep the process transparent and don't be afraid to talk about how disciplinary decisions are made.

Emphasize Professional Planning

Ensure adequate time, standardization and attention is given to vital planning processes. Shortcuts lead to free styling and eventual violations.

While there is no specific formula that tells us the exact amount of time necessary for us to properly plan an event, we all have a sense of when we've planned inadequately. Trying to do a job or task without adequate time to complete it in accordance with standard operating procedures is asking for trouble. Foster a healthy respect for the power of professional planning by taking planning seriously and setting a minimum planning time for high risk events. Even then, empower yourself and other personnel to follow their instincts if they feel the situation calls for more planning time.

Walk the Talk

Hold yourself to a higher standard. A single act of deviance by any member of an organization can result in loss of respect and compliance from subordinates, peers and supervisors. This is true in families as well, where a parent or sibling can significantly influence behaviors through the force of their own actions.

It may seem obvious to say that even a minor deviation from the straight and narrow road of compliance as a leader has an exponential effect on subordinates' willingness to do the same; but it is a point that cannot be over stated. Hold yourself to a higher standard. A single act of deviance by a formal or informal leader can result in a significant loss of respect from subordinates and peers.

Select Personnel Carefully for Unique Events or Special Missions

Select your most mature, experienced personnel for high risk/low frequency events.

It is appropriate to stack your deck when you have a known high risk situation at hand by selecting your most trusted, mature or experienced personnel for unique events or special missions. Remember, time pressure and high workload increase the likelihood of all types of violations occurring. By selecting your best personnel, you are using the ace up your sleeve.

Beyond *Violation Producing Conditions*, there are other drivers of noncompliance, including a tendency in recent years to over regulate and over proceduralize every nook and cranny of the decision space in our lives.

Red Rules and Brown Rules

In the late 1990s I was presenting a human factors course to a group of pilots that worked for a small company owned and operated by a seasoned pilot with over 50 years of flying experience. During the course of that presentation, I made the comment that "everyone needs to follow the rules, because we need to keep in mind that the rules are written in blood." The obvious metaphor is that others have died doing something that required a new rule so that it would not reoccur to those who followed. As I made this comment, I noticed the owner of the company standing in the back of the room visibly wince when I said the words "written in blood." I made a mental note to see what I had said wrong later.

At lunch I had my chance and approached the corporate patriarch. "Sir, I noticed your reaction when I was talking about flight discipline, was there something wrong with what I said?" He pulled me aside and replied slowly, "Tony, I understand better than most about rules written in blood. In point of fact, I have lost two family members in aviation accidents that should not have happened." Now I felt remorseful and understood his reaction, or so I thought. "Oh, I'm so sorry, I had no idea," I said sheepishly.

But what he said next really surprised and enlightened me. "That's not the problem I have with what you said, Tony. You had no way of knowing about my family and things like that happen. What really upsets me aren't the rules written in blood, it's the rules that are written in *crap*." I was a bit taken back. "What kind of rules might those be?" I inquired, trying to make some sense of his comment. "Oh, you know, the ones the bureaucrats write to cover their butts, or the accounting staff writes to make their job easier and my job harder. Those aren't rules written in blood, they're crap rules."

Two things amazed me about his insight. First, this man had the sophistication to make the fine discrimination between "red rules" and "brown rules." Secondly, I was truly impressed by the fact that he had the wisdom not to make that comment in front of his pilots who did not share his experience and connoisseurship. At two levels, this World War II veteran had a far better grasp on noncompliance than I did.

The main point I took from this is that perhaps we need to take a closer look at something called *decision space* and try to put a few guidelines on who should control it and why.

Protecting Your Decision Space

Too many rules breed a creeping cynicism, which in turn breeds noncompliance. Most organizations and individuals (unless they are teenagers) do not make a habit of questioning authority about new policies or procedures. We might grumble a bit, but for the most part we take it in stride … and often continue our actions as if the new policies did not exist.

We need to reach a point where two types of professional discipline become second nature habits. The first is the *organizational discipline* to keep the brown rules to an absolute minimum and enforce rules across the board. The second is the *personal discipline* to comply.

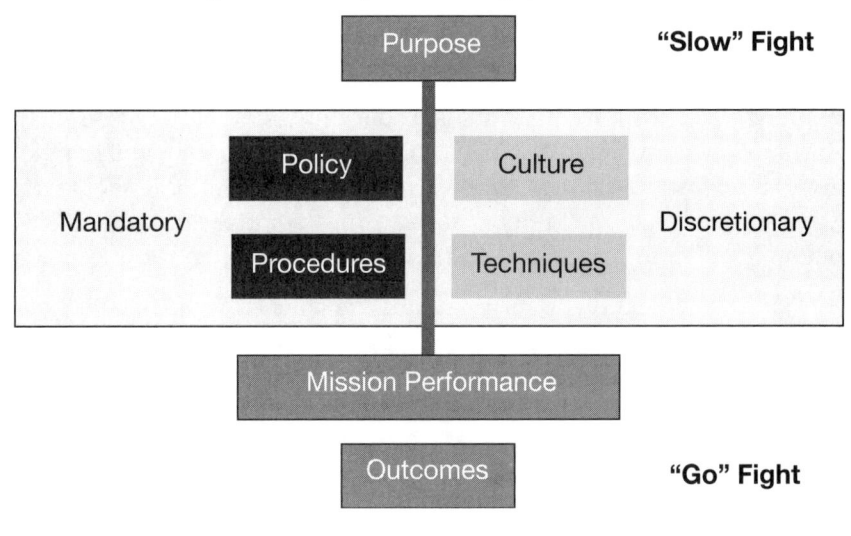

Figure 4.2
Decision Space

In this way we can protect and balance both the organizational and individual decision space. In Figure 4.2 we can see this concept illustrated. Policies and procedures flow from the purpose of the organization and should be clearly understood and by definition are mandatory. But not everything can be anticipated in advance, so the ability of thinking humans to adapt and improvise is an equal, if not greater portion of most performance equations.

The ways in which individuals and teams creatively solve real time challenges in support of mission accomplishment are often referred to as *cultural norms* and *techniques*. In a perfect world, policies and procedures will never conflict with cultural norms, but far too often they do. Anyone who studies noncompliance knows that culture will nearly always trump policy, at least in the long run.

In day to day operations, policy, procedures, culture and personal techniques all combine to get the job done and achieve desired outcomes. This is referred to in the diagram as the "go fight" and is waged by front line individuals and their first line supervisors, operating as a team to achieve organizational objectives within existing guidelines. But crafting, communicating and training actions are the role of supervisors, trainers and other staff members. This requires critical evaluation of what should be written in stone and what should be left to personal discretion. This is the "slow fight" and is the piece of the compliance iceberg that lies beneath the waterline.

Beyond over proceduralization, we also have the problem of rules with no room to apply judgment – often referred to as *zero tolerance policies*.

Zero Tolerance Boomerangs

There are certainly areas where we don't want to leave the compliance decision fuzzy. We don't want the scientists who handle doomsday viruses to play fast and loose with the rules. We don't want drunk pilots flying our airliners or drugged out surgeons changing our heart valves. But in some cases, we have blurred the line between true danger control and ease of administration, and in so doing have made some red rules turn brown, at least in the eyes of many.

Many of these so called zero tolerance policies begin with good intent; examples include keeping guns and drugs out of our schools. But inside that good intent we create systems that defy logic and poison the well of fairness which often results in an unintended consequence – loss of faith in the system of rules. Here is one example:[12]

> "Anyone who studies noncompliance knows that culture will nearly always trump policy, at least in the long run."

> John Turner couldn't understand what had happened to him. The twelve-year-old honor student was arrested during a school recess, handcuffed,

---

[12] From *Zero Tolerance for Noncompliance: Ten Steps Toward Lifelong Behavior Modification* by Berit Kjos. Found at www.crossroad.to/text/articles/zerotol.html

taken to juvenile hall, fingerprinted, and forbidden to call his mother. He had to sign a $250 bond and was subject to steeper punishment, along with a lifelong police blot on his personal computerized data file if found guilty. What could a good sixth grader do to deserve such bad treatment? *He hit back*, after being insulted, bullied and hit by another student.

John's school had adopted a policy called "zero tolerance" and in Ohio, the policy brings swift punishment on innocent victims as well as aggressors; both are summarily suspended. So when a young girl in Ohio was beaten by two other girls on her way to the school bus, all three girls were sentenced to equal punishment, a ten day suspension.

Intent to do wrong, a key element in criminal justice, is irrelevant.

I could list hundreds of similar examples. Suspensions for bringing nail clippers, a bottle of *Advil*, or a family heirloom pocket watch pen knife, into schools. The argument here is not whether it is helping or hurting the school violence problem – but rather what we are saying to our best and brightest children about rules.

My point is not to debate the rightness or wrongness of these policies, but once again, to point out the attitudes towards rule breaking that they foster. Forewarned is forearmed.

Neither Simple nor Easy

Compliance is a multifaceted and complex equation that includes our attitudes towards rules in general and rests on our ability to explain in concrete, non-threatening terms both the rationale and boundaries of organizational and personal decision space. But even at the highest levels of our most sophisticated organizations, this is not always understood.

In a speech to U.S. Air Force personnel at Joint Air Base Balad (Iraq) in late October, 2008 Air Force General Norton Schwartz, the new Chief of Staff said

> There is one way to do the nuclear mission, and that is the Air Force way. There is one way to do aircraft and missile maintenance, and that is the Air Force way. We collectively need to back a little bit toward something called compliance. We must, as an Air Force … do the right thing and do the right thing right. That's as simple as it gets.

Simple? Probably not.

Easy? Not a chance.

Compliance has many enemies. Any attempt to oversimplify this cornerstone of performance is doomed to frustration and eventual failure. There is an old military axiom that says "Beginners chat about tactics while professionals ponder logistics." Translation: It takes a sustained – and sustainable – effort to win a war, and it will take more than a call to arms from the USAF Chief to make it happen. So what firepower does the Air Force need to bring to bear on this target to make General Schwartz's vision a reality? And what can the rest of us learn from their challenge?

Here are a couple of new ways to look deeper at the challenge of creating and sustaining a *Culture of Compliance* in any organization, big or small.

Not All Noncompliance is Evil

We should all comprehend that there are different types of noncompliance, each with a different cause, and therefore a different remedy.

It is vitally important for individuals at all levels to comprehend the various types of noncompliance, some of which can actually be beneficial to us, if we take the time to learn from them. Currently, in our professional discipline courseware, we teach four distinct types of noncompliance, culled from the work of Professor James Reason and other experts:

- **Routine** – frequent and unofficially condoned violations of procedures – everybody's doin' it, nobody cares
- **Optimizing** – people who have discovered truly "better ways" of getting the job done outside the lines
- **Situational** – "Just this once" type violations based on a unique set of circumstances
- **Rogue** – People who violate policies and procedures for self-gratification and to feed their egos

Routine violations lead to a dangerous condition known as the *Normalization of Deviance*. *Rogue* violations are festering wounds and decay an individual or organization from within. But *Optimizing* and *Situational* violations can be used to create new and better processes and procedures (Optimizing) or to share a unique occurrence so that it does not surprise someone the next time it occurs (Situational).

The bottom line is that treating all noncompliance the same points to a lack of understanding of human behavior by everyone involved, lost trust, and a poor culture and organizational climate.

Compliance in "3D"

While researching my book *Flight Discipline*, I discovered that cultures of compliance leverage three key areas: (1) Personal and professional discipline (not to be confused with *punishment*), (2) diligence, and (3) attention to detail. Greatly simplified, this **3D** approach is outlined as follows:

Personal **Discipline** – Doing the right thing. When General Schwartz directs his airmen to "do the right thing," this is really an issue of professional ethics – a prerequisite for voluntary compliance. Therefore, we must begin any quest to change the status quo with the understanding that voluntary compliance is not automatic for many in our society, who were brought up to believe that breaking rules is cool, and that everyone does it. As we discussed in the beginning of this chapter, before someone can be expected to do the right thing – they must value "rightness" for its own sake.

Beyond the ethical issues, the next logistical underpinning for compliance is **Attention to Detail** – thoroughly accomplishing all tasks with concern for all the areas involved, no matter how small, repetitive or routine. The chilling words of Cameron Diaz to Tom Cruise in the final scene of the movie *Vanilla Sky* make this point clearly. Cruise, lamenting how his near perfect life was destroyed by a single momentary lapse in judgment, asks how "one little thing" could have such enormous consequences. Diaz's reply, "Don't you know silly, there is nothing bigger than the little things," has a distinct ring of truth for all corners of our lives, personal and professional (to get the full impact of this line, you really need to see the movie). Passion for details is a clear indicator of a high reliability individual or organization with a commitment to compliance.

The final "D" in the 3D approach is a deceptively simple word – **diligence** – which is the detail work done with concentration and care *each and every time*, all the way until the last step is done, the last part stops moving, and the handoff, debrief and paperwork is completed. In the words of Atul Gawande, M.D. in his outstanding book *Better: A Surgeon's Notes on Performance*, "*Diligence* seems an easy and minor virtue ... it is neither. It is both central to performance and fiendishly hard."[13]

Empowering discipline, detail and diligence at the level of each individual are just starting points for any organization serious about motivating and enabling their people for world class compliance. Next steps should include

---

13   Atul Gawande, *Better: A Surgeon's notes on Performance. Introduction.*

a scrub of policies and procedures for clarity and relevance, and a hard look at how they are trained and evaluated, as well as developing close-looped quality assurance and supervision.

There is no question that the first shot of this battle for a return to rigorous compliance was on target, and if General Schwartz was serious about this call to arms, his organization will follow up with a warfighter's relentless pursuit of the objective on all fronts.

Last Words on Compliance

Perhaps the most dangerous aspect of the noncompliance challenge is that we don't fully comprehend the extent and severity of the issue. This creates the illusion of compliance that masks the problem and severely inhibits efforts to fix it.

The second major issue is that many leaders in organizational settings don't really want to know the extent of the problem. If you know you have noncompliance in your organization, you are duty bound to do something about it, and as we have seen, this can be an extremely difficult challenge. So we often choose the softer, easier path of "see no evil, hear no evil."

In this manner we disrespect both the intellect and integrity of our most valuable resource, people. We can do better.

It is time to change directions and look at how high performing individuals sometimes do not find happiness and contentment in the team setting.

FIVE

The "Me" in Team

*"Be careful lest in casting out your devils that
you cast out the best thing that's in you."*
– Nietzsche

I'm a big fan of motivational posters, but one that bothers me as trite is the one with the picture of some type of team sport that says *"There is no "I" in Team."* I get what they're trying to say – that when we lose ourselves inside a team effort, we all do much better – but something about it just doesn't ring completely true. Perhaps it's because I am who I am – a self-centered, me first, baby boomer. Or maybe it's because I see a good bit of that in everyone, regardless of their generation.

I've been involved in high performance teams since my youth; first in sports as both a player and a coach, and then in the military, public service and now the private sector. I have won team championships and individual awards at multiple levels, but throughout it all I have found nothing to dissuade me from thinking that in most situations, the most you can expect from anyone is that they will act in their own self-interest. Certainly there are altruistic people out there, and most all of us have done a few selfless acts, but in most situations people do what is best for them. And I don't think that is unnatural, evil or even an obstacle to high performing teamwork. On the contrary, the key to effective teamwork and collaboration is tapping into this need.

> "... there may not be an "I" in *team*, but there sure as heck is a "Me" if you unscramble a few letters."

Most teamwork training and *How to Build a Great Team* books spend considerable time and effort on how to get individuals to serve the team. But inasmuch as this book is about personal error control, we will turn this approach on its head and talk about *how can the team serve the individual*. Once we unlock this door, we can expect team and individual performance to improve symbiotically. So in this chapter, we will look at interactions between individuals and groups in a team setting and attempt to shed some light on how we can improve our own individual decision making. In so doing, we might learn a little about effective collaboration along the way.

Edgar Cayce (1877–1945), a fascinating man called the "Sleeping Prophet" made this point about understanding the power of the individual ego in the team environment well. "In any influence, the will, a self, the ego, the I AM is the greater force to be dealt with, but as numbers do influence (as in the team environment), a knowledge of same (the dominance of the individual ego) certainly gives an individual a foresight into relationships."[1]

Literally speaking, there may not be an "I" in *team*, but there sure as heck is a "Me" if you unscramble a few letters. The bottom line is that individualism and group dynamics impact performance at both levels, and not always in a positive manner. Make no mistake, team failures occur at both ends of the individual-team spectrum.

Well, it appears we have once again stepped into dangerous and politically incorrect waters, so let's keep paddling and see if we can avoid being burned at the stake as heretics by the teamwork mafia.

Do Teams Really Improve Performance?

There is little doubt that in terms of pure knowledge content and scope, none of us is as smart as all of us. However, group dynamics impact free thinkers in some interesting and often negative ways. Not surprisingly, when free thinkers won't fully engage – teamwork falters and the end result is often less than optimal.

Edward de Bono, one of the world's foremost lateral thinkers had this to say about why clever people don't always perform well in team environments.

---

[1] Found at www.Edgarcayce.org

Thinking is often regarded as an extension of the ego. Clever children in school base their egos on being clever and on being right all the time. They dislike group work because they cannot then show the rest of the class where the good idea originated. When the ego and thinking are treated as the same thing there is a reluctance to be wrong and a need to defend a point of view rather than to explore the situation.[2]

The obvious point here is that if some of the smartest among us do not operate well in groups and find themselves unwilling to contribute or otherwise distracted by ego concerns, then the whole (team) may well be *less* than the sum of its parts. This is one of the rationales behind how the military academies prepare incoming cadets. These kids are some of the best and brightest the country has to offer, typically in the top 5% of their high school classes. Immediately upon arrival, they put them through basic training designed to first break them down and wipe out as much individualism as possible. The next four years is dedicated to building them back into highly functional members of a team. This is obviously not possible in most environments, so we need to do what we can to increase awareness of the challenge of high achievers.

"… group dynamics impact free thinkers in some interesting and often negative ways."

In some cases, high achievers actually sabotage teams by withholding key insights or manipulating others in their own inside game of ego gratification. There are numerous documented instances of flight crews and surgical team members being interviewed in the aftermath of an incident, who have admitted to willfully withholding key observations and information because of these group dynamics issues.

It is a simple reality that many individuals do not do their best problem solving or decision making in a team environment. They feel tamped down and bridled by cumbersome team processes. They don't like waiting their turn to speak, or perhaps lack the social skill set to be diplomatic with their criticism of the ideas and contributions of others. Simply put, they work better alone. Hopefully, these types find careers and families that tolerate – and perhaps even complement – this personality type, but we know this is not always the case.

---

2   Edward de Bono, *The Happiness Purpose*, 1977 found at http://www.edwarddebono.com/Passage-Detail.php?passage_id=88&

In other situations, these high performers end up in charge of teams, where their egos and enthusiasm tend to overwhelm normal team processes. The following example illustrates just such a case, where the Commander of a nuclear submarine, discovers the perils of poor teamwork.

Personal Accountability in the Team Setting:
The Tragic Tale of the *Ehime Maru*

When situations arise that trigger a team to press outside of a known and approved plan, the team skills and decisions of those in charge are critical in realigning the situation and bringing it back inside the boundaries of the original plan or a manageable contingency. This can often be successfully accomplished through the application of training and sound decision making, especially with highly experienced professionals in the team environment. However, there are occasions when even the most experienced, capable people fail, especially when they fail to understand the need for a clearly defined understanding of *personal accountability in the team setting*.

Let's see how these lethal conditions affected the world of a very accomplished submarine Commander and his crew. This is a case study about span of control, responding to warning signals, and the prudence of intentionally setting yourself up for a situation where you insert your own agenda in place of normal team protocols.

"It is a simple reality that many individuals do not do their best problem solving or decision making in a team environment."

> [3]On February 9, 2001 the U.S. Navy submarine *USS Greeneville* left the naval base at Pearl Harbour to conduct a public relations mission under the command of Commander Scott Waddle, USN. The mission was in support of the Navy's Distinguished Visitor (DV) program, designed to provide high influence civilians, members of Congress, journalists, and other "opinion makers" a close up look at nuclear submarines to demonstrate the submarines' capabilities, with the overall goal of building public and political support for the nuclear submarine program.
>
> The *Greeneville* departed Pearl Harbor on time at 8:00 AM local time with a crew of 106 in addition to the 16 distinguished visitors. The sub-

---

3   United States Navy (2001-04-13). "Record of Proceedings, Court of Inquiry Into the Circumstances Surrounding the Collision Between *USS Greeneville* (SSN 772) and Japanese M/V *Ehime Maru* that Occurred Off the Coast of Oahu, Hawaii on 9 February 2001"

marine reached its dive point south of Oahu a little behind schedule, at 10:17, and submerged beneath the waves. The first order of business was to serve the DVs lunch. They were scheduled to be served in two sittings, the first from 10:30 to 11:30 and the second from 11:30 to 12:30. But the schedule began to slip almost immediately as the lunch service ran late. After lunch, the real show was to take place where the crew would demonstrate the operational abilities of the submarine and then return the DVs to Pearl Harbor for a reception that was scheduled to begin precisely at 2:30 PM. As the lunch ran late, *Greeneville* officers repeatedly reminded their Commander that they needed to begin its demonstration maneuvers or the DV's would be late back to port for their 2:30 reception. Almost 30 minutes behind schedule, at 1:10 PM, Commander Waddle entered the submarine's control room and prepared to execute the demonstration.

Meanwhile, the *Ehime Maru*, a 191 foot Japanese fishing trawler, headed out for the day's mission to train Japanese high school students interested in pursuing fishing careers. A total of 35 people were on board *Ehime Maru*: 20 crewmembers, 13 students, and two teachers. As the *Greeneville* was finishing its late lunch service, the *Ehime Maru* was proceeding at 11 knots into the area where the *Greeneville* was conducting the DV cruise.

As per regulation, Commander Waddle checked the submarine's sonar contacts and noted that there were several surface vessels – one of which was the *Ehime Maru* – in the vicinity, but none closer than seven nautical miles away. According to several crewmembers, Commander Waddle became increasingly frustrated when informed that equipment preparations would further delay the start of the demonstration. Finally, at 1:15 PM, (46 minutes behind schedule) the *Greeneville* began the demonstration, including high-speed, full-rudder, 35-degree turns side to side, as well as rapid up-and-down movements. Commander Waddle personally directed the maneuvers, and according to his testimony the DVs "were loving it." Commander Waddle adds, "I could barely suppress a smile as I watched the expressions of joy and amazement on the faces of our distinguished visitors." The investigation report reveals that during the maneuvers, several civilians in the sonar room were talking with the sonar technicians, who were at the same time trying to keep track of any active sonar contacts in the vicinity.

Following the high-speed maneuvers, Commander Waddle called for the *Greeneville* to perform an emergency dive followed by an emergency main ballast blow, a maneuver that brings the submarine from a depth of about 400 feet to the surface in a matter of seconds. This maneuver is so aggressive that the entire bow of the submarine leaps above the waves upon surfacing. Due to high risk nature of this maneuver, regulations required the submarine to go to periscope depth to check for ships or dangerous obstacles on the surface. Standing orders called for the submarine to hold a steady course for a minimum of three minutes to reestablish sonar contact with any vessels in the area (possibly disrupted by the high speed maneuvers beforehand). In this case, however, Commander Waddle held a steady course for only 90 seconds, half the duration of the standing orders requirement.

Although the *Ehime Maru* was closing in on *USS Greeneville's* location, Commander Waddle failed to see the ship. Regulations further mandated that a three-minute, 360-degree periscope scan be conducted before executing the emergency main ballast blow maneuver. Aware that they were still behind schedule, Commander Waddle abbreviated the scan to less than 1½ minutes. He noted that the haze was still present, and sighted no ships in the vicinity. Satisfied that the area was clear, the Commander ordered the maneuver executed, and they threw the control levers as instructed and the submarine began its rapid ascent toward the surface.

At 1:43:15 PM, the *Greeneville* surfaced directly under the Japanese vessel, her rudder slicing *Ehime Maru's* hull from starboard to port. The Japanese crew heard two loud noises and felt the ship shudder. *Ehime Maru's* bridge crew looked aft and saw the submarine come out of the water next to their ship. Within five seconds *Ehime Maru* began to sink. Within five minutes, the *Ehime Maru* stood almost vertically on its stern and sank to the bottom of the sea as her crewmembers scrambled to abandon ship.

The court of inquiry issued numerous opinions, including that the accident was caused by "a series and combination of individual negligence (s) onboard the *USS Greeneville*, "artificial urgency" by Commander Waddle to rush the submarine through its demonstration schedule as it began to run late, failure to follow standard procedures, the abbreviated periscope search, distractions and obstruction caused by the presence of the civilian guests, crew training deficiencies, overconfidence and complacency.

Much like Mr. Robinson, the retired Marine Warrant Officer we discussed in Chapter 1, Commander Waddell got caught up in the emotion of the moment. But unlike Mr. Robinson, who was on his own to manage the moment, Commander Waddle had a team around him and procedures to follow. Both failed to manage the moment with tragic implications that will haunt them for life.

It is also worth noting, that at the time of the collision, the *USS Greeneville* had nine of the 13 watch stations in and around the control room manned by substitute personnel, and one of the sonar operators was unqualified to stand watch.

So as we begin to look at the error producing conditions present inside teams, we must understand the need for all members, especially leaders, to utilize their specialized knowledge and expertise. We will now turn our attention to some of the more common group dynamic pitfalls.

Group Dynamics Pitfalls

Group work is rarely flawless. In fact, groups pose special problems to decision making and foster their own unique types of error producing conditions for the individuals who populate them. Our focus here will be at two levels. First, how group dynamic pitfalls impact the thought processes of individuals and secondly, the teamwork issues that undermine high performance.

Five specific pitfalls are discussed below, beginning with the *Strength of the First Idea*.

Strength of the First Idea

"I know what we need to do so let's get on with it."

This problem occurs when the first idea – or someone's pet idea – is latched onto by everyone in the group as **the** solution. From the individual perspective, this might be driven by expediency (as in "let's get this over with") or ego driven superiority thoughts (as in "I can't believe I'm trapped in a room with these dimwits"). From the group perspective, it often occurs before the group becomes comfortable with either the challenge or each other, and everyone is simply eager to get back into their individual comfort zones.

A second problem is that this phenomenon often occurs under *time pressure* which compounds the challenge dramatically, which was undoubtedly a contributor to the mistakes made in the control room of the *USS Greeneville*. In many situations decisions must be made quickly, but in these circumstances group members must keep in mind that people will be less likely to raise objections if they feel that doing so would result in delaying the process. Personal and team errors are usually an inevitable result of this pitfall.

Problems

- **Pet idea (or first idea) dominates thoughts and actions.** Once this train starts rolling downhill, it's tough to go back to look at alternatives. At this point the group has too much time and energy invested in pursuing and executing the first idea to have much desire to look at new ideas, which leads to our next problem.

- **Exclusion of new ideas leads to lost situation awareness through channelized attention and fixation on one course of action.** Framing and solving an ill defined problem is tough, so once the group moves to the planning and execution phase, the individuals in the group stop the analysis of the problem. This may occur before all the potential negative implications of the proposed course of action can be brought to the table.

- **Short circuits information gathering and brainstorming.** Once team members sense the fact finding and options analysis phase is over, they turn their minds towards next steps and are reluctant to go back and test new ideas. This results in cutting off legitimate alternatives before they are evaluated.

Checklist for Recognition and Prevention

- Begin with an agreed position to put multiple options on the table before "moving to solution."

- Recognize time pressure if a rapid decision must be made, and communicate the risk it poses to the group. For example, "Let's make sure that we don't fall into the trap of grasping the first idea just to meet our timeline."

- Promote big picture thinking, and explore multiple available options.

Of course, there are many times when the first idea is the best idea, but you will never really know unless and until the idea is vetted and tested in the group setting with all players actively involved. So the individual error lesson here is to be aware of your ego driven tendencies, and recognize when they are inappropriate for the task, time and talent on hand.

Sometimes it's not the strength of the first idea, but rather the reputation of one of the team members that gets in the way of good group decision making.

Excessive Deference/Halo Effect

"I've heard a lot about this person; they are brilliant and will know what we should do."

The *halo effect* occurs when we give too much credence to first impressions or previous experience that may not be relevant in the current situation. A classic example of the halo effect is when celebrities are used to endorse products that they have no actual expertise in evaluating, and with which they may not even have any prior affiliation. In the case study of the *Ehime Maru*, the unquestioned authority of Commander Waddle was an example of this type of group behavior.

> "A classic example of the halo effect is when celebrities are used to endorse products that they have no actual expertise in evaluating...."

A corollary to the halo effect is the *reverse halo effect* where individuals are perceived to have little or nothing to offer based on erroneous first impression or on irrelevant past experience.

The halo effect has also been called the *Association Fallacy* which asserts that qualities of one thing are inherently qualities of another, merely by an irrelevant association. The two types are sometimes referred to as *guilt by association* and *honor by association*. An example might include something like, "She went to Harvard, so a simple program management job is child's play for her." Of course, program management skills likely have very little to do with where you went to college, but once the inference is made and accepted, a potentially false set of expectations are put into play.

Problems

- Carry over from other experience – or a single first impression – may not be appropriate for the task or problem at hand.
- Charisma or reputation from one environment often cloaks incompetence in a new situation.
- Reverse halo effect often inhibits valuable contributions from those who are perceived by the rest of the team as having little to offer.

Checklist for Recognition and Prevention

- Trust but verify; no one is perfect.
- Respect everyone's previous experience, but back them up and monitor their performance as you would anyone else.
- Avoid generalized feedback. Use specific constructive comments and trend information to provide usable feedback.

Our next challenge occurs when <u>no one</u> wants to step up to the challenge of critical thinking inside the team.

Groupthink

"Go along to get along."

This occurs when people in a team setting feel that it is more important to fit in than to solve a real problem. Non-assertiveness and a desire to go along with most any idea presented prevent team members from suggesting their own improvements or criticizing or commenting on the ideas of others.

Groupthink results in many potential contributions or solutions never being placed on the table for evaluation or inclusion in the plan. At best, this results in a decision or plan of action that **appears** to be supported but may not be "optimized" since there is little attempt by anyone to make it better.

At worst, the groupthink process reaches a point where the final decision is one that is **not supported by anyone** in the group, and the team succumbs to the emotional need to complete the task without any conflict.

Problems Caused

- Poor group dynamics inhibit creative contributions from out of the box thinkers. In order to get the most out of everyone in a group setting, there must be some critique and give and take on challenging ideas.
- The appearance of consensus or unanimity around the proposed solution masks the weakness of the team effort and can lead to false commitment to a bad plan.
- Groupthink often results in one of the rare cases where a lone individual can outperform a team.

Checklist for Recognition and Prevention

- Talk about groupthink up front. Assign someone the task of wearing the "black hat" and challenging ideas. This opens the door for others.
- If this is not done and you begin to see groupthink creeping in, state your intent to act as a "devil's advocate" to combat it. Use a statement such as "I don't necessarily disagree, but I'm going to challenge that line of thinking just to make sure we aren't falling into groupthink here."
- Sense and fight the first emotion that inhibits your contribution to the group process.
- Treat pros and cons of ideas equally, particularly if it is your idea under discussion.

Another problem that can exacerbate *groupthink* is when team members lack the confidence to voice their opinion.

Lack of Assertiveness

"My viewpoint is not important and won't be listened to anyway."

The lack of assertiveness is crippling to both group and individual planning and decision making and likely results in more compromised results than any other phenomena. As a communication style, *assertiveness* is distinguished from *aggression* and *passivity* in how people deal with personal boundaries.

Passive communicators do not defend their own personal boundaries and thus allow overly aggressive people to unduly influence them. They are also typically not likely to risk trying to influence anyone else due to their passive disposition. Aggressive communicators do not respect the personal boundaries of others and are likely to attempt to dominate a group.

A person communicates assertively by not being afraid to speak his or her mind or trying to influence others, but doing so in a way that respects the personal boundaries of others. Even in strict vertical hierarchies such as the military setting onboard the *USS Greeneville*, appropriate assertiveness is an essential insurance policy against poor individual decision making.

Problems Caused

- Break down of group process around personalities and communication styles before the mission focus of the group can ever get started.
- Emotional jetlag – An offended individual mentally stays at the place the error was made but the situation keeps moving, resulting in them "checking out" of further discussion or problem solving.
- Loss of problem focus as personal issues begin to dominate the discussion.

Checklist for Recognition and Prevention

- Commit yourself to contribute in a respectful but assertive manner.
- Expect aggression and counter it with logic and fact, not emotion.
- Recognize passive types and regularly invite them into the discussion, until such time as they feel safe in communicating openly with the rest of the group.

There are entire books and university courses on effective teamwork and it is a subject worthy of study. I offer one powerful tool and technique that has proven effective in multiple settings, including the dynamic and error intolerant world of combat aviation.

Team Communications Loop 5-Step Process

Group dynamics error traps can be avoided or mitigated by recognizing the role of each individual in the group and applying one common tool – the

Team Communications Loop (TCL). This tool takes the guesswork out of when and how to interact in a group setting. Through the use of this tool, even individuals who do not normally work well inside team environments can engage and contribute productively.

This continuous process is illustrated at Figure 5.1.

1. **Ask** probing and clarifying questions to promote both your own understanding and that of the group as a whole.

2. **Advocate** a position, either your own or in support of someone else. Try to phrase advocacy in positive terms, but don't hesitate to oppose or refute bad ideas or shallow thinking.

3. **Resolve** differences with logical, rational group processes, not emotion or volume.

4. **Decide.** Make or contribute to decisions seeking consensus ("I don't fully agree but I can live with that") vs. unanimity ("Does **everyone** agree?). Don't allow one person to dominate the decision process or veto a good alternative that the rest of the team is in support of.

5. **Review** both the decision and the process used to arrive at it. Realize that most group processes will continually reach mini-decisions and solutions along the way to final consensus.

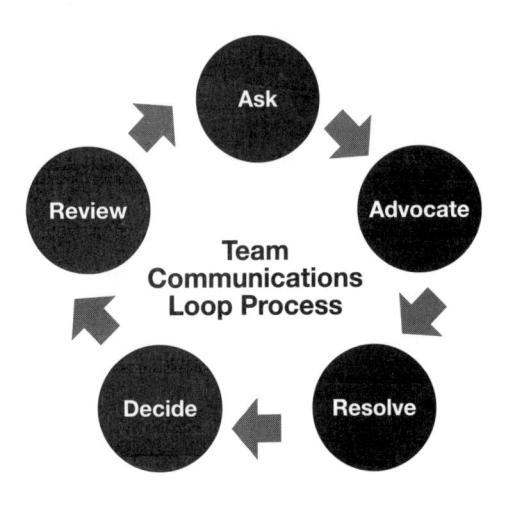

Figure 5.1
Team Communications Loop

Tap the Individual – Feed the Team

People who cannot work well in the group setting are at a tremendous disadvantage in the 21st century workplace, or even in many social environments. Regardless of your enthusiasm – or lack thereof – for participating in a team project, you should be aware of your strengths and weaknesses with regards to team operations and work to improve them. Following this initial step, all of us need to be aware of the needs and tendencies of others in the group to assist them in contributing as well.

> "Teamwork is not the solution for every problem...."

High performers should not be made to feel unappreciated. There is absolutely nothing wrong with trying to find a win-win situation for those who routinely seek credit and personal satisfaction from their work. Contrary to popular belief, ambitious and ego driven achievers can find happiness inside the team environment, but it might require a little give and take from both sides.

As Nietzsche reminds us with his quote at the top of this chapter – we can't afford to "cast out" high achievers and free thinkers inside the restricting confines of an overly structured team. But we must also be aware of the benefits of bringing multiple talents into play against difficult challenges in situations that demand team approaches. Teamwork is not the solution for every problem, but poor teamwork or non-participative individuals practically guarantee a poor outcome, something we should all recognize before we throw every problem or challenge into committee.

Armed with the background of why we need a personal perspective on performance, it's time to see how we can leverage our own uniqueness for a lifetime of personal performance improvement.

SIX

Proof of Life: Error Control in Action

"Good luck can't last a lifetime unless you die young."
– Despair poster

In the movie *Proof of Life*, Terry Thorne (a character played by Russell Crowe) is confronted with a nearly impossible task – to locate and recover a kidnapped executive in the jungles of South America. As he and his partner Dino (played by David Caruso) discuss the apparently insurmountable challenge they face, the following exchange takes place.

> Dino: *Do not get me wrong, I would love to come out of this a winner, but I have been over this and over this a thousand times and **it's impossible**.*[1]
>
> Thorne: *So we're on then?*
>
> Dino: *Absolutely.*

I love this scene. There is something about trying to accomplish what others say is impossible that puts a determined smile on the face of many high

---

[1] Original term omitted for this book's PG-13 audience, it's well worth renting the movie to get the full impact.

achievers. These are the people Theodore Roosevelt was talking about when he said these immortal words, often referred to as the "Man in the Arena" speech.

> It is not the critic who counts: not the man who points out how the strong man stumbles or where the doer of deeds could have done better. The credit belongs to the man who is actually in the arena, whose face is marred by dust and sweat and blood, who strives valiantly, who errs and comes up short again and again, because there is no effort without error or shortcoming, but who knows the great enthusiasms, the great devotions, who spends himself for a worthy cause; who, at the best, knows, in the end, the triumph of high achievement, and who, at the worst, if he fails, at least he fails while daring greatly, so that his place shall never be with those cold and timid souls who knew neither victory nor defeat.[2]

In the final analysis, as the "man in the arena" we have to take responsibility for fixing the human error challenge in our own lives. There are a few bottom lines in this regard. First, reading a book – even this book – won't do it. We have to have knowledge, and armed with this knowledge, we must act. Second, a good attitude or "caring" about our performance or safety is not enough. The world is full of well meaning screw-ups armed with little but good intent. Clever slogans are not enough. Being a part of a high performance culture is not enough (but it helps). In order to improve and take responsibility for our performance, we need move from thought processes and culture discussions into action. We need to *do things* differently.

This chapter is designed to provide a means to gain traction on the road to high performance by providing the tools to implement personal performance analysis and modification. It is science based and will prove its worth at the only level that really counts – *you*. The approach and tools provided are incremental, meaning you can do as little or as much as you desire or need. Some will get all they currently want from the heightened awareness of the material in this book. Others will go deeper, each according to their needs.

The Science Behind the System

When it comes to changing long established personal behaviors, you are only as committed as you are convinced; therefore, it is very important that you take the time to understand that this program for personal error control is based on solid research and sound scientific principles. You are conduct-

---

[2] Theodore Roosevelt, "Citizenship in a Republic," Speech at the Sorbonne, Paris, April 23, 1910

ing the final part of that research with this guide. Once this understanding is in place, your chances for success improve greatly, as the program is not something being done *to you* but *by you*. Here is how it works.

Early Detection of Hazards, Risks and Opportunities

Empowered accountability works for a couple of very simple reasons. First, it reaches deeper into both the individual and the system, a subject we will speak to in detail Chapter 11, *The Business of Error Control*. On an even more basic level, the tools and techniques provided give everyone the opportunity to identify hazards and risks at an earlier point, thereby expanding the time and options available to counter the threat.

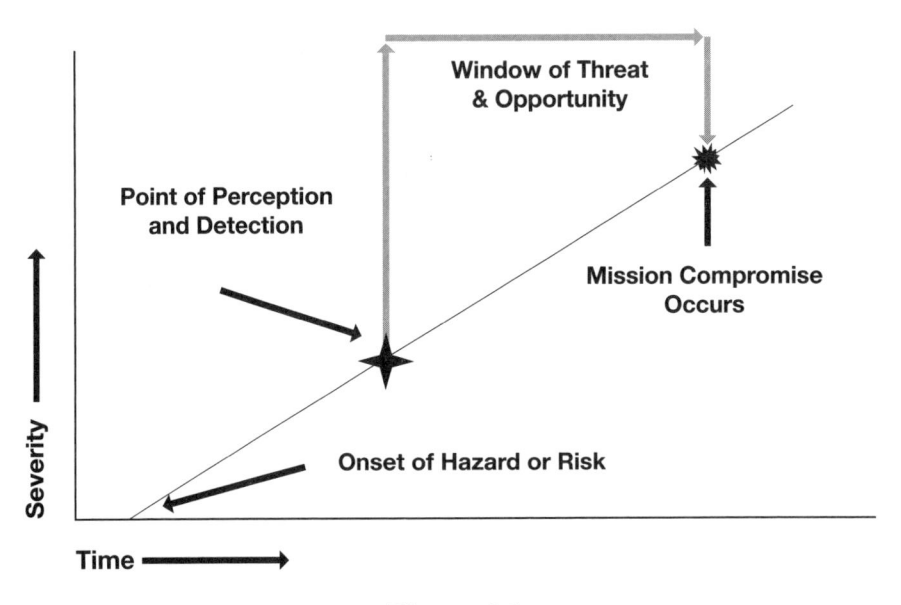

Figure 6.1
Window of Threat and Opportunity

Figure 6.1 illustrates a common situation, where a hazard (internal or external) exists somewhere in our environment. For discussion purposes, let's use the example of the aggressive driving tragedy between Clifford Robinson and Christy Antonuccio in Chapter 1. The onset of the hazard, through the eyes of Mr. Robinson began much earlier when he was previously cut off at the intersection. As his frustration grew, the severity of the risk grew. This is illustrated by the diagonal line. The timing of the event trigger (in this case when Ms. Antonuccio cut him off) is unknown – and unknowable – to him.

In this event, Mr. Robinson did not recognize and react to the risk until <u>after</u> the trigger event occurred, and not in time to prevent a tragic consequence. The *window of threat and opportunity* was exceeding brief.

The point here is that while we do not have any control over when the trigger event will occur, we <u>can</u> enlarge the playing field if we identify the risk at an earlier point in time. This concept is illustrated in Figure 6.2. Although many safety programs have an active hazard identification process, they do very little for us in our day to day lives. However, when recognition of error producing conditions and threats get embedded as a *routine life skill*, then we have a sea change of error and risk control both at home and in the work environment.

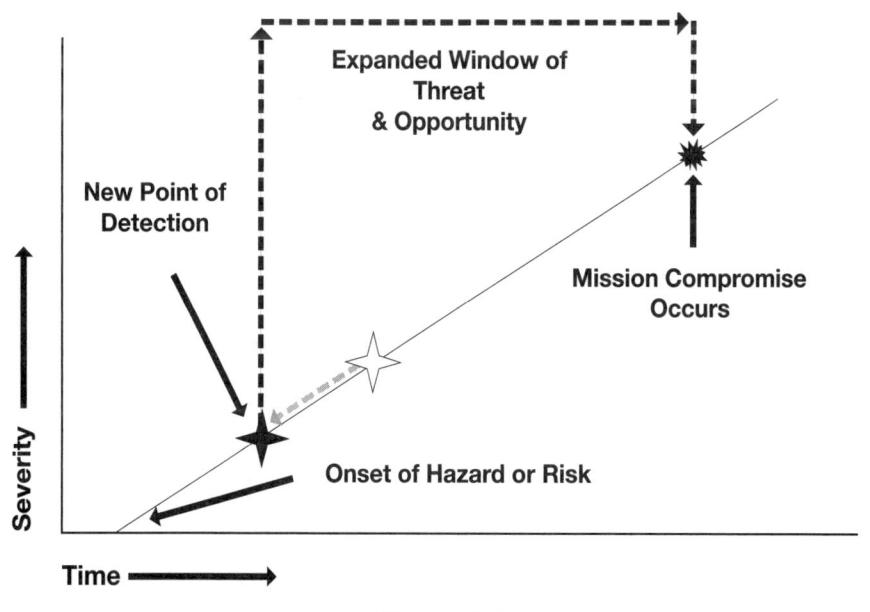

Figure 6.2
*Expanded Window of Threat and Opportunity
Through Early Detection*

In addition to identifying hazards and risks earlier, the blue threat process also works to increase the window of opportunity to leverage *positive opportunities*. The next step is to refine this capacity by drilling down into our individual performance patterns. In the previous chapters we have provided a solid working knowledge on human error in general, now let's examine the five basic steps to the blue threat error control process.

Let's take a high level look at each:

Step 1. Read and Comprehend the Blue Threat Language, Terms and Processes. This first step is vitally important. A good place to start is by pausing to read the *Blue Threat Proverbs* in Chapter 12. Then return to this spot and take a few hours to work through the pages between here and there to learn the landscape and terminology of the empowered accountability approach.

Step 2. Use the Blue Threat Tools to Identify Personal Error Patterns (PEPs). Let's begin with a not so obvious premise. As a unique individual human being, you have different unique strengths and weaknesses than others; so it follows that you make different types of errors than others. As an individual intent on reducing the number and negative consequences of your errors, you must first grasp the nature of error in general, and then utilize tools and techniques to accurately identify your personal error patterns. In this chapter, we simplify this vital initial step through a behavioral science based patented process called Identify, Categorize, Analyze, and Neutralize (I CAN™). Once you verify these personal performance patterns, the next step is to identify where you can intervene to render them non-threatening.

Step 3. Identify Error Control Centers of Gravity (ECG). Experts on error and high reliability have battled for decades against the apparent random nature and variability of human error. Both of these issues disappear when the sample size is reduced to one (1) – you. That is the essence of the blue threat approach; as an individual, you can both predict and prevent personal error patterns and consequences if you are prepared to see and counter the precursors to your PEPs in real time daily life. In short, you learn to take control of events that used to appear randomly to disrupt your plans or otherwise negatively influence your performance. The final step is to apply interventions to control error and improve performance.

Step 4. Apply Appropriate Interventions. Once error control centers of gravity are known, applying appropriate countermeasures at these leverage points is an intuitive process. Even so, this book provides clear guidance ranging from simply heightened awareness of the problem to specifically designed personal operating procedures (POPs) to counter tougher challenges. More on POPs later.

Step 5. Review and Refine. Not every intervention will result in the desired impact. In fact, most of your initial behavior and thought modification efforts will change as you put them into practice. Some challenges that require deep intervention early will eventually become a habit you no longer need to think about. Review cycles are built into the blue threat process. Use them.

Standing on the Shoulders of Giants: A Note on Sources

The tools for identifying and tracking error patterns have been selected after a deep and thorough literature search of over 400 sources and consolidated into what we hope is an easy to use and reliable process for assisting you in your efforts to identify and systematically reduce the number and consequences of your unique performance robbing behaviors. The primary sources are listed in the references section.

Levels of Effort and Impact:
As Little as You Want – As Much as You Need

As a continuous improvement program, the blue threat process occurs across several distinct levels. It is important to note that even though you will be taught how to use all levels effectively, we have found that most people do not often progress from one level to the next until they perceive a need to do so. Although it will not yield optimum results, this "go slow" approach is perfectly acceptable and in line with the overall philosophy of personal readiness and accountability inherent in every aspect of this program.

Figure 6.3, *Levels of Effort and Outcomes from Personal Error Control*, illustrates the four levels of blue threat competence. Please understand that when we refer to competence and incompetence in this figure, we are not talking about your professional competencies, but rather your ability to predict and control your performance degrading behaviors.

Let's begin where most of us are, in the realm of the uninformed status quo, mostly oblivious to the patterns of situations, thoughts and actions that lead us astray. This doesn't mean we are stupid, but rather that we have not yet received the necessary information with which to identify and counter the complexity of human error. With the initial information in this book, you gain an enhanced awareness of error types and the risks they pose in your environments. At this point, you are still at risk, but you are cognizant of the dangers posed by human error from yourself and others and are immediately more vigilant.

When you are ready to move further into your continuous improvement error control initiative, you can start the process of tracking and analyzing your personal performance behaviors using the *Blue Threat Report and*

Analysis Tool (BRAT)™ described in detail later in this chapter. At this stage, an individual can predict and prevent performance degrading behaviors but must do so with conscious effort and discipline.

The next breakthrough point in the personal improvement process comes when you have enough data points and analysis indicating an area of concern that you feel needs to be specifically addressed by creating procedures to deal with the challenge. For example, through the BRAT™ process you determine that your aggressive driving tendencies are getting worse and decide you need to do something to correct the problem before something bad happens. This chapter provides specific instructions on how and when to develop and execute a personal operating procedure (POP) at the error control center of gravity (ECG).

The final stage is practice, where the awareness, process and procedures begin to become a way of life. At this point you are well inside the normalization of excellence criteria and have fully ingrained both the process and the comprehension required to continue it for a lifetime of improvement.

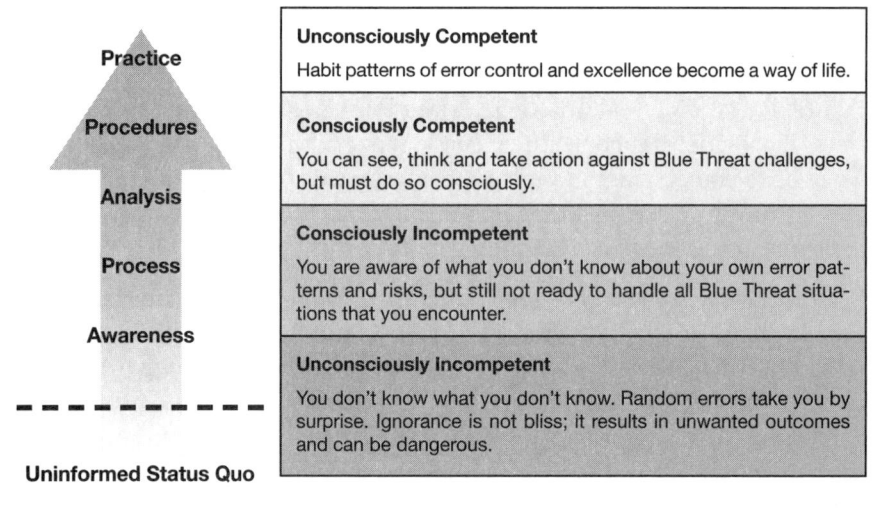

Unconsciously Competent
Habit patterns of error control and excellence become a way of life.

Consciously Competent
You can see, think and take action against Blue Threat challenges, but must do so consciously.

Consciously Incompetent
You are aware of what you don't know about your own error patterns and risks, but still not ready to handle all Blue Threat situations that you encounter.

Unconsciously Incompetent
You don't know what you don't know. Random errors take you by surprise. Ignorance is not bliss; it results in unwanted outcomes and can be dangerous.

Arrow levels (bottom to top): Uninformed Status Quo — Awareness — Process — Analysis — Procedures — Practice

Figure 6.3
Levels of Effort and Outcomes from Personal Error Control

Now it is time to look at some specific tools for developing the data we need to begin a systematic and data-driven improvement process.

Instructions for Blue Threat Tools

Completing and analyzing the *Blue Threat Report and Analysis Tool* (BRAT™) on the following page is the single most vital part of the blue threat program. At first, you may find it difficult to find the time or energy to complete it (it typically takes about 10–15 minutes per day and I use the process as my evening ritual), but once you have done a few and made this a part of your daily regimen, you will see that the time invested is well worth it and can even be enjoyable. Using this approach, you will become your own error detective with a sample size of 1 – you. An example report and analysis tool is contained in the Appendix.

Getting Started: Pacing is Important

At first blush, the BRAT™ may seem a bit overwhelming. For this reason, many have found it helpful to ease into the process by beginning the tracking with simple narratives and adding additional sections of the form as you become more conversant and comfortable. In point of fact, this is exactly the way I developed and beta tested it. Others will dive in at the deep end and begin to use the entire process from the beginning. There is no right or wrong way.

The process for personal error reduction is grounded in the science of behavioral change, so there is one indispensible requirement. *First you need to desire the change.* This is accomplished by what the social scientists call cognitive dissonance – a fancy name for wanting something better than the status quo. The error tracking system is designed to show you the numbers and types of errors you are currently making to make you aware that the status quo is something that is not satisfactory – and that you are very likely making many unnecessary errors that can be prevented. Here are the basic steps to get started.

1. **Keep something to record notes on** errors and events that occur during the day on your person at all feasible times. Some use a small notebook to capture a keyword to remind them later, others their Personal Data Assistant, such as a Palm Pilot or Blackberry. The initial format does not matter nearly as much as capturing events as soon as possible after they occur, while they are still reasonably fresh in your mind.

2. **Capture the event in a simple three stage format:** What was happening? What did I (or someone else) do? What happened (or could have happened) as a result? Don't write a book, just get down the basics and perhaps what you were thinking about it as the event occurred.

Blue Threat Report and Analysis Tool (BRAT)™
EVENT AND/OR ERROR REPORT

Date/Time_____ **Ref. #**_____
☐ Error Avoided/Opportunity Achieved

Error Category
☐ Defective Outcome ☐ Waste/Inefficiency ☐ Missed Opportunity

Background—What was going on?
_____
_____
_____
_____

Action taken?
_____
_____
_____
_____

Consequence/Potential Consequence?
_____
_____
_____
_____

Risk Assessment Guide

Probability of Recurrence	Potential Severity
A—Very likely to occur routinely	1—Death, serious injury, or failed mission
B—Probably will occur at short intervals	2—Minor injury, damage to mission
C—May occur but infrequently	3—Lower quality, time or resource waste
D—Unlikely to occur again	4—Minimal threat, inconvenience

    Probability of Recurrence   **A B C D**
    Potential Severity   **1 2 3 4**

Immediate Follow-up Actions (if required)
_____
_____

Error Producing Conditions
☐ Physiology/Fatigue
☐ High Risk-Low Frequency Event
☐ Time Pressure
☐ Low Signal to Noise Ratio
☐ Normalization of Deviance
☐ One-Way Decision Gate
☐ Information Overload
☐ Poor Communication
☐ Faulty Risk Perception
☐ Inadequate Standards
☐ Previous Error
☐ Distraction
☐ Broken Habit Pattern

Violation Producing Conditions
☐ Mission Expectations
☐ Power + Ego
☐ Unlikely Detection
☐ Poor Planning
☐ Leadership Gap
☐ Poor Role Models/Copycat
☐ Unique/Special Event

Hazardous Attitudes
☐ Anti-Authority
☐ Impulsiveness
☐ Invulnerable/Bulletproof
☐ Too Competitive/Macho
☐ Resignation
☐ Pressing Too Far
☐ Vanity/Ego Protection
☐ Emotional Jetlag
☐ Along for the Ride
☐ Procrastination/Delayed Decision

Mental Bias
☐ Expectation Bias
☐ Confirmation Bias
☐ Specialty Bias
☐ Framing Error
☐ Fundamental Attribution Error
☐ Other_____

Group Dynamics Traps
☐ Strength of the First Idea
☐ Excessive Deference/Halo Effect
☐ Groupthink
☐ Lack of Assertiveness

Situational Factors
Time
Location
Team members
Type of event
Other

Blue Threat Report and Analysis Tool (BRAT™)

Remember: the goal here is to get you to realize how you get into error prone situations so you can recognize and proactively avoid them or reduce the risk they pose to your performance.

3. **Identify and check the box** for any error producing conditions, violation producing conditions, hazardous attitudes and mental biases that were present when the error or event occurred.
4. **Transfer any notes** from other formats to the BRAT™ form on a daily basis. Most successful efforts set aside some dedicated time in the afternoon or the evening for this purpose. If you did not record any errors/events in the previous day, this is a good time to reflect and ask the question "Did I miss anything?"

Remember, this entire process is growth based, and designed for you to implement as desired or required. You may not be interested in personal data collection yet, but someday you might be. Keep the motto of the blue threat process in mind – *as little as you want – as much as you need*.

Trend Analysis (I CAN™)

Trending personal behavior data is not rocket science – although some would have you believe otherwise. It is, however, necessarily systematic to avoid any internal bias that undoubtedly exists surrounding your own perceptions of your daily performance; therefore, you must proceed within the following steps to maintain the reliability of the results. There are four relatively simple steps in the Identify, Categorize, Analyze, and Neutralize process.

1. **Identify.** After collecting sufficient data, which should be at least one week's worth of BRAT™ reports, transfer the data to the roll up analysis on your BRAT™ Tally Sheet (Appendix). Record the events and their reported conditions (EPCs, VPCs, hazardous attitudes, etc.) on the BRAT™ Tally Sheet to track frequency.
2. **Categorize.** First, use the risk assessment guide found on the BRAT™ Report to categorize the error risk in terms of probability of recurrence and potential severity and determine any immediate follow-up actions that may be necessary. Then, estimate the average potential severity (see Figure 6.4) for each of the marked error conditions on the completed BRAT™ Reports and record them on the BRAT™ Tally Sheet. This requires some estimation on your part based upon the error reports. This should provide the basis of your error control risk priority.

3. **Analyze.** Using the completed BRAT™ Tally Sheet as a tool, prioritize your errors from highest to lowest based on risk/frequency and conceptualize a mitigation strategy for correction. This step is highly dependent on your individual circumstances, so the process for developing mitigation strategies is intentionally left open ended. Document your error control interventions and be sure to update and refine each strategy as it evolves. Note: There are no special forms required for this step, but development of a hand written or electronic error control journal is very useful for this purpose as well as for record keeping and continuous improvement.

4. **Neutralize.** Follow up on each error control effort and mitigation strategy with a personal debrief session during your routine error recording sessions. Ask yourself three simple questions:

    a. Did I encounter the specific error threat today?

    b. Did I actively employ my planned mitigation strategy?

    c. Was the strategy effective or do I need to refine it?

Probability of Recurrence	Potential Severity
A – Very likely to occur routinely	1 – Death, injury, or failed mission
B – Probably will occur at short intervals	2 – Minor injury, damage to mission
C – May occur but infrequently	3 – Lowers quality, time waster
D – Unlikely to occur again	4 – Minimal threat, inconvenience

Figure 6.4
Risk Assessment Guide

Notes: Use this process to track the numbers and relative severity of your errors. Make sure to think through the potential for damage and danger, not just the consequences from this single event.

Severity estimates are what could have happened – not the actual consequence of the error. For example, running a red light would code out as a "1" even if you were not broadsided and killed doing it.

From Error Management to Error Control

When trying to communicate a new idea and advocate a new conceptual approach, words are important; so let's start our discussion on error countermeasures with a couple of key definitions.

Manage (*mán·age*) transitive verb

to oversee processes for running something such as a store, department, or project; to guide and control business affairs

Control (*con·tról*) transitive verb

to exercise power or authority over something; to limit or restrict somebody or something in expression, occurrence, or rate of increase

Error *control* – not error management – should be our goal. Human error is responsible for the loss of hundreds of thousands of lives each year – it's more dangerous than a pit bull with a mean streak. You don't manage that kind of threat – you control it. Or at least you should. The next steps in the blue threat process teach error control through proceduralization. In the same way that checklists and standards are developed and enforced in industrial settings such as aviation, manufacturing and healthcare, we can take the guess work out of many situations by developing and implementing personalized versions.

The Personal Operating Procedure (POP) is a valuable tool that is well worth the preparation time to specifically target personal error reduction centers of gravity (ECG). The guidelines for developing a POP closely parallel those used by aircraft manufacturers and in other high risk industries in developing checklists to standardize performance when training and judgment are not enough to guarantee safe and effective operation.

POPs allow individuals to create simplified "cookbook" methods to combat frequent error producing conditions and situations and also provide details about the appropriate precautions. In general, a POP is what is referred to as a *cognitive forcing strategy* which, in layman's terms means it requires a conscious decision and makes it easy for a person to respond in a specified, predetermined manner in the presence of the temptation to do otherwise. It's not like you will go to jail if you violate a POP, but it does force a conscious reflection before making a decision to deviate, avoiding the complacency and apathy that often accompanies poor decisions.

For example, my personal blue threat analysis process revealed a growing aggressive driving problem over three consecutive months. Awareness and informal methods of control were not having the desired effects. When confronted with a particularly obnoxious aggressive driver, prior to creating and implementing a POP, the tendency to let my emotions take over was creating problems and potentially hazardous situations. Following its implementation, I recognized the need to make a conscious decision about each occurrence and had a pre-packaged solution – a readily available option – in how to respond.

> **Situation:** Routine and numerous reoccurrences of aggressive driving were identified on self reports with increasing frequency and severity over a six week period. This 4-step POP was developed and implemented.
>
> **Title:** Reduce Aggressive Driving (4 steps)
>
> **Date:** 1 Aug 2007
>
> **Review due:** 1 Nov 2007
>
> 1. I will practice proactive courtesy on the highway and
> 2. Add 20 minutes (or 10%) to my estimated travel time so as not to get in a hurry and frustrated.
> 3. When confronted with aggressive driving behavior by others, I will give right of way when feasible and not respond with aggression to their behaviors – no matter what.
> 4. I will respond with a smile and "after you" gesture to replace my former middle finger response.

POP Example

After implementation of this procedure, the urge to respond aggressively to other drivers nearly disappeared, and the frequency of BRAT™ reports in this area dropped by 90% and has remained there. Now when I am confronted with aggressive driving by others, I actually get a sense of satisfaction for having conquered it in myself.

The best approach to creating a POP is to analyze the problem, write the procedure and test it. Be brief and succinct; the shorter, the better. A typical POP contains the following elements:

- Situation description
- Title of POP
- Original issue date

- Revision/review date (usually done at 30 days, 90 days and one year for a new POP, and then annually thereafter)
- Step-by-step procedure with identification and emphasis of "critical steps"

Examples of topics that lend themselves well to the POP format include common error patterns associated with:

- Time
- Place
- People
- Specific sequence of events that are frequently encountered

Review, refine and discard the POP when no longer useful or needed. Also, remember that most POPs will need to be refined to reach their maximum effectiveness. Some may initially be overly restricting and you can relax as you bring the challenge they were meant to address under control. Others may not be written strongly enough or you may have to broaden or narrow the scope or break them down into steps to make them easier to remember or execute in real time scenarios. It is also useful to keep all personal operating procedures in the same book or file so you can refer to them often and refresh your commitment to compliance. When the desired behavior becomes *habit*, the procedure is no longer needed and should be discarded – or at least put into mothballs. Recall the discussion from Chapter 4, on over proceduralization being a leading cause of noncompliance. Don't become part of this problem. For a true *Blue Threat Ninja*, personal operating procedures should be a temporary solution on the road to forming lifelong habits of excellence.

Get Started

I'm pretty convinced that the last seven words ever uttered by humans on this Earth will be "we've never done it this way before," an appropriate but sad epitaph for those who would rather die than change. Empowered accountability takes courage to try some new things, and time to adjust and optimize new ways of viewing yourself and your interactions with the world.

There are scores of experts out there that will tell you that fighting human error is a fool's errand and an impossible task. So like Terry and Dino in *Proof of Life*, who relished the impossible challenge, I'll ask you …

"So we're on then?"

SEVEN

Common Enemies: Error Producing Conditions

"I don't know why Pinocchio ever wanted to be a human, he's better off with a wooden head."
– Orson Scott Card

Being human comes with some amazing capabilities matched pretty evenly against some tough worldly challenges. In this chapter, we are going to look at some of the more common performance robbing conditions, some which are environmental and others of our own making. We began the knowledge quest by discussing compliance and its foes in Chapter 4, followed by the process to take theory to action in Chapter 6. In this chapter, we will provide another layer of core information in the form of descriptions and tools for recognizing key *error producing conditions*, which are proven precursors and multipliers of human error.

It is critical to keep in mind that these elements are not sufficient to cause error in and of themselves. They are simply *conditions*; they must be combined in some way with *you and your environment* before they can manifest in any negative outcome. This is where and why most "information only" self improvement and human factors programs fail. Only by integrating this new information into an active process like the one you learned in the last chapter, can you use this information to its full advantage.

A little bit of knowledge can be a dangerous thing. Likewise, knowledge about error producing conditions without the tools to implement it in the real world is *inert* and in many cases might even make a situation worse. Here is an example.

Consider the "turn in the direction of the skid" information provided to you about recovering from a loss of directional control on a slippery road. Without this information, correcting the skid is intuitive. As the rear end of the car starts to slide to the left, the front end of the car is no longer aligned with the highway and is angled to the right. You naturally – and correctly – turn the wheel to the left. But if you *over think* it, a delay ensues while you try to remember what you were taught, and when you are sliding out of control, thinking is not your best course of action.

The response to human error inducing conditions and circumstances in your real world is far less intuitive than recovering a sliding vehicle. We are much better off with the knowledge than without it, but there is still the potential to assume that knowledge is sufficient and stop before we learn how to implement the new information in our daily routines. This can get us trapped in two ways. The first is where we are unable to apply the new information in real time and much like the sliding driver we begin to *over think and under do*. This leads to the second problem, which is the frustration which results from being able to better see what is happening to you, but only after it is too late to do anything about it.

The NIFITI™ (nih-fée-tee) Technique

In order to provide an easy means of applying this new information, we have developed three simple steps to put the theory into action. *Name It, Frame It, Tame It* – or what we refer to as the NIFITI™ technique. Here is how it works.

> **Name It** is the recognition stage where you identify the error producing condition as hazardous and put it into a common language that you and other team members will recognize. That gives everyone a common reference and an instant understanding of the risk. For example, using this technique, you can begin to recognize *time pressure* events in everyday activities both at work and at home by saying the words either to yourself or to others.
>
> **Frame It** means to put the challenge in context with the threats it presents. Is this a potential threat to your decision making? Will it push you to continue a course of action that isn't wise? Often these two steps are enough to trap or mitigate the threat.

Tame It. This last step may involve a variety of actions ranging from stopping the sequence of events until further information is obtained or analyzed, to taking immediate action to correct a situation spinning out of control. In any case, following these three steps provides an excellent real time threat buster for error producing conditions that you can see coming.

Here is an example of how this works: A surgical team is running late getting started on what should be a routine gall bladder removal. During the pre-brief the surgeon states,

I know we are getting a late start, but time pressure (name it) is one of the leading causes of error during routine procedures like this one (frame it) so we are not going to rush anything. If anyone sees the need to slow down, report an observation, or ask a question, it is your responsibility to bring it to my attention. Don't be looking at the clock (tame it).

As you can see, the *Name it – Frame it – Tame it* approach is a powerful, simple and elegant solution to move from knowledge to action. OK, let's dive into the new information.

Error Producing Conditions (EPC)

The concept of error producing conditions comes primarily from the work of J. T. Williams in the late 1980's but is still used in many fields to assess the potential impact of errors. The technique is used in the field of human reliability assessment (HRA), for the purposes of evaluating the probability of a human error occurring throughout the completion of a specific task. The following list is modified from the early work of Williams and has been tested as a tool for personal error control.

The EPCs that follow are roughly ordered from most likely to cause error to least likely.[1] It is not a complete list, but it does give us a place to begin to look for reasons why we make the mistakes we do. If we can learn to see and avoid EPC's, or even to decouple them from each other, our performance should improve immediately.

---

1 Note that these probabilities do not reflect anything about your personal environment of error proneness and must be integrated. This prioritized list comes from an academic study (see footnote 2) that provides a general frame of reference and ordering consideration for you to comprehend the relative differences in the EPCs.

Fatigue/Physiological Degrade

Fatigue is the principle precursor to human error across all industrial settings. It is universally recognized as Public Enemy #1 in high risk endeavors. Depending on the severity of the fatigue and the complexity of the task, fatigue has been shown to raise the probability of error by up to a factor of 50.[2] Fatigue has been called the "chronic disease of the 21st century" and sadly, it is mostly self-inflicted.

Jonathan[3] died almost instantly when his truck ran off the road. He had fallen asleep at the wheel of his delivery truck after taking a second job to make ends meet. Most of Jonathan's work days were in excess of 16 hours, but he had the weekends to catch up and only needed to do it for a few more weeks to climb out of the financial jam he was in. It wasn't the first time he had fallen asleep on the drive home. His wife recalls, that during the previous six weeks he had mentioned repeatedly "not remembering the drive home." I told him he was going to kill himself, she lamented, before breaking down into tears....

"... the *Name it – Frame it – Tame it* approach is a powerful, simple and elegant solution to move from knowledge to action."

Elements of the Error Producing Condition (EPC)

- Fatigue effects are task dependent – routine physical and intellectual tasks are affected least; vigilance and decision making are affected most

- In routine conditions, fatigue effects are masked by apparent competency and apathy associated with decreased vigilance

- Total Mental Fatigue Factor = Sleep debt (ideal sleep vs. actual sleep x number of days) + hours of continued wakefulness + effects of circadian rhythm

- People are very poor judges of their own fatigue or level of impairment

---

2 All probability statistics in this section are based upon the Human Error Assessment and Reduction Technique (HEART) by J. T. Williams. HEART is a technique used in the field of human reliability assessment (HRA), for the purposes of evaluating the probability of a human error occurring throughout the completion of a specific task. Found at Federal Aviation Administration (FAA) Human Factors Workbench. Online at www.faa.gov

3 All case studies in this section are based on actual events. Names and some event sequences have been changed to protect the identity of the participants.

Action Steps for Recognition and Prevention

- Protect your sleep as a performance resource – 8 hours is the magic number
- Estimate your level of fatigue as quantifiably as possible using the equation for Total Mental Fatigue Factor
- Use alternative planning strategies to move "headwork" up front whenever fatigue effects are likely to impair decisions later
- Do not increase your tolerance for error – stay inside standards and fight the urge to take shortcuts with an iron discipline
- Nap if possible; 20–30 minutes can significantly improve mental performance, more can lead to "sleep inertia" upon reawakening

High-Risk/Low Frequency Events

First time events make amateurs of us all and can injure or kill in a hurry if the risk is great enough. They are known to raise the probability of error by up to a factor of 17. Situations that are novel or only infrequently encountered, and yet are perceived as important or even considered mission essential, often result in perception, execution and unsound decision making errors.

It was Jim's first big international business trip. He wasn't a heavy drinker but was excited and eager to show his more experienced sales colleagues he could party with the big boys. They hit the hotel Happy Hour at 5. By 8 pm he was feeling no pain and agreed they should go downtown where the real action was. By midnight he was under arrest in a foreign land....

Elements of the Error Producing Condition (EPC)

- Some high risk/low frequency (HR/LF) events provide discretionary time, others demand immediate action or response
- HR/LF events often lead to a perceived need to "get this over with" and subsequent self-induced time pressure. As events unfold, stress increases beyond the point of optimal performance, further deteriorating your ability to perceive, execute and make knowledge-based decisions
- Lack of an experience base negates intuitive recognition of dangers

Action Steps for Recognition and Prevention

- List potential HR/LF events for your personal level of preparedness and environment; simulate or mentally rehearse responses to these HR/LF events if actual training to proficiency is not an option
- Recognize potential HR/LF events within any major change in your planned sequence of events
- Consciously address the increased risk of an active HR/LF scenario
- Remember, the first decision is how to dedicate your most valuable resource – time; if appropriate, take actions that "buy time" to expand your options and ability to analyze and plan
- Remember that in true HR/LF emergencies, errors are to be expected more frequently and resiliency is vital to bounce back and keep moving

Time Pressure

Time pressure seems to be everywhere these days and leads to procedural shortcuts and attention management problems caused by multi-tasking beyond cognitive capacity and expanding risk thresholds to "make it work." Ironically, many time pressure events are self-induced or agreed to in advance. It is known to raise the probability of error by a factor of 11.

Evan was running late for a meeting he could not afford to be late to. This would be the third time in the last month and people were starting to notice. Normally, the three hour trip across western Kansas on I-70 was an 80 mph run with straight roads and little construction. His radar detector was the latest technology, and with luck he should get to the meeting with a half hour to spare. Now a freak September ice storm had made the radar detector unnecessary, he could barely manage 50 miles per hour and on top of that the road was clogged with overly cautious flatlanders. He was half-way around the Ford van when he hit the ice on the overpass and lost control. He hit the guardrail hard and the world turned upside down – again and again. When it all stopped, he climbed out of the broken windshield, said a quiet prayer of thanks and shaking badly, surveyed the damage. "At least I'll have a legitimate excuse this time," he thought.

Elements of the Error Producing Condition (EPC)

- Causes a scheduling shift in near-future events, negating the planned sequence and any pre-planned tactics or strategies
- Often results in the "necessity" to abandon normal procedures or restrictions to meet new timeline
- Negates recognition primed decision making[4] (RPDM) by stepping out of normal habit patterns and routine

Action Steps for Recognition and Prevention

- List potential time pressure scenarios that you routinely encounter and develop techniques and discipline to reduce these known scenarios
- Avoid self-imposed time pressure in all situations
- Recognize a time compression encounter as the 1st step of the "Lost Situation Awareness Triangle" (time pressure – broken habit pattern – distraction); aggressively fight to stay inside normal habit patterns and avoid distractions
- Aggressively manage the task scheduling for any unfolding time pressure scenario or major mid-mission change event
- Strive to get ahead and stay ahead – if feasible, move elements from high-workload segments to an earlier timetable for accomplishment
- Always ask "what's next?" to keep mentally ahead of the curve; manage time – all the time – and give time pressure events the respect they deserve

Low Signal to Noise Ratio (LSNR)

LSNR occurs when important cues are lost in the "background noise" of events, preventing timely recognition and actions. Unless the signal is amplified, repeated and perceived, lost situation awareness often occurs. LSNR is known to raise probability of error by a factor of 10. Depending on the situation, it can have life and death consequences.

---

4   Recognition primed decision making is the intuitive capacity built from experience. It is described eloquently and in detail in Dr. Gary Klein's outstanding book *Sources of Power*.

It was great to see everyone in the family again. Brothers, sisters, aunts, uncles and all the kids had gotten back together at Karen's suburban home for a mini family reunion. They all had agreed to "keep an eye" on each other's kids, but when one of the young mothers said "has anyone seen Tommy?" the entire crowd went on high alert looking for the three year old toddler. Moments later, a scream came from the next door neighbor's back yard. Somehow, Tommy had managed to go out the screen door, cross the neighbor's yard, climb through a construction fence and had fallen into the pool next door. The ambulance came quickly and the emergency room did their best, but after 48 hours of consulting with neurologists and clergy, the parents pulled their child off life support....

Elements of the Error Producing Condition (EPC)

- High <u>and</u> low workload can both contribute to low LSNR. High workload increases mental "noise level" – low workload (complacency) reduces sensitivity to the signal through boredom or apathy

- Signal recognition is dependent on both focus (what you have in your scan) and "mental bandwidth" (amount you are capable of scanning)

- Engineering solutions try to amplify the signal and reduce the associated noise levels – human approaches can do the same

Action Steps for Recognition and Prevention

- Identify specific high/low workload areas where LSNR might cause you to miss an important cue

- Discuss countermeasures such as sterile (mission only) communication periods, heightened awareness, specified monitoring, and challenge and response communications procedures

- Avoid "tunnel vision" or preoccupation with single anomalies that can disrupt your normal scan pattern or cause you to "focus more and see less"

- Consider other alternatives for signal "amplification" and noise reduction during critical operational phases, such as an "if you see something – say something" approach to promote assertiveness throughout the work team for missed signal amplification

Normalization of Deviance (NOD)

also known as "Routine Noncompliance"

Originally used to describe the events and culture in NASA that preceded the crash of the Space Shuttle *Challenger*, it now applies to any situation where individuals or organizations ignore existing guidance as a matter of routine. NOD is known to raise the probability of error across an entire organization by negating the margin of safety provided by policy and procedures.

Ben had gotten away with the "lighter fluid on the smoldering charcoal" trick a hundred times. In spite of the multiple warnings on the back of the bottle, and his wife's constant reminders that he was an idiot for doing it and setting a bad example for the kids, it was still the best way he knew to get the charcoal ready in a hurry. For some unknown reason, this time was different and as he released the pressure on the plastic container after squirting a good bit into the fire, the flame followed the stream back into the container and exploded. He survived the event, but every time he looks in the mirror he gets a cruel reminder of his poor decision....

Elements of the Error Producing Condition (EPC)

The Normalization of Deviance typically occurs in four distinct phases

1. An event occurs outside of good judgment or policy without a negative consequence
2. Because nothing bad happened, the deviation is allowed to continue
3. Eventually, the deviation becomes not only condoned, but expected
4. An accident occurs outside of existing guidelines, and someone is found to be willfully negligent and held accountable

Action Steps for Recognition and Prevention

- With an honest and open process, list all areas where you, your family, your work team or organization currently operate outside of existing policy or procedural guidance
- Review *Violation Producing Conditions* (VPC's) in Chapter 4 and implement appropriate controls
- Determine a path forward to create or restore integrity of good judgment, policy and procedures or obtain appropriate waivers

- Establish a continuous improvement process to seek higher levels of effectiveness and efficiency within existing guidelines; negate the need to deviate for mission accomplishment

One-Way Decision Gates

One-way decision gates occur when there is no obvious way to reverse an unintended or unwise action. One-way decision gates are known to raise the probability of error by a factor of 8.

Sharon had completed her mountain flying checkout and was headed through the pass on a VFR flight plan up to Leadville (Colorado) to get her "Sharon has landed at the highest field elevation in the U.S." certificate, along with lunch and a tank of Avgas before heading back home before dark. As she made her turn into the mountain pass, she suddenly realized she had made an dreadful and irreversible error by flying into a box canyon that was too narrow to turn around in and too high for her single engine aircraft to climb out of. The wreckage was found three days later 75 feet below the rim of the canyon....

Elements of the Error Producing Condition (EPC)

- One-way decision gates are the point in a course of action beyond which reversal is not possible. Examples include firing a weapon, jumping from an aircraft, or failing to disengage from a course of action in time to execute an alternative

- Points of no return are often not recognized for what they are until it is too late. Recognition requires an "enlightened eye" for seeing future options opening or closing, much like a chess master

- Final chances to avoid one-way decision gates are called *exit strategy SOPs* (standard operating procedures) and include such events as missed approach points for pilots and weapons release decisions for law enforcement officers

Action Steps for Recognition and Prevention

- List all potential one-way decision gates that occur in your operational environment

- Simulate or mentally rehearse responses to these events to develop the "enlightened eye" of the chess master

- Assess future consequences of all unplanned events or decisions during periods of rapid change and or high risk activities
- Develop, plan, brief and execute exit strategy SOP's as if your life (or someone else's) depended on it – it often does
- See one-way decision gates coming before you get to them and recognize them for what they are

Information Overload

Description: Effects of information overload include anxiety, poor decision-making, difficulties in memorizing and remembering, and reduced attention span. Information overload is known to raise the probability of error by a factor of 6.

Marybeth was having a typical soccer mom day; helping out with the Church newsletter in the morning, two dentist appointments for the boys while the car was getting its annual inspection, a quick lunch and then drop the oldest off at the bus for his All Star travel team baseball game by 3. They arrived at the school at 2:55 with no bus in sight. Something wasn't quite right, so as she grabbed her cell phone to call Allison (another mom), she noticed two missed calls from earlier in the day. As Allison answered, Marybeth heard the distinct sound of an aluminum bat hitting a ball in the background as she was informed that the bus left at 1 pm and the game was nearly over. She will never forget the look of disappointment on her son's face when she told him he'd missed his all star game....

Elements of the Error Producing Condition (EPC)

- Overabundance of low quality, fragmentary information has been called "data smog" due to its potential to obscure essential information at critical decision points (See also *Low Signal to Noise Ratio*)
- At some point in the information gathering process, the decision making enemy switches from *uncertainty* (not enough data) to *confusion* (too much data). Recognizing this point is key to recognizing the presence of this EPC
- These effects merely add to the stress caused by the need to constantly adapt to a rapidly changing situation. Sooner or later, the mistakes begin

Action Steps for Recognition and Prevention

- Learn to recognize your personal symptoms of information overload – channelized attention, confusion, frustration, etc. Use memory aids and lists

- Strive for precise communications; a concise message communicated at the appropriate time to the appropriate person (See also *Communications/Information Transfer*)

- Fight to find a "data appropriate" zone where information can be communicated, assessed and effectively utilized in real time

- Upon recognition of information overload, immediately confirm real time priorities, then return to working the problem in a controlled manner

- In real time operations, develop a comfort level with "adequate" information as opposed to "complete" information. Remember, time is your ally and enemy – data requires analysis and analysis eats time (See *Time Pressure*)

Poor Communications/Information Transfer

Description: Regardless of the setting, imprecise, incomplete or misunderstood communications increase the potential for individual error in all situations. This EPC is known to raise the probability of error by a factor of 5.5.

Rex worked as a maintenance technician in charge of equipment repair on his company's stamping presses. After a week of vacation, his first task back was to replace the heavy magnetic plates on a piece of company machinery. Previously, when Rex had performed this task, it was necessary to remove a clamp and use full strength with a pry bar to remove the plate. Unknown to Rex, the plates were no longer sealed in the same manner and the plates could be removed without the aid of any mechanical device. When he attempted to remove the face plate with the full force of the pry bar, it came off MUCH quicker than he had expected. The 45 pound plate fell down on his foot breaking it in four places. The company was found at fault for not notifying all employees of the change in procedure and Rex received a significant insurance settlement plus full pay for the four months it took to recuperate from the preventable injury.

Elements of the Error Producing Condition (EPC)

- Faulty communications are listed as contributory or causal in over 50% of industrial accidents
- Typical breakdowns include late/incomplete information transfer during changeover or "handoff" operations or following a period of vacation or other "off time"
- Bias, noise, time pressure and vagueness also play key roles in limiting understanding in real time operations
- Communications apathy leads to perceptions of understanding where it may not exist

Action Steps for Recognition and Prevention

- Speak clearly, to the point and at a point in time when the receiver is ready to listen and act upon your information
- Confirm understanding by repeating or clarifying key communications
- Challenge poor communications on important issues. Example: "Are you saying our schedule is no longer valid?"
- Be aware of and account for bias you may have about an issue, desired outcome or the person delivering the message
- Listen aggressively for meaning – question key points to ensure understanding
- If time permits, analyze key pieces of information by looking at all the relevant factors and walking the other person through your analysis of the issue at hand – summarize for comprehension

Faulty Risk Perception

Risk management begins with hazard identification. Individuals who become comfortable with certain risk factors may not recognize them as hazards until it is too late to act. Faulty risk perception is known to raise the probability of human error by a factor of 4.

Robert was getting back into the swing of things following a painful divorce. It had been over a year since the divorce and one of his friends had set him up with Karen, a petite 30-something school teacher "who liked to party." After a quiet dinner, they hit a local night club, shared a few drinks and ended up back at his new apartment for a night of unprotected intimacy. Within a week he knew something was very wrong, and an embarrassing visit to his medical practitioner confirmed a full blown case of gonorrhea. With friends like that....

Elements of the Error Producing Condition (EPC)

- Risk optimizing requires a clear and realistic picture of both risk and reward; know the mission – know the true risk
- **Risk** = Exposure and Probability x Severity x Impact on mission or people
- A hazard becomes more risky when it is unknown, unaccounted for or underappreciated
- Risk severity is often determined by situational factors outside of our direct control or experience

Action Steps for Recognition and Prevention

- Seek optimum risk level, balancing risk and reward and avoid underestimating or overestimating the risk or reward
- Avoid the common tendencies to obsessively seek minimum risk level or maximum mission accomplishment mental models
- List and rank order all routine personal and mission hazards and risk factors from "highest risk" to "least worthy of action;" review and update them often
- Force the risk-reward analysis and discussion during all changes or non-routine operations
- Search and destroy *Normalization of Deviance* sequences
- Once risks are identified, seek to control them through rejection, avoidance, delay, transfer, or by spreading them out over time – leave room for the unexpected
- Avoid the poor risk assessment traps of being either overly optimistic or too alarmist

Inadequate Standards

Ambiguity in a standard of performance has been shown to increase the occurrence of human error by a factor of 4. Often, this is caused by new or changed policies or procedures or by the existence of multiple sources of conflicting guidance. Other issues involve lack of clarity and cultural or language barriers in communicating the standard.

In November of 2006, the National Transportation Safety Board issued a formal recommendation that public transportation systems create rules restricting the use of cell phones and texting devices by drivers while operating public conveyance such as trains, trolleys and buses. Over the next three years over 40 people would be killed in a variety of accidents across all three areas directly due to driver inattention while operating cell phones or texting devices before any state or federal rule was put into place.

Elements of the Error Producing Condition (EPC)

- Inadequate standards leave interpretation up to the individual and lead to unnecessary variability in responses
- Conflicting standards force some degree of noncompliance in cases where they are mutually exclusive, e.g., different minimum equipment requirements
- Inadequate standards signal confusion or apathy from leaders and quality assurance personnel, often leading to noncompliance from line personnel

Action Steps for Recognition and Prevention

- Seek clarity from appropriate supervisory level whenever and wherever standards are conflicting or unclear
- Fuzzy standards can be mitigated by clear written and verbal statements of intent by executive leadership, supervisors and standardization personnel
- Absent supervisory guidance or response to a request for clarity, think through and determine how you plan to operate under a personal SOP congruent with the intent of the guidance
- Communicate your personal approach to fuzzy standards to your supervisor, peers and subordinates

Distraction

Distraction occurs in many forms and has been defined as *a departure from whatever current need or plan a [person] is attending to.* Managing personal distractions is like managing any other part of your performance challenge. You first need to be clear – get a handle on what they are. Distractions are a big part of our life, and being conscious about them is the first step to managing them.

The first performance goal is making *unconscious* distractions, *conscious* distractions. In the words of time management expert Tony Clark, "Personal distractions can be very loud and demanding. Just make sure they play their part on your terms."

Eighteen year-old Whitney was just home from spring break and was pumping gas at the 7-Eleven when a Ford Explorer cutting through the parking lot lost control and hit a pick-up truck, which then hit the gas pump, pinning Whitney between her minivan and the gas pump. The pump spewed fuel and sparks from the accident made the pick-up truck and the minivan burst into flames. Whitney was unable to escape and died screaming in the ensuing fire. The driver of the Explorer was charged with Careless Driving Involving Death. Following the investigation, police said there was no evidence that drugs, alcohol or car malfunctions were involved in the accident. A moment of distraction on a routine drive through the 7-Eleven parking lot was all it took to set off this tragic sequence of events, ending an innocent life.

Elements of the Error Producing Condition (EPC)

- Distraction is typically caused by one of three things: lack of ability to pay attention, lack of interest in the object of attention, or greater interest in something other than the object of attention
- Internal distractions can be viewed as "preoccupation" and are within our direct control
- External distractions are not within our direct control, and must be dealt with through attention management, communication and focus tools
- *Interruptions* are often the first flag that a distraction is present
- Distractions are often a key element of procrastination

Action Steps for Recognition and Prevention

- Recognize any interruption from a planned work flow as a signal a distraction is present

- Learn to "button up" preoccupations by taking positive steps to resolve them or temporarily compartmentalizing them in your mind to prevent continuous distraction
- Use attention management strategies such as *attention steering* and *memory flags* to keep your focus on what is important
- Communicate the risk posed by the distraction to yourself and the group to increase awareness

In addition to these eleven EPC's, there is one more serious trigger event we need to recognize as a serious error producer.

The Twelfth Offender: The First Mistake

The Twelfth Offender is error itself – and the distractions, broken habit patterns and loss of focus that often follow in the wake of an initial error.

How many times have we seen a flawless figure skating performance deteriorate into a nightmare before our eyes, simply because the skater seeking a perfect performance could not retain their focus after one small slip or fall? Or for baseball little league fans, how often do you see the "error disease" spread from one infielder to another until an entire team collapses in one embarrassing inning?

There are reasons behind this phenomenon, and once understood, they can be fought.

Errors possess their own momentum. Left unchecked, they build upon each other until a previously normal situation spins chaotically out of control. In sports, it's called "choking." In human factors and accident investigation terminology, this sequence of deteriorating performance is called "an error chain" and it is broken by applying a few easy rules of thought and action.

Though she was generally considered to be the world's best figure-skater for many years, Michelle Kwan was twice upset by American teenagers in the Olympic Games – first by Tara Lipinski in 1998 and then by Sarah Hughes four years later. In both cases, Kwan could not recover after early mistakes. Failing to skate anywhere near her best, she lost her opportunity to become an Olympic Champion even though the judges were clearly pulling for the four-time world champion to win.

Elements of the Error Producing Condition (EPC)

When I asked myself, "When am I most likely to make an error?" the answer was simple – *right after I just made the first one*. Like many of you who grew up professionally in high risk industries, I have a very low tolerance for error. When I make a mistake, it angers me, frustrates me and it distracts me.

Action Steps for Recognition and Prevention

- First, give yourself a reasonable expectation of making an error or two. To continue with the baseball metaphor, even World Champion professional teams lose 30–35% of the time. The key to championship performance is to not let a loss of perfection knock you off stride. Stay focused, especially in the first few seconds after you recognize the first error, as this is the danger zone where your attention gets hijacked

- Secondly, address and correct the error at the appropriate time and place – which might be **never** – but certainly not when doing so would potentially interfere with the ongoing task at hand

- Finally, bounce back and learn from the errors you make. If you study and track your own error patterns, you will quickly see how certain sequences of errors can be anticipated, recognized, avoided or mitigated before they do harm to you or your performance

Summary

Predictable is preventable. Armed with adequate knowledge and a will to improve, error producing conditions can be seen in advance. Use the NIFITI™ technique to heighten awareness and increase vigilance and make certain to account for your personal and professional environments as you process this new knowledge into action.

In our next chapter, we are going to look at hazardous attitudes and their impact on our performance and normally sound judgment.

EIGHT

Blind Spots: Hazardous Attitudes and Mental Bias

> *"The greatest discovery of my generation is that a human being can alter his life by altering his attitudes of mind."*
> – William James

Often, it is not external error producing conditions that cause us to error, but rather an internal mindset that turns us into our own worst enemy. These conditions are referred to under a variety of names across a few different disciplines. For our purposes, we will limit our discussion to a relatively few bad actors known as *hazardous attitudes* and *mental bias traps*.

As we go through our lives, our attitudes change based on our experiences, training, the situation and the people we live and work with. With some personal insights, we can mold and manage attitudes by teaching ourselves how to recognize and react. To a certain extent, managing hazardous attitudes and uncovering mental bias traits is a skill like any other, and the more you practice, the better you become. You may not be able to control many things in your life, but you can control your attitude and account for personal bias. Armed with this skill set, you will make fewer errors in the heat of the moment.

Hazardous Attitudes (Hazats)

Here is the short list of essential information about hazardous attitudes. First of all, they are not a permanent part of our personality. If you believe the smart people who make their living studying such things, personality is a relatively fixed aspect of our being sometime before puberty. Attitudes, on the other hand, are malleable things that come and go, change shapes, and dramatically impact how we see and interact with our world.

"The second important aspect of hazardous attitudes is that all of us have them on occasion...."

The second important aspect of hazardous attitudes is that all of us have them on occasion, some more than others. No one is immune to occasional *impulsiveness* or its fiendish doppelganger *procrastination*. Most men (and quite a few women) will admit to a periodic episode of *over competitiveness* or an occasional *anti-authority* moment.

Hazardous attitudes annoy us when we witness them in others, but most of us have a difficult time seeing them in ourselves. This is a mistake we will fix here. Left unchecked, hazats are dangerous and potentially lethal if we allow them to filter our perceptions or hijack our decision making.

Here is the good news. Hazardous attitudes and the mental bias traps follow a few basic forms. They are easy to recognize with just a little knowledge and a desire to improve. We will provide the knowledge here, and hopefully a little motivation to improve as well.

The final bit of good news is that if we can recognize these attitudes and mental bias traps, we can neutralize them before they can compromise the mission or do us any harm personally or professionally.

We will begin with one of my favorite hazats, and one I am still guilty of on occasion.

Anti-authority

"No one tells me what to do!"

This hazat generally manifests itself as rage against the organization, co-workers, or even family members. Anti-authority attitudes are often found in people who may pride themselves on being a loner or a renegade, or might have just had something happen to them that they perceive as an injustice such as being passed over for a promotion or snubbed in some other manner.

Lt Col Bud Holland was a B-52 pilot who crashed an aircraft at Fairchild Air Force Base in Spokane, Washington while performing prohibited maneuvers in preparation for an air show in the early 1990s. His attitude that <u>no one</u> was going to tell him how to fly or what he was allowed to do in "his aircraft" was pervasive for over three years before the tragic ending took three other senior officers and family men with him to the grave.

Problems Caused

- Disdain for people and positions manifests itself as disdain for policies and regulations
- Acts of rebellion become acts of recklessness
- Undermines leadership
- Destroys morale and followership in others

Checklist for Recognition and Prevention

- Evaluate specific reasons behind frustrations
- Communicate clear expectations of standards
- Don't pander to or validate complaints
- Report acts of noncompliance so the system can deal effectively with the problem, which is often progressive

"Anti-authority attitudes are often found in people who may pride themselves on being a loner...."

Impulsiveness

"I (we) need to do something about this now!"

This attitude short circuits logic so you may not fully understand the scope of the problem(s). Impulsiveness is when the person urges action before collection and analysis of useful information. Often, impulsiveness strikes when we want to exert influence on a situation that is spinning out of our understanding and/or control. Mark Dykeman, an IT professional and blogger at *broadcasting-brain.com* offers the following advice and tool for combating impulsiveness.[1]

---

[1] Modified from http://broadcasting-brain.com/2008/12/18/think-again-a-checklist-for-weighing-the-impulsive-act/

Before you pull the pin, before you leap off the cliff, before you charge into battle, before you commit to an irreversible course of action ... think again and ask yourself the following questions.

1. Do you understand the situation well enough to do what you are about to do?
2. Are you reacting in anger, fear, or hurt?
3. Do you really understand the consequences?
4. Have you told the people who need to know what's about to happen?
5. Do you know what the costs will be?
6. Has anyone else tried something like this before and been successful?
7. Is this something you need to do – or simply want to do?
8. Is there a better way?
9. If you answer "no" to any of questions 1–7 and "yes" to question 8, maybe you'd better stop and think again.

"Often, impulsiveness strikes when we want to exert influence on a situation that is spinning out of our understanding and/or control."

Problems Caused

- May not have adequate experience or knowledge to support reliable intuitive decision making
- Premature actions may proceed through one-way decision gates
- Self induced time pressure is the first step in the loss of situation awareness (SA)
- Short circuits team inputs and supervisory or peer intervention or assistance from others

Checklist for Recognition and Prevention

- Encourage multiple options as a matter of routine
- Ensure adequate planning time to think through and brief multiple scenarios
- Encourage actions that will "buy time" instead of reduce it
- Seek all available information before deciding a course of action

- Stay conservative until planning and analysis are complete

Invulnerability

"It can't happen to me!"

The keys to recognizing this attitude in yourself and others lie in a healthy respect for your own mortality. Watch out for signs of a bulletproof mentality and remember even Superman is vulnerable to kryptonite. Another signpost to recognize this hazardous attitude is the tendency to shrug off close calls. Every near miss is a tremendous learning opportunity and should be viewed as such. Merely emerging unscathed is not proof of invulnerability or superior skill. It may be just luck.

> "Watch out for signs of a bulletproof mentality...."

Timothy Treadwell was a self described naturalist and grizzly bear "expert." He camped among the coastal grizzly bears of Katmai National Park in Alaska for over a decade. He gave hundreds of presentations in which he claimed the bears were not naturally aggressive and argued that they were misunderstood. He gave them cute nicknames and called them his "buddies." At the end of his 13th season in the park in 2003, he and his girlfriend Amie Huguenard were killed and partially devoured by one or possibly two of his "buddies."

Problems Caused

- Attitude insulates from legitimate fear
- "It hasn't happened yet" becomes "it can't happen"
- Feeds normalization of deviance phenomena through ever greater risk taking
- Breeds unwarranted confidence to handle novel situations
- Breeds a casual attitude towards compliance as they see themselves as providing for safety margins – not policy or regulations

Checklist for Recognition and Prevention

- See a close call as a "near miss" (or better said "near hit") that requires action to prevent recurrences and not validation of someone's superior skills, judgment or good fortune
- Maintain a healthy respect for new situations and first time mistakes

- Remind yourself and peers that their actions jeopardize others as well as themselves
- If someone (maybe you) has cheated death a few times, realize the law of averages is catching up with you

Too Competitive/Macho
"That's nothing. Watch this!"

The Macho man has an "I'm better than you" attitude and may be ultra-competitive. The Macho man's need to be the center of attention can drive them to write checks with their words and actions that their skills and abilities simply can't cash. You don't want to be anywhere near these people when those checks bounce.

> "The Macho man's need to be the center of attention can drive them to write checks with their words and actions that their skills and abilities simply can't cash."

Jim's over competitive attitude was always simmering. He couldn't resist the urge to "one up" every story or add his two cents worth on why someone else's achievements weren't so great. But when his temper flared on the basketball court during a recreation league game, resulting in an intentional elbow to a workplace colleague's face, it was the last straw. He was let go the following week.

Problems Caused
- Often overly aggressive people who feel they have to "one up" everyone in inappropriate competitions
- Wrong agenda: "Me" instead of "us" leads to lost focus on mission or organization's goals
- Safety and mission compromised by over-competitive attitude

Checklist for Recognition and Prevention
- Avoid inappropriate competitions and challenges
- Keep authority gradient[2] clear

---

2 *Authority Gradient* is the term used to describe the level of power a person in charge exhibits over his or her subordinates. In smooth working teams of adults, a good leader will have a shallow authority gradient; with over competitive or immature types, a more steep gradient is usually necessary.

- Tolerate only as long as the macho person's words and actions do not endanger either the mission or anyone's safety

Resignation

"Why bother, man? We're doomed."

In high risk environments, people do not have the luxury of simply giving up on a task and walking away. This hazardous attitude manifests itself in a passive acceptance of fate regardless of the time and options still available. *Resignation* often turns into continual whining and no initiative towards solving the problem. It can also be contagious in a group setting.

In one of the most amazing survival stories ever told, both resignation and incredible resilience were demonstrated. During a fateful climb on Mount Everest in 1996, guide Rob Hall led a group of climbers including 50 year old American doctor Beck Weathers. A series of events and bad weather turned the trip into tragedy.

> "Resignation often turns into continual whining and no initiative towards solving the problem."

During that climb, Weathers began to suffer from vision problems and was left alone for a whole night with both hands and his face exposed to the elements in a terrible blizzard. His fellow climbers said that his frozen hand and nose looked and felt as if they were "made of porcelain" and left him there after resigning themselves that he would perish on the mountain and they had to look after their own survival. But Weathers survived another freezing night alone in a tent unable to drink, eat, or even keep himself covered with the sleeping bags he was left with. When Weathers realized no one was coming for him, he decided he would not die in place and pulled together enough willpower to crawl over the frozen terrain to a nearby camp. Following the ordeal, Beck had his right arm amputated halfway below the elbow. All four fingers and the thumb on his left hand were removed; his nose was amputated and reconstructed with tissue from his ear and forehead and he lost parts of both feet to his injuries. He continues to practice medicine, and deliver motivational speeches because he would not resign himself to fate when the odds appeared insurmountable. Weathers authored a book about his experience, <u>Left for Dead</u>, which was first published in 2000.[3]

---

3   Beck Weathers, Left for Dead: My Journey Home from Everest

Problems Caused

- Quits trying to solve problem, encourages others to do the same
- Makes the situation seem out of control
- May stop monitoring duties or providing expected input to program or project team
- Their incessant whining annoys and distracts, often at critical phases of a problem

Checklist for Recognition and Prevention

- Re-engage the whiner and try to keep on some task. Don't pander to the whining or you will only get more
- Assign specific duties and instructions to monitor their progress and avoid slipping back into resigned attitude
- Reinforce critical role as team member, for example, "Snap out of it. We need positive attitudes and everyone working together to get this done"

Pressing Too Far

Also known as "Mission Hacking" or "Get there-itis"

"We're going to get this done come hell or high water."
or, **"I've got somewhere I need to be!"**

Pressing usually manifests itself when someone is rushing to get something accomplished regardless of the potential hazards. They may be unwilling to discuss alternatives and may be harboring a hidden agenda (a soccer game they need to get to, another appointment, desire to please a boss) that is overcoming their personal and professional discipline. The result is often unwise and unnecessary risk. This is often a difficult hazardous attitude to decode, as striving hard for a goal is also the mark of a high achiever. The difference between a logical high achiever and one who is *pressing too far*, is when the goal becomes <u>too</u> powerful for rational risk assessment.

After graduating from Emory University, top student and athlete Christopher McCandless abandoned his possessions, gave his entire $24,000 savings account to charity and hitchhiked to Alaska to live in the wilderness. McCandless was an American wanderer who adopted the name "Alexander Supertramp" and hiked into the wilderness with little food and equipment, hoping to live a period of solitude. Almost four months later, he died of starvation near Denali National Park. Jon Krakauer wrote a book about his adventures, published in 1996, entitled Into the Wild, which was later made into a movie.

> "The difference between a logical high achiever and one who is *pressing too far*, is when the goal becomes too powerful for rational risk assessment."

Problems Caused

- Pushes to get through or complete a task in spite of increasing or unwarranted risks
- Does not want to discuss or evaluate risks or alternatives
- Likely has a hidden agenda that may conflict with the overall objective

Checklist for Recognition and Prevention

- Uncover the hidden agenda if possible, and acknowledge a hidden agenda might be there even if it can't be uncovered
- Communicate your understanding of the desire to press on
- Force feed the risk-reward discussion and consider multiple alternatives

Oversized Ego/Vanity

"I'd rather die than look bad!"

Not surprisingly, you can both die and look bad doing it. In point of fact, many have done so. In his excellent book, *Deep Survival – Who Lives, Who Dies, and Why*, Laurence Gonzales says that it's a shame we can't die more often because it's such a learning experience. He also says that he doesn't want to die a dumb death that leaves people shaking their heads and putting "Here lies a moron" on his headstone. You may develop an attitude that says you can't stand to fail in front of others and that if anybody can do this, it's you. This lowers your defenses and inhibits your ability to respond appropriately to threats. People experiencing this attitude will push past normal procedural and regulatory limits to prove themselves to someone else. What you may end up proving was not what you intended.

One of the most frequent killers of amateur and professional pilots is the pressure to land in bad weather (low cloud decks or high crosswinds) because another pilot has already done so. This attitude of "if he can do it, so can I" is fallacious for many reasons, including rapidly changing weather conditions, or the type of aircraft or equipment on board. Yet in many a pilot's mind, it becomes a false matter of skill and courage. Good judgment is not cowardice, and true skill is often shown in the decision <u>not</u> to attempt a poor bet and to successfully execute an alternative option.

"... you can both die and look bad doing it. In point of fact, many have done so."

Problems Caused

- Pushes past procedural and regulatory limits to prove themselves to others
- Often has difficulty accepting the need to discontinue the plan of action
- If they succeed outside of the limits, they are likely to do so again and again

Checklist for Recognition and Prevention

- Don't engage or encourage competition
- Stay mission focused and remind Ms. Ego that the job is why you are there
- Execute "Exit Strategy SOP's" with an iron discipline
- Remember that many have done both (died and looked bad) and "Here lies a moron," is a humbling epitaph
- The old adage that "discretion is the highest form of valor" is a great counterpunch to this hazat

Procrastination

"When I get the feeling to do something, I lie down until the feeling goes away." – Poster caption

Procrastination is a behavior that is characterized by deferment of actions or tasks to a later time, often resulting in errors or degraded outcomes caused by lack of time or a poor attitude towards accomplishment. The word itself comes from the Latin words *procrastinatus* (forward) and *crastinus* (to tomorrow). Procrastination is only remotely related to time management or prioritization, as procrastinators often know exactly what they <u>should</u> be doing, even if they cannot get around to doing it.

> "... procrastinators often know exactly what they <u>should</u> be doing, even if they cannot get around to doing it."

Three criteria are often used to categorize procrastination. For a behavior to be classified as procrastination, it must be *counterproductive*, *needless*, and *delaying*.

For the third year in a row, Ron missed his tax deadline. He hadn't collected the documentation very well since he changed jobs and was unsure he could ever get the paperwork together that he needed. The IRS didn't care about his problem, however, and on a routine audit they discovered seven years worth of delinquent or inaccurate taxes. Two years later, the government took his house and began wage garnishment proceedings.

Problems Caused

- Pushes important challenges back in time, giving you less time to accomplish them correctly
- Compounds the error equation by adding time pressure
- Reinforces itself as a bad habit

Checklist for Recognition and Prevention

- Realize you are delaying something unnecessarily
- Discover the real reasons for your delay. List them if necessary. Use your list and break up big items into manageable tasks
- Dispute those real reasons for your delay and overcome them. Be vigorous in your assault on your task list
- There are often three simple reasons people procrastinate. We convince ourselves that the task is:
    1. *Too difficult* – the task seems hard to do; we naturally tend to avoid difficult things in favor of those which seem easy to us.
    2. *Time-consuming* – the task will take large blocks of time, and large blocks of time are unavailable right now.

3. *Missing information, knowledge or skill* – you wait until you have all the pieces of the puzzle before you start (which might be never).

The antidotes? Tell yourself, "*this isn't so tough, it won't take as long as I think it might, and I am sure that I can get the rest of the pieces of the puzzle as I need them.*" The final step – get started, now.

Beyond hazardous attitudes that manifest themselves in the forms described above, there is another serious risk to sound analysis and decision making. Mental bias – an unconscious filtering of information that degrades our ability to get at ground truth in our environment, is also recognizable and can be countered in real time.

Bias Blind Spots

Mental bias – or mindset – induces error by narrowing our perception, analysis and response options. They run the gamut from negative "stereotypes" to intuitive mental shortcuts. Bias arises from various life experiences, as well as self interest, loyalty and risk estimations. Some social scientists have questioned whether all of the "biases" are in fact cognitive errors, as some typically develop as decision making shortcuts. There is no doubt, however, that left unchecked, bias blind spots can negatively impact our perception, interpretation and actions – often resulting in unnecessary errors and undesirable outcomes.

"*... left unchecked, bias blind spots can negatively impact our perception, interpretation and actions....*"

Poor decision making is often the outcome of *a bias blind spot* – the failure to recognize and compensate for one's own mental biases. This is where the I CAN™ (Identify, Categorize, Analyze, and Neutralize) process of personal performance tracking and analysis can be extremely useful. As we become more aware of our tendencies to take these mental shortcuts, we can consciously identify when they are most likely to occur and control the hazardous mindset in real time by stepping back for a longer, deeper look.

Additionally, we can become more comfortable inviting others into our decision process to gain an outside perspective, keeping in mind that another's perspective may also come with personal bias, but likely not the same ones as yours. Although there are dozens of cognitive biases identified by researchers, we will look at a few of the most troublesome. Before looking at each in detail, here are a few steps you can take to prevent any form of cognitive bias from becoming a problem.

Action Steps for Combating All Forms of Mental Bias

- **Become aware of your bias blind spots.** Know what is pushing your buttons when you are making observations and decisions. Use this error tracking system to identify your personal blind spots.

- **Give all new situations the respect they deserve.** Test your assumptions and don't fall victim to seeing what you expect to see or want to see.

- **Look outside of your own specialization for explanations and options.** The cliché that says "if all you have is a hammer, everything looks like a nail" is an accurate assessment of this bias blind spot. Open your toolkit by being able to break out of your own specialization.

- **Recognize changing situations as a rationale for reassessment.** In real time operations and life, change is the one constant. Don't get locked into having to be right in every situation. Correcting a wrong perception, analysis or decision makes it right in the long run.

- **Invite others into your decision process.** By asking for input from other team members, you are far more likely to be challenged on areas of personal bias and avoid a costly error.

Expectation Bias

"I've seen this a thousand times."

Expectation bias is an error in analysis caused from the fact that you were expecting a certain result of your perception, analysis or selection of course of action. In short, you "see" what you expect to see (or hear, feel, read, etc.) instead of what is actually there. *Expectation bias* has been called the "expert's curse" as it often occurs to highly experienced people while practicing routine or familiar tasks.

This can lead to a series of issues, beginning with a selective search for evidence. We tend to gather facts that support our expectation but disregard other facts that support different conclusions. Even worse, we can then experience selective perception, where we actively screen-out information that we do not think fits our (erroneous) model of reality.

Do power lines cause cancer?

In 1979, a firestorm of controversy erupted over a study that claimed to "prove" electromagnetic fields (EMF) around power lines caused increased cancer rates.[4] *Subsequently, dozens of studies have found that this is not the case, but people believe what they want to believe and when a friend or family member is diagnosed with cancer, they point to the fact that a power line runs close by. Following an exhaustive study in 1995 that conclusively disproved the EMF-cancer link, Robert L. Park, Ph.D., executive director of the American Physical Society wrote, "Will this report end the controversy? Of course not. An entire industry (including researchers) is now dependent on the fear of an EMF hazard."*

In 1995, the society's executive council concluded: "The scientific literature and the reports of reviews by other panels show no consistent, significant link between cancer and power line fields. This literature includes epidemiological studies, research on biological systems, and analyses of theoretical interaction mechanisms. No plausible biophysical mechanisms for the systematic initiation or promotion of cancer by these power line fields have been identified. Furthermore, the preponderance of the epidemiological and biophysical/biological research findings have failed to substantiate those studies which have reported specific adverse health effects from exposure to such fields."[5]

Yet people continue to see what they are conditioned to see, their thinking limited by their own preconceptions, the media, or the influence of others – unfortunate and unnecessary.

"Expectation bias has been called the expert's curse...."

Problems Caused

- Unwillingness or inability to look beyond the scope of our past experience base
- Rejection of the unfamiliar as irrelevant
- Ineffective teamwork due to "halo effect" based on your high level of previous experience
- Misperception of reality may go unrecognized for prolonged period of time and drop out of your short term memory

---

4   Wertheimer N, Leeper E. Electrical wiring configurations and childhood cancer. American Journal of Epidemiology 109:273-284, 1979

5   American Physical Society, Executive Council Statement, April 23, 1995

Checklist for Recognition and Prevention

- Keep a beginner's mindset – try not to fall into perfunctory habits of perception or response based on familiarity or previous experiences
- Increase awareness by highlighting where and when expectation bias has or is likely to occur. Hint: Anywhere you routinely experience the same thing over and over
- Routinely ask, *what might be different than I think it is?*

Specialty Bias

"I'm uniquely qualified to handle this (and you're not)."

Also known as *professional bias* this mindset seeks to see and solve all issues through the lens of an individual's own field of specialization. For example, a human factors expert may only see the human solution to every problem, while an engineer may see a technological one.

> "Source credibility bias blocks input from others who eventually figure out we won't listen to them."

Specialty bias has an evil twin called *source credibility bias* where we reject inputs if we have a bias against the person, organization, or group to which the person belongs. This usually occurs because they are not a part of our group or specialization. For example: "You're not a pilot/surgeon/artist, you couldn't possibly have a solution to this problem."

In high end medical practices, practitioners are trained to identify problems in their own field of specialization, as well as being compensated by the number of procedures they perform. As a result, many are influenced to diagnose patients with a bias toward their own specialization, sometimes resulting in misdiagnosis and unnecessary treatment, up to and including the removal of organs.

*In many ways this is similar to another type of specialty bias by financial brokers who specialize in a few products they evaluate as the best for you. What you have to determine, is that when experts try to tell you what is best for you, make sure you understand they are influenced and potentially biased by what is best for **them**.*

When anyone questions their motives, we see source credibility bias enter the arena, and are quickly informed by those "in the know" that outsiders have no right or validity to question their expert opinions.

Problems Caused

- When we fall victim to *specialty bias* we often underestimate our own level of uncertainty on a topic. When others we trust fall victim to it, we often place unwarranted confidence in their opinion
- This can lead to the illusion of understanding and control, and it snowballs into underestimating future risks because we tend to believe we have more control over events than we really do
- *Source credibility bias* blocks input from others who eventually figure out we won't listen to them
- If we have a successful outcome in spite of our specialty bias, we develop the habit of being unwilling to change thought patterns that we have used in the past in the face of new circumstances

Checklist for Recognition and Prevention

- Realize that challenges come in many variations, and multi-disciplinary approach is nearly always beneficial
- Use lateral thinking skills to force the problem analysis out of your comfort zone
- Routinely ask, *what might be different than I think it is?*

Need to be Right (Confirmation) Bias

"I told you so."

This bias is also known as *confirmation bias* and crosses all boundaries. It manifests itself in the need to confirm earlier perceptions, analysis and decisions and leads to a defensive posture of having to prove "rightness" even if the situation has changed dramatically. *Confirmation bias* is everywhere in our lives, and often it is thrust upon us by others.

Amateur parapsychologists are masters of the confirmation bias game. After a long winded explanation of some very high tech equipment to measure any-

"Seeking confirming evidence is something we do naturally, but it's not very smart."

thing from changing temperatures to low frequency electromagnetic effects, these pseudo-scientists wander around measuring entirely natural phenomena and use every variance on their equipment to "prove" the existence of ghosts or spirits from beyond. With completely unsustainable statements such as "One theory is that when spirits manifest themselves, they disrupt the electrical flow and draw heat from the surrounding area, resulting in cooler local temperatures. See, there is another example of it here in the east corner of this basement ... obviously we have some activity here."

I'm not saying that ghosts don't exist; just that these means of detection are classic examples of a cognitive bias we are all occasionally influenced by.

Problems Caused

- Overbearing attitude that always searches for "proof of rightness" impairs social interaction and can label someone as a "know it all" no one listens to, even when they might be right
- Confirmation bias can lead to suppressed evidence or any data that might prove your personal or pet theory wrong
- Confirmation bias leads to poor self assessment. We tend to attribute our success to our abilities, knowledge and talents, but we attribute our failures to bad luck and external factors
- Poor assessment of others. We attribute other's success to good luck, and their failures to their mistakes or ineptitude

Checklist for Recognition and Prevention

- Don't verbally form or state your opinion on a subject too early. Once something is mentally committed to or stated in public, the emotional need to be right escalates dramatically
- Check your attitude and actions carefully when feeling emotions like *pride* and *self-satisfaction*
- Begin your self assessment or situation assessment with the assumption that you are likely to deceive yourself by overestimating your contribution to the successful outcome – or underestimating your responsibility for a failed one
- Routinely ask, *what might be different than I think it is?*

Seeking confirming evidence is something we do naturally, but it's not very smart. Understanding the fact however, can help us reach rational conclusions by properly analyzing perceptions and evidence and not simply seeing what we want to see.

Fundamental Attribution Error

"This always happens when those guys are involved."

The *fundamental attribution error* occurs when the victim or a participant in a negative outcome is seen as the primary cause for the event. When we fall victim to this mindset with regards to people, we are often overestimating the internal factors (or causes) of a situation and minimizing the external factors.

For example, a teenage driver is sideswiped while driving safely and is wrongly blamed. "It had to be your fault, everyone knows that teens are dangerous drivers and the other driver had never had a ticket or accident in his life."

Fundamental attribution error tends to attribute failures to personal qualities rather than situational causes. Some researchers feel this is a natural tendency because we tend to hold people, rather than situations, in the center of our attention. When we observe other people, the person is the primary reference point while the situation is overlooked as if it is nothing but mere background. Whatever the reason for the bias, it is real and can easily derail our decision making and subsequent actions based upon those biased decisions.

Fundamental attribution error is a foundational cause of racism and stereotyping in the world. The example of the Harvard professor who accused the Cambridge police officer of coming into this house "because he was a black man in America" did not consider all the information about the 911 call about a potential break in at the location. He only saw a white police officer and leapt to the conclusion that this was racial profiling. Likewise, those who see elevated crime rates in minority communities as evidence of inferior values or character are guilty of this same error producing bias.

Problems Caused

- Faulty generalizations – in order to simplify a complex world, we tend to group things and people. These simplifying generalizations can seriously bias decision making processes

- Blame game – we tend to ascribe causation to people we don't respect or like even when the evidence isn't convincing or only suggests a weak correlation between cause and effect
- Premature termination of search for contrary or confirming evidence – we tend to accept the first human centered explanation as the only logical explanation for the outcome

Checklist for Recognition and Prevention

- Learn to question initial assumptions on cause and effect as a matter of routine and be sure to consider both human and environmental factors
- Learn to value and weight situational factors appropriately. They usually play a larger role than we give them credit for
- Withhold judgment when tempted to assign blame for an outcome – get and weigh all the factors
- Routinely ask, *what might be different than I think it is?*

Framing Error

Keep an open mind; plan for the unanticipated.

A *framing error* often occurs in two situations. The first is when we are confronted with a situation and we mentally anchor to our first explanation or analysis, thereby "framing" the initial problem incorrectly. Follow-on perceptions, interpretations and decisions are unduly influenced by this initial "brain lock," and our view of subsequent information is severely narrowed and filtered. For example, a police officer seeing a man in civilian clothes running with a gun may initially anchor to the thought "criminal" when perhaps the situation might be different.

The second type of *framing error* occurs when we shape our plans around an expected or hoped for outcome, and thereby set ourselves up for mismanaging the unexpected if and when it does occur. For example, a pilot flying an instrument approach in a low cloud deck has two ways of planning his actions:

> "I will fly the aircraft to decision height, and then continue the normal landing if I have the runway environment in sight."

Or, alternatively, "I will fly the aircraft to decision height, and then execute a missed approach if I do not have the runway environment in sight."

By framing the plan for the more difficult and less expected outcome (the missed approach), the aircrew avoids the stress of the unexpected and is pleasantly surprised when they break out of the clouds and execute a normal landing.

> "By anchoring too early to an explanation for events, your mind naturally closes out disconfirming information."

Problems Caused

- By anchoring too early to an explanation for events, your mind naturally closes out disconfirming information
- Planning only for the expected sets you up for a high stress, time pressured error if the unanticipated does occur

Checklist for Recognition and Prevention

- Always search for disconfirming evidence
- Plan for the more difficult or unanticipated event, and consider framing your verbal plans in those terms
- Routinely ask, *what might be different than I think it is?*

Summary

There are dozens of hazardous attitudes and bias types we can fall victim to, and we have only scratched the surface here. A free society relies on its citizens to make rational judgments in many situations such as a trial by jury. However, a capitalistic society uses as many of these weaknesses to sell us every possible manner of service or goods. So, we are caught in the middle between conflicting demands (rational decision making) and known patterns of bias that others routinely use against us. The deck is stacked against us, but armed with an understanding of both the types of hazardous attitudes and bias we face, as well as the seriousness of the risks they pose, we can see and counter them more effectively each day.

Now we are going to change directions and take a hard look at how our spiritual beliefs may help shape our performance.

Part Three

Empowered Accountability: Implications and Applications for the Real World

"The first step towards empowered accountability is the cold slap of reality that comes when you stop making excuses and realize you were personally responsible for a bad outcome."

– Tony Kern

NINE

A Few Matters of Faith

*"Find God's grace in every mistake and
always give more than you take."*
– Rascall Flatts, *My Wish*

Discussions about faith and spirituality make people nervous. Many of you are probably already asking yourself what a chapter on *faith* is doing in a book about empowered accountability and error control? That's a fair question. I have a couple of good answers. First, it squarely addresses the issues of ethical decline and narcissism we brought up in Chapter 4. Secondly, nearly all faiths address the issue of *compliance*, and provide encouragement for personal accountability. Finally, after eight chapters focused almost exclusively on the individual perspective, I thought it might be time to point out that the doors to improved personal performance also open outward.

Spirituality is globally recognized by both secular and religious authorities as a legitimate component of personal performance and well being. With that on the table, my purpose here is to speak to both believers (in God) and non-believers from an interfaith perspective with the same intent as the rest of this book – to give you a competitive edge against error in your life and to help you improve your performance across the board. If a few non-believers cast their eyes a bit more towards the heavens as a result – so much the better.

I'm a Christian. As such, I believe that my actions on earth impact the quality of my afterlife. I share this basic belief with Moslems, Jews, Hindus, Buddhists, Baha'i and a variety of other mainstream faith groups. As a Christian, I believe in self-improvement, rejection of destructive behaviors, and making the world better for others. In addition to the previously mentioned faiths, I share these beliefs with Taoists, Sikhs, Buddhist, Jainists and followers of the Shinto path. Zoroastrianism, one of the world's oldest religions, share these common themes in pursuit of outcomes including physical and moral purity, the resistance of evil, and the religious duty to care for both the material and the spiritual aspects of their existence. Even many of the so called *pagan* and *neo-pagan* religions share a good bit of common ground with believers when it comes to personal responsibility for doing good things and avoiding wrongdoing. When we roll all of the followers of these faiths together, well over three quarters of world's population is involved in some form of faith based instruction, so I think faith is not only a legitimate topic for our discussion, it is an imperative one.

We will steer well clear of deep theological or doctrinal discussions for two very good reasons. First, I am not an expert on my own faith, let alone other religions. Unlike many men and women "of the cloth" who write *How to be a Better Christian* books, I approach this topic as a humble and highly imperfect practitioner of my faith, yet one who sees the Divine in day to day things. Secondly, a discussion on how spirituality contributes to error control does not require us to dig too deep into any theology or religious doctrine. When it comes to personal responsibility, it really doesn't matter which holy book you consult. It's all up front and pretty easy to find.

Most faiths take the position that God is ultimately in control yet man is responsible for his own actions. Faith based wisdom then, is not just *knowing* the right thing to do but having the character and will to *do it*. This common ground is our launching pad for discussing matters of the spirit.

Faith in Action

In the New Testament book of *James*, the brother of Jesus tells us that "Faith by itself, if it is not accompanied by action, is dead.[1]" Francis of Assisi,[2] made the same point when he said "Preach the Gospel at all times, and when necessary, use words." If actions do indeed speak louder than words, it begs a couple of relevant questions:

---

1 James 2:17 (NIV)
2 Saint Francis was the founder of the *Order of Franciscans*, a Catholic group formed in the early 1200s.

- What are the relevant actions of faith?
- How does error control and personal improvement manifest itself in our spiritual quest?

Let's begin with the question of *actions*. For our purposes, I have isolated three requirements for action from across the spectrum of faiths.

- Acknowledgement of wrongdoing (sin)
- Repentance
- Personal action to change current behaviors and eliminate wrongdoing in the future

Living in Sin City: The Acknowledgment of Wrongdoing

Let's start where I seem to end up far too often, talking about *sin* – or wrongdoing in the eyes of God. For the purposes of this discussion, I will continue to use the word *sin*, even though it is not universally recognized by other faith groups. I will also rest heavily on my Christian background in discussing the concept of sin.

Sin is often used to mean an action that is prohibited by a divine code or considered wrong, and can refer to either a state of mind or a specific action. We live in a culture where the concept of sin has far too often become entangled in legalistic arguments over right and wrong. Although the list of things one can do to sin is far too long for this book, let's start with a few lists we might be able to agree on – or at least are familiar with.

The first are the Ten Commandments of God, or *Decalogue*, a list of religious and moral imperatives that, according to Judeo-Christian tradition, were authored by God and given to Moses in the form of two stone tablets on the mountain referred to as either *Sinai* or *Horeb* (Exodus 19:23; Deuteronomy 5:2). They are recognized as a moral foundation in Judaism, Christianity, and Islam.

1. And God spoke all these words, saying: "I am the LORD your God, you shall have no other gods before Me"
2. You shall not make for yourself an idol
3. You shall not take the name of the LORD your God in vain
4. Remember the Sabbath day, to keep it holy
5. Honor your father and your mother

6. You shall not murder
7. You shall not commit adultery
8. You shall not steal
9. You shall not bear false witness against your neighbor
10. You shall not covet your neighbor's house; you shall not covet your neighbor's wife, nor his male servant, nor his female servant, nor his ox, nor his donkey, nor anything that is your neighbor's

The second list comes from the Old Testament book of Proverbs,[3] and states that there are "six things the Lord hates and the seventh His soul detests" namely:

- Haughty eyes
- A lying tongue
- Hands that shed innocent blood
- A heart that devises wicked plots
- Feet that are swift to run into mischief
- A deceitful witness that utters lies
- Him that sows discord among brethren

A final list that became all the rage in the European Middle Ages is colloquially called the *Seven Deadly Sins*. The Roman Catholic Church developed and recognizes *Seven Virtues* that can be used to counteract these sins. The sins and their associated virtue include:

Sin	**Virtue**
Lust	Chastity
Gluttony	Temperance
Greed	Charity
Sloth	Diligence
Wrath	Patience
Envy	Kindness
Pride	Humility

---

3   Proverbs 6:16-19

The Science of Sin

Beyond willpower, character, good and evil, there are some very scientific reasons why people sin. Using advanced technology such as functional magnetic resonance imaging (FMRI), a technological wonder that measures which parts of the brain are activated by certain types of stimuli, we are discovering that the brain's reward system is activated in different ways depending on the nature of the sin.

In the September 2009 edition of *Discover* magazine, researcher Kathleen McGowan outlines several fascinating findings from recent research. Not too surprisingly, the sins of *lust, gluttony* and *sloth*, which feed our physical desires are the most difficult to suppress. *Lust*, for example is said to activate multiple pleasure and emotional centers in the brain simultaneously. "It sets nearly the whole brain buzzing," says one researcher.[4] The sins of *pride, wrath* and *envy* activate less powerful parts of the brain. And as much as we would like to find it, McGowan says there is no single "sin center" in the brain, but we are learning more every day about how the reward systems in our minds "lead us into temptation."

> "Although many religious doctrines downplay or even attack science as heretical, in this case science reveals precisely what most faiths teach...."

On the other side of the coin, there are other parts of our brain that attempt to "deliver us from evil." These networks activate when we make the effort to fight back against temptations. Inhibitory control networks in the front of the brain activate when we make the effort to resist. "The two sides battle it out, the devilish reward system versus the angelic brain regions that hold us in check."[5]

Although many religious doctrines downplay or even attack science as heretical, in this case science reveals precisely what most faiths teach, that there is a battle waging inside each of us between good and evil and it begins not in what we do, but in what we *think*.

---

4 "Seven Deadly Sins" by Kathleen McGowan, *Discover Magazine*, Sept 2009. p 50.
5 ibid.

Thoughts and Deeds

Divine law is what it is – unapologetic and directive. It is also important to note that sin goes beyond simply doing wrong things but also includes *thinking* wrong things. Jesus told the religious ruling Jews of His day in the Book of Matthew (Matt 15:18–20),

> But the things that come out of the mouth come from the heart, and these things defile a person. For out of the heart come evil ideas, murder, adultery, sexual immorality, theft, false testimony, slander. These are the things that defile a person; it is not eating with unwashed hands....

Wow, this is a pretty high standard of morality and behavior and frankly, this doesn't sit well with many in the modern world, who would prefer some softer tones and a bit more wiggle room. The Apostle Paul, however, puts the legalistic view of sin in perspective when he says "we all fall short of the glory of God" and further in Romans 3:20, "Therefore no one will be declared righteous in His sight by observing the law; rather, through the law we become conscious of sin." That is our first goal – to become conscious of our spiritual wrongdoing in the same manner as we will become conscious of our other performance robbing thoughts and actions.

> "Divine law is what it is – unapologetic and directive."

I feel a bit more comfortable knowing that I am in good company when it comes to sin (all of us have strayed) but I have no hope of changing if I don't first recognize that I have erred.

As we review the descriptive and prescriptive lists of sins we see one striking similarity between every sin – *willful personal behavior*. By definition, sin involves an error of controllable thought or deed. Some may argue that these lists do not accurately reflect their own virtues or values. This fact is regrettably acknowledged. If this is the case with you – substitute or supplement your own doctrinal or personal values to the list. But in order to differentiate *right* from *wrong*, we must have some place to start and it can't change to suit your desires of the moment.

No matter what the contents are of the list you believe in or have generated, when we stray from the path, the first step of the improvement process is to acknowledge the sin.

Paul refers to the process of recognizing sin and being responsible for it as *godly sorrow*. "*Godly sorrow brings repentance that leads to salvation and leaves no regret, but worldly sorrow (without repentance) brings death."* Further, Paul tells us why this recognition step is so vital. He writes in 2 Corinthians 7:10–11. *"See what this godly sorrow has produced in you: what earnestness, what eagerness to clear yourselves, what indignation, what alarm, what longing, what concern, what readiness to see justice done."*

Look at Paul's word choice; *earnestness, eagerness, indignation, alarm, longing, concern, readiness.* Those are words of **action**. To cut to the chase – acknowledgement of wrongdoing is our first step towards spiritual growth and our call to action. Following recognition and acknowledgment, the next action step on the list might be the toughest of all.

Repentance: A Much Maligned and Misunderstood Term

Repentance is an often misunderstood word that conjures up images of the *Saturday Night Live* "Church Lady" or fire breathing preachers damning half the congregation to eternal hellfire. The roots of the word hint that these concepts might be slightly off base. Let's look at the concept across a few faith systems.

- In Hebrew, the concept of repentance is contained in two verbs: בוש shuv (to return) and םחנ nicham (to feel sorrow), indicating a recognition and reconciliation for wrongdoing.

- In Christianity, the Greek translation is the word (μετάνοια), a compound word beginning with meta (after), and noeo' (thinking, perceiving or observing). Put together, the word means "to think, perceive, or observe differently after."[6] The concept of repentance is not isolated to the Judeo-Christian world.

    "By definition, sin involves an error of controllable thought or deed."

- The Arabic word for repentance, Tawbah is mentioned repeatedly in the Holy Qur'an[7] and literally means "to return." In an Islamic context, it refers to the act of leaving what Allah has prohibited and returning to what He has commanded.

To keep it simple, let's just say that repentance is a reflective change of thought and action to correct a wrong; which is pretty much what we have been talking about in this entire book up to this point.

---

6   Merriam-webster.com/dictionary/metanoia
7   Sura 9: verses 102 to 106.

So far we can say that the practice of personal error control is in complete harmony with the teachings of the vast majority of major faiths in the world. We can even go beyond that and safely state that personal acknowledgement of wrongdoing and repentance is a mandatory aspect of these faiths. Now let's look closely at the tie-in between empowered accountability and spiritual growth.

Getting Personal: Seeking Wisdom and Self Discovered Truth

Blue Threat Proverb 13 states, *You are only as committed as you are convinced.* A 10-year old's baseball coach told him the key to being a great hitter is to believe in your heart that you are the greatest hitter that has ever picked up a baseball bat and stood at the plate – look for a pitch in the strike zone and hit it right back over the pitcher's head. In simple terms, be absolutely convinced of who you are and what you are capable of doing, and then do it. After a few successful trips to the plate, the belief is strengthened and the continuous reinforcement of the positive behavior takes hold. The concept of positive thinking, personal engagement and self discovered wisdom works the same way in spiritual growth. There are many relevant faith-based teachings to support this position.

> 'Repentance is an often misunderstood word that conjures up images of the *Saturday Night Live* "Church Lady"'

Buddhism, as traditionally conceived, is a path of salvation attained through insight into the ultimate nature of reality though many specific practices including the cultivation of self awareness, mindfulness, and self discovered wisdom.

A principle tenet of the Baha'i faith emphasizes

> The fundamental obligation of human beings to acquire knowledge with their "own eyes and not through the eyes of others." One of the main sources of conflict in the world today is the fact that many people blindly and uncritically follow various traditions, movements, and opinions. God has given each human being a mind and the capacity to differentiate truth from falsehood. If individuals fail to use their reasoning capacities and choose instead to accept without question certain

opinions and ideas, either out of admiration for or fear of those who hold them, then they are neglecting their basic moral responsibility as human beings.[8]

Perhaps the wisest man ever was King Solomon, the primary author of the Book of Proverbs which begins:

> These are the wise words of Solomon son of David, king of Israel. They teach wisdom and self-control; they will help you understand wise words. They will teach you how to be wise and self-controlled and will teach you to do what is honest and fair and right (Proverbs 1:1-3).

Solomon goes into some detail about applying wisdom and discipline to everyday life. Examples include:[9]

> Listen carefully to wisdom; set your mind on understanding. (Proverbs 2:2)
>
> Hold on to wisdom, and it will take care of you ... If it costs everything you have, get understanding. (Proverbs 4:6-7)

"... the practice of personal error control is in complete harmony with the teachings of the vast majority of major faiths in the world."

Believers hold that the ultimate source of wisdom comes from God, often revealed in the world. They draw strength and serenity from prayer, and strange as it may sound, even non-believers can benefit greatly from prayer and meditation in their quest to improve.

Prayer and Meditation

Prayer is the act of addressing and communicating with a higher power, who I will continue to call God. Praying has many different forms. Prayer may be done privately and individually, or it may be done with others. Some prayers are very structured, others pray through open meditation, *listening* rather than thinking or speaking petitions.

Meditation is a mental discipline by which one attempts to get beyond conscious and reactive thinking into a deeper state of relaxation or awareness. It may or may not involve any higher power. Both prayer and meditation have great potential for improving decision making and helping to control error, albeit for different reasons.

---

8   Found at http://info.bahai.org/article-1-3-2-17.html
9   Holy Bible, New Century Version for all Proverbs in this section

Many faiths combine the two. For example the Baha'i faith teaches that meditation is necessary for spiritual growth, alongside obligatory prayer and fasting, saying:

> Meditation is the key for opening the doors of mysteries to your mind. In that state man abstracts himself: in that state man withdraws himself from all outside objects; in that subjective mood he is immersed in the ocean of spiritual life and can unfold the secrets of things-in-themselves.[10]

When it comes to prayer, some traditions are more directive than others. Islam for example, holds prayer as one of the five pillars, commanded by Allah. Judaism and Christianity are less prescriptive on frequency and duration, but still strongly call for "the duty of prayer." In one form or another, nearly all organized faiths advocate and acknowledge the value of prayer. As the Psalmist wrote, "Give ear to words Oh Lord, consider my meditation" (PSA 5:1 KJV).

Jonathan Edwards is widely regarded as America's greatest theologian. In the early to mid 1700s, he was a colonial American Congregational preacher and the first president of the College of New Jersey (later to be named Princeton University). Over 200 years ago, he delivered a powerful sermon on the benefits of prayer for Christians. His message is timeless and relevant to our purposes here.

> "A principle tenet of the Baha'i faith emphasizes the fundamental obligation of human beings to acquire knowledge with their own eyes and not through the eyes of others."

The following is excerpted from Jonathan Edwards' sermon, "Hypocrites Deficient in the Duty of Prayer"

> Consider the great benefits of a constant, diligent, and persevering attendance in prayer.
>
> Prayer is one of the greatest and most excellent means of <u>nourishing the new nature, and of causing the soul to flourish and prosper.</u> (emphasis added throughout in underlined text)

---

10 '*Abdu'l-Bahá*. Bahá'í Distribution Service. pp.175. http://reference.bahai.org/en/t/ab/PT/pt-55.html.

- Prayer is an excellent means of <u>taking off the heart from the vanities of the world</u>, and of causing the mind to be conversant in heaven.

- Prayer is an excellent <u>preservative from sin</u> and the wiles of the devil, and a <u>powerful antidote</u> against the poison of the old serpent.

- Prayer is a duty whereby strength is derived from God <u>against the lusts and corruptions of the heart, and the snares of the world</u>.

That is a lot of benefit from a single solitary practice that requires no resources but our time and attention. From a more contemporary point of view, prayer has been associated with both physical and mental wellness.

According to a study by Dr. Anne McCaffrey of the Harvard Medical School, one-third of Americans use prayer to facilitate physical healing. Sixty-nine percent of the 2,000 people surveyed said prayer greatly improved their health.[11] Additional studies have linked prayer and spirituality to positive health outcomes with high blood pressure, asthma, heart attacks, headaches and anxiety. "It's not a fringe thing," says McCaffrey. "I think very mainstream Americans are using prayer in their daily lives."

Of course, none of this means that either prayer or spiritual health is a substitute for traditional medicine, or that prayer will ensure physical well-being. But it does seem that either the prayer itself or the lifestyle that accompanies it has positive results in the real world. Here are a few other benefits of prayer that cross the secular boundary:

> "... prayer has been associated with both physical and mental wellness."

- Prayer gets us outside of ourselves which helps us reflect on multiple aspects of our lives more objectively.

- Prayer for others strengthens relationships by bringing the importance of people other than ourselves into sharper focus.

- Prayer focuses the mind, first by helping to block out the mental noise of day to day activity and secondly, through some advanced meditative techniques used in faiths such as Buddhism.

---

11 "Health Benefits of Prayer" found at http://archive.newsmax.com/archives/articles/2005/7/29/04002.shtml

The bottom line here is that each of us is responsible for our own spiritual assessment and growth. Using the tools in this book, coupled with prayer and the scriptural teachings of your faith, will allow the discovery of wisdom based upon your unique situation, life, and spiritual background.

With our spiritual compass aligned by acknowledgement of wrongdoing (sin), repentance and a personal approach to seeking the truth, we can now turn our attention to something really scary.

Spiritual Warfare Perspective

Many people believe that the devil himself roams the earth with a pack of demons who are looking for souls to devour and send to eternal damnation in the fires of hell. The doctrinal position of some Judeo-Christian traditions is that Satan and other demons, are spiritual entities that regularly manifest their presence in the earthly realm. They exist to deceive humanity and have the mission to thwart God's purposes on earth.

> "... each of us is responsible for our own spiritual assessment and growth."

In the Gospel of John, Jesus himself refers to Satan as "a murderer from the beginning" and "the father of lies" (John 8:44). In other scriptures, the devil is described as a "roaring lion, seeking whom he may devour" (1 Peter 5:8). Men are said to be "taken captive by him" (2 Timothy 2:26). Christians are warned against Satan's "devices" (2 Cor 2:11), and called on to "resist" him (James 4:7). If Satan is simply a symbolic representation of our dark side or a construct of our imagination as some suggest – he sure gets a lot of attention from some pretty heavy hitters.

The adversary has a lot of tools in his toolkit to work on our lives in a negative way. Some have simplified the attacks of the enemy by calling them "the 5 D's of Diablo." Whether you believe in his existence or not, each of these impact personal performance and it's a good idea to stay aware of them:

- **Deception** (lie to you about the reality of the way things really are)
- **Discouragement** (get you so down on yourself and others that you can't function)
- **Distraction** (keep you away from your main purpose in life by placing others things in your way)
- **Disqualification** (encourage you to fall into complete immorality and thus lose your integrity and voice in the world)

- **Death** (kill your will to live or bring about spiritual death and separation from God through sin and destruction)

Whether or not you believe that the devil is real or symbolic, there is little doubt that evil roams the world and often preys on the innocent. All major faiths repeatedly warn against carelessness in dealing with the forces of evil, be they natural or supernatural.

Alistair Begg, the head of the *Truth for Life* ministry and Senior Pastor at Parkside Church near Cleveland, Ohio, says that in spite of all the temptations in the world and the fact that there are malevolent forces trying to coax us across the lines of Godly behavior, "at its core, every sin is an inside job." He goes on to say that Godly people must be truly prepared to protect themselves and their loved ones because "every morning is a call to battle stations."[12]

> "Whether or not you believe that the devil is real or symbolic, there is little doubt that evil roams the world...."

So how do we fight a giant like sin? Perhaps we can find some guidance in a case study of a young boy faced with a gigantic challenge.

Into Action: Felling Giants

According to the First Book of Samuel and a more brief report contained in the Qur'an, a few years back there was a pitched battle shaping up in the Valley of Elah, on the southern plains of modern day Israel. The Philistine army was on the march and ready to make war. Their opponents were the outmanned Israelites under King Saul. Both sides set up camps across from each other in the valley, and the Philistines sent Goliath, their champion to challenge the Israelites to send a warrior to fight him in a winner take all battle. If Goliath were defeated, the Philistines would become the subjects of Saul's army. If Goliath won, the converse would occur. For forty days, in both the morning and evening, Goliath bellowed his challenge, but no man from Saul's army came forward, and for good reason. Depending on the version of the story, Goliath stood a minimum of six and a half feet tall.[13] In a one on one battle with this heavyweight, it appeared the Israelites were doomed.

---

12 Spiritual Warfare series available at https://store.truthforlife.org/index.php?main_page=product_music_info&products_id=1460

13 The Dead Sea Scrolls text of Samuel, gives the height of Goliath as "four cubits and a span," approximately 200 centimeters or about six feet seven inches. Later manuscripts read "six cubits and a span," which would make him about 290 cm or nine feet six inches tall. Either way, one big man.

Into this picture steps David, the youngest of eight sons, not yet fully grown and an extremely unlikely hero. Tired of the giant's boasting, David approaches the King and offers to fight. Saul answered, "You can't go out against this Philistine ... You're only a boy. Goliath has been a warrior since he was a young man" (1 Sam 17:33).[14] But David talked a good game, and after explaining that he had already killed both a lion and a bear, Saul relented, and dressed him in traditional adult armor. After trying to move around a bit in the heavy helmet and breastplate, David said to Saul, "I can't go in this (heavy armor), because I'm not used to it." Then David took it all off. He took his stick in his hand and chose five smooth stones from a stream. He put them in his shepherd's bag and grabbed his sling. Then he strode on the battle ground to meet the Philistine giant.

As Goliath came near to attack him, David picked up his pace and ran to meet him. He took a stone from his bag, put it into his sling, and let it fly. The stone hit the Philistine squarely and sunk deep into his forehead. Goliath fell face down on the ground. (1 Sam 17:48–49) Finishing the job, David took Goliath's sword, cut off his head and carried it to King Saul. Nice work.

I know some of my Christian and Jewish friends will likely take issue with my interpretation of this story. *It was the power of God that felled Goliath*, they will say, working through the boy David. They argue that David knew he would be victorious and said as much to Saul. OK, I could almost buy this line of thinking if David had taken *one* stone, but he took *five*. I don't think David felt as if he was assured of victory. He knew he was going into a fight.

> "... at its core, every sin is an inside job."
> – Alistair Begg

From my perspective, here are the lessons of David vs. Goliath that we can utilize in our spiritual growth in support of our empowered accountability objectives.

Be courageous enough to move past conventional wisdom. David saw an alternate road to victory. None of the soldiers saw it, nor did the King, not because they weren't smart guys, but because they weren't shepherds skilled with a sling. David saw Goliath not as a giant he was too small to defeat, but as a target too big to miss.

---

14 Holy Bible, New Century Version

Go on the offensive. One of the most fascinating parts of this story to me is verse 48, "David ran quickly to meet him." Once he was committed to the fight, he took the fight to the enemy without hesitation; quickly and forcefully. This is an important point in our overall error control effort. Far too many so-called threat and error management approaches wage purely defensive battles, waiting for the error to show up. Not only is this not a good strategy, it's boring.

> "David saw Goliath not as a giant he was too small to defeat, but as a target too big to miss."

Choose weapons you trust and personally control. In the hands of an expert, a sling hurling a half pound projectile is an extremely lethal weapon. Niccolo Machiavelli,[15] in *The Prince*, states that we should all learn this lesson from David. "Fight with our own weapons, using our own strengths, and do not try to borrow or hire those of others, who may someday fail us in our hour of greatest need." What are your best weapons?

See your size and individuality as strength, not weakness. David did not see himself as a boy fighting a giant. He saw himself, quite accurately, as a tribal shepherd with world class sling skills, up against a slow moving target with a bare forehead. He took five stones, but probably had a pretty good idea it wouldn't take that many to get the job done. Goliath had at least one brother, so maybe David kept a stone or two for him or anybody else that wanted a piece of him (2 Sam 21:19).

Throw straight at a target you can see close up, but not too close. David fought the battle at a distance that kept him out of Goliath's reach but close enough to use his weapon of choice effectively. There are lessons here for us. If in our battle with sin and error we get <u>too close</u>, we put ourselves in harm's way. If we fail to get close enough to see our target accurately, we risk not getting the job done at all. The key is to find the right level of engagement to see and fix the challenge without falling victim to it.

---

15 Since the day he penned his thoughts, politicians and powerbrokers have been fascinated by Machiavelli's approach to power. His very name invokes the term Machiavellian —the use of all available political means to seize and hold power.

Sin and personal error are giants we can slay. Perhaps we cannot conquer all sin/error in all places at all times, but we can use a new set of tools to take the fight to the enemy and dramatically improve our success rate.

Let's now turn to the next chapter and look at lessons from those who have made their last mistake.

TEN

Speaker for the Dead[1]

"All that we know about those we have loved and lost is that they would wish us to remember them with more intensified realization of their reality. What is essential does not die but clarifies."
– Thornton Wilder, American playwright and novelist

What would those who have made their last mistake tell us if they were able to? How would they explain what happened to them in a way that could help us in personal and insightful ways that the cold narrative of an accident review or police report cannot?

I am not a psychic. I make no claims to have heard anyone from beyond the veil in any real sense, yet I cannot forget the men I have known who failed to come home at night from what should have been a routine day. Common themes and key messages from these tragic and untimely deaths echo in my head – and in my heart – like whispers from beyond.

This chapter is my attempt to communicate the thoughts that might come forth if the dead could leave us one last message. Some might feel it is pre-

---

1 *Speaker for the Dead* (1986) is the title of an excellent science fiction novel by Orson Scott Card. It is the sequel to the Hugo Award winning *Ender's Game* and looks at the deep understanding that can come from serious reflection on causes and consequences of death. It's not as grim as it sounds and I highly recommend the book.

sumptuous for me to put my thoughts in their name. When my old friends and I meet again, they will undoubtedly critique my words as woefully inadequate and incomplete. I ask their indulgence and pray I will not stray too far off centerline.

I've been to too many funerals. I don't like them, not only because it reminds me of my own mortality and the loss of a friend or family member, but also because too often in death we invent a new person, one we want to remember free of fault or flaw. Of course no one lives that way, and I've always felt it inappropriate and even disrespectful that we try to remember only the good times and sound decisions instead of the real person. We all fully understand the need to comfort families in times of grief. As close friends of the recently deceased, we are almost a part of those families, so it is understandable why we try to paint over this apparent stain of human error on the legacy of these fine men and women.

A second reason we tend to dismiss or understate the errors that kill our friends, family, and colleagues is that these people – and the mistakes they made – are very often a reflection of ourselves. Up until the moment of truth, we were near equals. Now we are alive and they are dead. Does that mean we truly were better (drivers, pilots, firefighters, etc.) than they were? Or does it mean we suffer the same vulnerabilities? One is a much easier pill to swallow and requires no further action on our part.

> "By adopting a condescending attitude towards the dead ... we tacitly approve our status quo."

By adopting a condescending attitude towards the dead (as in, "How could they have made that kind of dumb mistake?") we tacitly approve our status quo. Subconsciously, we might even feel a little superior. Armed with hindsight bias, we can clearly see their errors in a cause and effect chain that they did not. We think this would never have happened to us. This is the ultimate disrespect.

We have all made mistakes that *could* have killed us. Reaching for a dropped object while driving, accidently touching a live electrical wire, climbing too high on an unsupported ladder, crossing a busy city street against traffic or becoming distracted during some other type of high risk activity.

I've never been big on the whole concept of *luck*, but for some reason, I have survived the very same errors that have killed others. I prefer to think of this good fortune as *playing the odds*, and the longer we go without learning from others or correcting our own errors – the more likely we are to join the growing list of those who have passed from this world in an untimely fashion due to avoidable human error.

What would the dead have us know?

In this short section, we will listen to the hypothetical voices of a few people who have suffered untimely deaths due to human error. In some cases it was their own error that caused the tragedy, in other cases they were literally "just along for the ride" but did nothing to stop the chain of events. In each of these cases, I either personally knew the victims or am very familiar with the event that took their lives.

"It all happened so fast."

> "We have all made mistakes that *could* have killed us."

Bobby and Tom were young, good looking and having the time of their lives. Fresh out of high school where they were both star athletes, the two best friends were living life in the fast lane, literally. Then one night a simple combination of fatigue and momentary distraction caused the driver to drift off the right hand side of the paved highway onto a poorly maintained dirt shoulder. The startled driver overcorrected, the vehicle rolled and less than three seconds later, a giant oak tree provided the endgame. I spoke at the funeral, where hundreds of grief stricken friends and family were shocked by the suddenness of it all.

Every year a variant of this accident takes the lives of hundreds of drivers and passengers. The scenarios are talked about in driver's education classes, and organizations like the National Transportation Safety Board attempt to better educate the public at large. But until we internalize the risk as individuals, and practice "managing the moment" we remain as vulnerable as we have always been to this type of sudden loss of control. This is only one of hundreds of scenarios at work, home, and the highways in between where life can go from green to mean in a nanosecond.

I believe that Bob and Tom – and thousands of others who have fallen victim to these types of untimely deaths, would want us to know how quickly the relative calm of the moment can unravel into a life threatening scenario. I believe they would tell us to stay on our toes, especially when driving or in other realms where the laws of physics place us only seconds away from a tragic ending.

"I never saw it coming."

Mike was an experienced fighter pilot, just getting started on what appeared to be a highly successful career path. He graduated in the top 10% of his Air Force pilot training class and got his aircraft of choice – an A-7D and a *Project Season*[2] assignment to the National Guard. As an air to ground attack fighter, the A-7D was a blast to fly, a fast mover that flew in the low altitude structure, an environment that demands constant vigilance.

> "... life can go from green to mean in a nanosecond."

Because of the speed these and other high performance aircraft fly at low altitudes, the way in which you "clear your flight path" is much different than it is in an automobile. In a car, if you are going to make a left turn, you look 45–90 degrees to your left, depending on the track of the road and the speed you are travelling, and then guide your vehicle along the track. Not so in a high speed aircraft. Because of the speed, the ground track of a low altitude, fast mover is *always in front of you,* and at most you may need to look 5–10 degrees left or right of your current centerline, even for an aggressive high-G turn. At first this is unnatural, but those who fly at low altitudes are taught early on the dangers of simultaneously "turning and looking" (away from the actual flight path in front of the aircraft).

But in a tactical environment, there are a lot of things to look for – ground threats, other aircraft, and visual reference points to name just a few. The key survival tool is to look for these things when you are nearly straight and level and know you are well clear of any other aircraft or terrain. It appears Mike forgot this rule, just for a moment, and impacted a hill on a training range on a clear day with no other malfunctions.

The hill – like the oak tree in the previous example – didn't move. That hill had been in the same place for at least the last 12,000 years, yet it snuck up on Mike and killed him. One momentary distraction at a critical point in time was his final mistake. It took this highly skilled and well trained professional at high speed directly into a fixed object, one that he never saw coming.

I believe that Mike would likely tell us that as we get caught up in the high speed aspects of our lives (literal and metaphorical), we can never lose track of things that are important – even for a moment. We live closer to the edge than we realize.

---

2   *Project Season* was the name for a program that assigned active duty pilots to Air National Guard units.

"The risk doesn't change, but our attitude towards it does."

Tom was a seasoned professional firefighter from a family of seasoned professional firefighters, and when he was dispatched on a hot July day to fight a fire in northern Washington, it was just another in a long career of wildland fires. There were a few red flags, such as unseasonably high temperatures and historic low humidity rates, but for the most part, this one was much like many of the fires he had successfully engaged in the steep river canyons of the Pacific Northwest. They would be the third crew to work the fire, which was slowly burning in a river bottom area.

"One momentary distraction at a critical point in time was his final mistake."

Things got a little more interesting for Tom and his firefighting mates when they got cut off by a wall of flame while trying to disengage from the blaze just after lunch. But he had been in tight spots before, and as the crew retreated in their vehicle up the box canyon he put an experienced eye on the terrain to pick the best spot to "ride it out." They found just such a spot a few miles up the canyon road – a nice clear area with a sand bar in the middle of the river.

They were now well ahead of the fire and this looked like an acceptable safety zone. He had a few rookies on his crew that were getting pretty nervous, so he walked up the hill with a few of them and settled them down a bit. A few members of the team wanted everyone to get down to the road by the river and prepare for the worst, but the fire was crawling towards them up the river bottom at a relatively slow pace, there was plenty of time ... until there wasn't.

Suddenly, the fire behavior changed. The sky turned black and it began to rain ash. In the span of a few seconds things went from relatively calm to chaotic, and then the fire "blew up." Almost instantaneously, acres of land erupted into an inferno all around them. There was no time to get back to the road, let alone the sand bar in the river. Tom and those around him dropped onto the rocky slope where they were standing and attempted to get inside their reflective fire shelters. Two minutes later the fire had burned through, and Tom and three others around him lay dead on the ground.

I believe that if he had the chance, Tom would tell us that over the years, he had grown accustomed to the risk of wildland firefighting, and perhaps lost just a bit of respect for the wrath Mother Nature can wreak in the blink of an eye. I don't know if Tom ever read this statement from an Army Major talking about risk acceptance, but I believe he would agree with its sentiments.

Each new plateau of risk, when first attained, seems to be the last; but, as we grow accustomed to it, a new horizon beckons. What insulates us from fear as we approach the danger is simply habit, the familiarity of a point we have reached and all the points we've left behind. Until one steps too far, it's often hard to tell the difference between recklessness and skill.[3]

"I wasn't ready to go yet."

Gone too soon. A life interrupted. Taken from us in the prime of their lives. These and other statements reflect the cruelty of human error induced tragedy. One of the points we made in an earlier chapter is that when we first start out in life, we are usually armed with youthful health and enthusiasm, but lack the structured experience and lessons of life to clearly see trouble coming. However, the risk doesn't necessarily diminish with experience or age, but in fact may increase due to our dulled readiness and creeping complacency.

"... risk doesn't necessarily diminish with experience or age, but in fact may increase due to our dulled readiness and creeping complacency."

Regardless of the life stage of the victim, preventable death zeros out what might have been for these individuals and those close to them. As we state in *Blue Threat Proverb #1, human error is not a victimless crime.*

Don't cut your life short unnecessarily by remaining oblivious to the threat posed by human error.

"We don't want to have died in vain."

I believe the one lasting sentiment of those who have been taken from us too soon, would be that we learn from their mistakes, so that their deaths have some meaning. Beyond the cold facts contained in the police reports and lessons learned from accident investigations lies a far more subtle lesson – we must understand ourselves to fully comprehend the risks we pose to others. In each of these cases above, there were undoubtedly clues to avoiding the impending disasters before the events occurred. But to tune into these clues demands a level of insight rare in this world. It is not enough to know why things go wrong. We must get to the level of self awareness to comprehend – in real time – why things go wrong *to me.*

---

3   Major Chris Miller, United States Army

Tom, Bobby, Mike and Tom are merely examples of different people, from different worlds who all met the same fate due to their inability to see and avoid life threatening hazards. Some of the factors in each of these tragedies were certainly environmental, but surely some were personal.

Speaker for the "Almost Dead"

There is another group who have valuable lessons for us, those who have survived near death experiences. I am one such person. Ironically, even after a near death experience, many people fail at honest self-appraisal and instead of accepting responsibility and learning from the event, they will actually twist the interpretation of the event into one where only their skill and cunning saved the day. I know better. Here is a reflection on my event, taken from my *Commander's Intent* weblog.

The Gift of Borrowed Time[4] (posted 10 December 2008)

I let yesterday pass without comment, just like the 9,131 days that preceded it since 9 Dec 1983. On that memorable date 25 years ago yesterday, I was at the controls of a KC-135A air refueling tanker and was involved in a human error induced mid-air collision with an E-3 AWACS with a call sign of *Sentry 99*. Without going into grisly detail – miscommunication, poor risk management, oversized egos and an inexperienced 2nd Lieutenant with less than 500 hours flying time (that would be me) combined into a sequence of events that put two very large, fast moving aircraft at the same exact coordinates of time and space. It was a severe collision that ripped large pieces off of both aircraft. It is no exaggeration to state that it was an event no one should have survived. Yet we all did. For some unknown – and perhaps unknowable – reason, I was spared from an event that should have taken my life.

"A man who lives on borrowed time lives on trespass-ground."

From my perspective, I have lived on borrowed time since that moment.

Only from this side of the last 25 years can I gauge the magnitude of this gift. Sons that would never have been born, achievements that would have never been realized, love and life that would have never been experienced – all turned on that 11 seconds of metal on metal over the skies of the Persian Gulf.

---

4   Commander's Intent weblog, found at http://www.convergentperformance.com/gwoe/blog/2008/12/gift-of-borrowed-time.html

In 1898, *The English Dialect Dictionary* defined the phrase *borrowed time* this way. "A man who lives on borrowed time lives on trespass-ground." To me this means that those of us whose time on earth has been extended through no fault of our own, need to earn our keep.

I have had one or two other near death experiences since then, but none quite so spectacular. My quest since that fateful day has been to discover and fulfill the reason for this gift and to "pay my way forward." I'm not sure what this experience might mean to others, but I see a difference between those who see their time on earth as a right of birth vs. a gift. I have no such burden of expectation that life owes me anything. For me, it will always be the other way around. For that clarity and every future moment, I am grateful.

> "Perhaps the danger is even greater precisely because we no longer perceive the need to think about it."

Summary

If the dead could speak to us, I believe there would be two important lessons they would want us to know. The first is that we are more vulnerable to a quick demise than we think we are. Even in the affluent gated communities of today's first world countries, where we sit behind ADT alarm systems and drive cars with more airbags than cylinders; where safety and security systems wrap us in cocoons of perceived invulnerability – danger lurks. Perhaps the danger is even greater precisely because we no longer perceive the need to think about it. The *blue threat* is a clear and present danger and you are the only one who can defend yourself from the danger within.

The second – and more urgent – message the dead would have us know is that there is still time on the clock for us. We don't know how much time, but it is some finite amount. Time gives us the opportunity to do something to prevent the types of self induced and preventable tragedies that took them from us. Or they might use the words of the anonymous poet who said,

> "One day your life will flash before your eyes,
> make sure it's worth watching."

ELEVEN

The Business of Error Control

"Mistakes are like knives that either serve us or cut us, depending on if we grasp them by the blade or by the handle."[1]
– James Russell Lowell, American Poet

Whether we are managing our own finances, our family budget, or are the CEO of a Fortune 500 company, we are all business leaders in some regard. Whatever your situation may be, in business as in life, the dividing line between success and failure is often obscured, at least from this side of the crystal ball.

When failures do occur, 20-20 hindsight will usually show where we got off track. With the data smog of daily operations cleared, the errors we made and the lines we unknowingly crossed become all too clear, but by this time the damage has been done.

Empowered accountability is a new tool to help predict and prevent errors **before** they impact the bottom line; and to help guide us through the wilderness of mirrors that has become the modern business landscape. Put simply, errors rob profit and resources at every level of your material and human resource supply chain. Errors undercut quality, safety, and create waste into otherwise efficient systems. Noncompliance negates training, guidance, pro-

---

[1] Paraphrased from *"Mishaps are like knives, that either serve us or cut us, as we grasp them by the blade or the handle."*

188　BLUE THREAT: WHY TO ERR IS INHUMAN

"Errors undercut quality, safety, and create waste into otherwise efficient systems."

cess and procedures. Even worse, modern technologies can turn the single error of an individual into a costly and sometimes deadly chain of events. Then of course, the media may broadcast your failure around the world in a matter of minutes, permanently damaging your reputation.

In this chapter, we will first gain a better perspective on the true cost of human error. From there, we will show how empowered accountability leads to *professional reliability*. Finally, we provide some suggestions for near term inter-industry applications at multiple levels.

Pop quiz. What do the following 168 companies have in common?

Adams Childrenswear, A.F.C. Bournemouth, A J Purdy, Allco Finance Group, Aloha Airlines, Amtrak Express Parcels, AP Hydraulics, Apex Aircraft, ATA Airlines, Australian School of Business and Technology, B3 Technologies, Bennigan's, Bill Heard Enterprises, Bowie Castlebank (William Munro), Bradford & Bingley, Buffets, Champ Car World Series, Circuit City, Coast Air, Commander Communications, Countrywide Financial, Dawahares, Dolcis, eos Airlines, FreshXpress, Frontier Airlines, Glitnir, Gretna F.C., Halifax Town A.F.C., Harold's, Holley Performance Products, IndyMac Bank, International Race of Champions, iQon Technologies, Kaupthing Bank, Kaupthing Singer & Friedlander, Krispy Kreme Hong Kong, Landsbanki, Lehman Brothers, Lenox, Levitz Furniture, Lillian Vernon, Linens 'n Things, Luton Town F.C., Mattress Discounters, Mervyns, Meguro Sushi, MFI Group, Montres Villemont, Morgan UK, Motorworld, Nationwide Airlines, Northern Rock, Oasis Hong Kong Airlines, Olan Mills, Opes Prime, Peau Vava'u, Photo-Optix, The Pier, Pilgrim's Pride, RC Developments, Rosebys, Rotherham United F.C., Sanlu Group, Sharper Image, Shoe Pavilion, Silver State Helicopters, Silverjet, Skybus Airlines, Super Aguri F1, Tribune Company, Tropicana Resort & Casino, Trust Japan, Tweeter, U-Right, Value City, VeraSun Energy, Vivitar, Wachovia, Washington Mutual, WCI Communities, Wickes Furniture, Wilsons Leather, WiQuest Communications, Whittard of Chelsea, Woolworths Group, XL Airways UK, Yamato Life Insurance Company, Zavvi, Ziff-Davis, Zoom Airlines, 3D Realms, A1 Grand Prix Operations, AbitibiBowater, Allied Carpets, Apex Silver Mines, Arena Football League, Arcandor, Babcock & Brown, Bashas', BearingPoint, Birthdays, Boater's World, Central Park Media, Charter Communications, Christian Lacroix, Chrysler, Crabtree & Evelyn, Darlington F.C., Denver Newspaper Agency, Eddie Bauer, Empire Direct,

Extended Stay Hotels, Filene's Basement, Firedog, Fleetwood Enterprises, FlyLAL, Fortunoff, General Growth Properties, General Motors, Goody's Family Clothing, Gottschalks, Hartmarx, Idearc, Joe's, Journal Register Company, Karmann, KB Toys, Land of Leather, LDV Group Limited, Lear Corporation, LyondellBasell, Märklin, Magna Entertainment Corp., Merisant, Midway Games, Monaco Coach Corporation, Nortel Networks, Peanut Corporation of America, Philadelphia Media Holdings, Qimonda, Ritz Camera, Saab Automobile, Setanta Sports, SETA Corporation, SFCG Co., Silicon Graphics, Six Flags, Smurfit-Stone Container, Spansion, Spectrum Brands, SPV GmbH, SsangYong, Station Casinos, Steve & Barry's, Strathfield, Stylo, Sun-Times Media Group, Tronox, Trump Entertainment Resorts, Visteon, Viyella, Waterford Wedgwood, Young Broadcasting

This is the short list[2] of major corporations that failed (dissolved, bankrupt or otherwise placed into receivership) in the 2008–2009 recession. There are some pretty big boys on this list, including General Motors, Trump (as in *Donald*) Entertainment Resorts and a host of airlines and banks. Some were featured in Jim Collins best seller *Good to Great* as paragons of sustainable business excellence. Yet, when the winds of change blew, none of these organizations could stay afloat.[3]

As a small business CEO, I see more than corporate failures here. I see massive layoffs, home foreclosures, and thousands of personal bankruptcies. Most of all, I see failed leaders, flawed plans, failures to adapt, and broken dreams. In my nightmares, I see the name of my company on a similar future list.

The societal impacts of these business failures include seismic shifts in government policies, massive taxpayer bailouts and layers of new government oversight bureaucracies in the making. The effects of these actions will not be known for decades to come and will likely shape the business landscape for the first half of this century. If we added in the small and medium sized business failures, the list would stretch into the thousands.

Many of the leaders of these failed companies (CEO's, Boards of Directors, etc.) have claimed they were victims of forces they could not control. Perhaps

---

2   This incomplete list determined from multiple online and text sources believed to be accurate at the time of this publication.
3   Many of the companies have and will emerge from bankruptcy and receivership, but they are largely different companies when they come out of this process.

they are right. Each one of these failures has its own history and story to tell, but beyond any doubt, the role of human error at multiple levels of these organizations was significant.

One more thing is certain. The recent global economic meltdown put added incentive behind planning and efficiency efforts. Not all significant errors are made by executives. Errors suck the life blood from organizations through the simplest of means – including simple misunderstandings of roles and responsibilities, as cited in the study below.

Rivers of Red Ink

Errors cost money – lots of money. They reduce profit and steal resources from other worthwhile initiatives. In a *White Paper* released in June, 2008, global analyst firm IDC examined human error in the form of "employee misunderstanding" and its financial impact on 400 businesses in the UK and the US. An excerpt from the *executive summary* states in part:[4]

> Large enterprises are each potentially losing tens of millions of dollars to what is termed "employee misunderstanding," meaning actions or errors of omission by employees who have misunderstood or misinterpreted (or were misinformed about) company policies, business processes, job function or a combination of the three. Employee misunderstanding is a very different proposition to a deliberate disregard for the rules or a plain mistake, whereby an employee simply does something that they didn't mean to (like forgetting to back up computer storage or putting a decimal point in the wrong place).
>
> The financial cost of employee misunderstanding is immense. Our survey of 400 UK and US corporations estimates that the cost of employee misunderstanding in a 100,000-employee company **averages $62.4 million (£31 million) per year**. In total, UK and US enterprises are losing an estimated $37 billion (£18.7 billion) each year. Loss of business due to unplanned downtime was the largest area of loss attributed to employee misunderstanding.
>
> However, the cost of intangibles such as reputation, customer trust and the like could have even greater consequences. As recent losses of computer media in the UK have shown, the potential for a misunderstanding to have **major consequences lies not just with senior management – it can reside with the lowest-level (or even temporary) employees....**

---

4   Executive Summary. *$37 Billion: Counting the Cost of Employee Misunderstanding.* White paper. Found at www.cognisco.com/downloads/white-paper/uk_exec_summary.pdf

> Although this is clearly a matter that can have a major impact throughout the whole enterprise, businesses that we spoke to (on both sides of the Atlantic) are mostly unprepared. (emphasis added)

Hopefully, the picture is beginning to emerge that error control is about far more than safety or quality – it cuts across the board at the core economic health of our organizations.

The True Costs of Compromised Safety

Human error control is most often associated with safety or quality control efforts. This is fine as far as it goes, but often results in the issue getting less management attention than it might deserve if the true costs were known. Often, it is only in the aftermath of a serious consequence that the economics of error become clear. Figure 11.1 illustrates that even with good insurance coverage, much of the cost of an accident or injury still resides with the parent company.

There are two areas where future costs cannot be accurately estimated. The first is the likely rise in your long term insurance rates and the second area is the financial ripple effects of a damaged reputation.

To get at some hard numbers on the costs of human error, we will now look at three examples from the occupational spectrum. Whether you are the CEO of the world's largest corporation or just recalculating your personal finances following an insurance premium hike in the aftermath of a fender bender, errors cost big time.

Military Safety – Using data from the Department of Defense from the last long term study between 1975–1994, the following statistics are mind numbing:

- Over $50 billion lost to human error related accidents and incidents the 20 year period
- More than 2,000 aircraft destroyed in human error accidents
- More than 15,000 on and off duty deaths due to accidental causes

Since this time, equipment costs have soared and these numbers are undoubtedly higher. For example, the loss of a single B-2 Bomber in Guam cost over $1 billion dollars. But when it comes to the dollars and sense of human error, the military is not alone.

Figure 11.1
Hidden Costs of an Accident

INSURED COSTS
(The tip of an Iceberg)

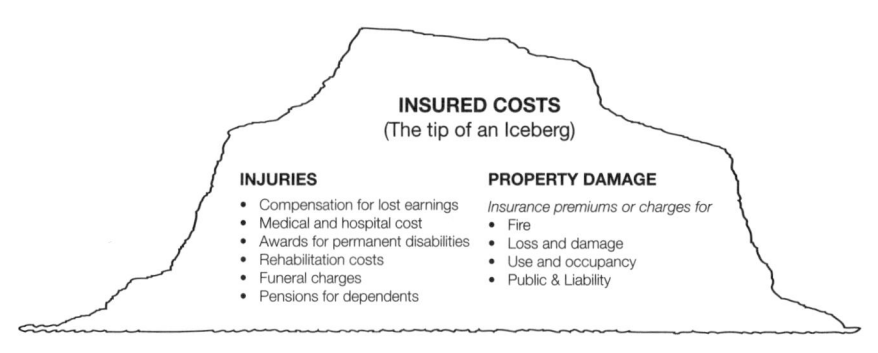

INJURIES
- Compensation for lost earnings
- Medical and hospital cost
- Awards for permanent disabilities
- Rehabilitation costs
- Funeral charges
- Pensions for dependents

PROPERTY DAMAGE
Insurance premiums or charges for
- Fire
- Loss and damage
- Use and occupancy
- Public & Liability

UNINSURED COSTS

INJURIES
- First aid expenses
- Transportation costs
- Cost of investigations
- Cost of processing reports

WAGE LOSSES
- Idle time of workers while work is interrupted
- Man hours spent in cleaning up accident area
- Time spent repairing damaged equipment
- Time lost by workers receiving first aid

PRODUCTION LOSSES
- Product spoiled by accident
- Loss of skill and experience
- Lowered production of worker replacement
- Idle machine time

ASSOCIATED COSTS
- Difference between losses and amount recovered
- Rental of equipment to replace damaged equipment
- Surplus workers for replacement of injured employees
- Wages or other benefits paid for disabled worker
- Overhead costs while production is stopped
- Loss of bonus or payment of forfeiture for delays

OFF THE JOB ACCIDENTS
- Cost of medical services
- Time spent on injured workers welfare
- Loss of skill and experience
- Training replacement worker
- Decreased production of replacement
- Benefits paid to injured worker or dependents

INTANGIBLES
- Lowered employee morale
- Increased labor conflict
- Unfavorable public relations
- Loss of goodwill

By permission of QANTAS Airways

Information Technology – No one really knows how much money is lost as a result of human error in the IT world because the ripple effects of even single point errors are nearly incalculable both in terms of direct costs and the reputation of the provider. Some human error problems are so pervasive, they occur across companies, industries and leap over supposedly hack proof systems. The following example from *Forbes* highlights the problem and cost of human error inside "highly secure" electronic firewalls.

When the *Anna Kournikova virus* was spreading wildly in 2001, it infected millions of computers and clogged e-mail servers by offering a racy picture of the teen tennis star to unsuspecting e-mailers. Or, in some cases, not so unsuspecting.

"A big proportion of the infections we saw were coming from people who had *actually gone out searching for the virus* because they wanted to see Anna Kournikova," says David Perry, global director of education for Trend Micro. "We didn't see this happening two times. We saw it thousands of times."

Today, some security professionals say, enterprise computer users haven't gotten much savvier. Perry says he still sees *as many as one in five virus infections coming from users who purposefully infect themselves out of curiosity*, just one of the many practices that undermine information technology security with varying combinations of naiveté and carelessness. And as cyber-criminals become more sophisticated and networks more intricately connected, that human error element leaves companies highly vulnerable to data leaks and intrusion in spite of billions spent on electronic protections.[5]

Once again, it's an issue of personal accountability costing industry billions of dollars. Even in some of the most professional fields, such as healthcare, we see this familiar refrain.

Healthcare – According to findings of the Institute of Medicine (IOM) report in 1999, around 100,000 Americans die each year because of human error inside the healthcare system. If accurate, **this makes human error in health care the eighth leading cause of deaths in the U.S**. Moreover, the total annual national cost of the medical errors is estimated at between $17 billion and $37.6 billion.

Emory Hospital's Chief Quality Officer Bill Bornstein is one of many thoughtful professionals who are grappling with the patient safety challenge. In an article titled *Medical Mistakes: Human Error of System Failure*, he spells out the ongoing debate about both the accuracy of the 1999 IOM report and the appropriate response to it.

---

5   *Accounting For Human Error*, Andy Greenberg, found at http://www.forbes.com/2007/08/30/behavior-employees-vulnerable-tech-cx_ag_0830secure.html

There are also questions about the accuracy of the (IOM report) numbers. In July, the *Journal of the American Medical Association* ran point-counterpoint articles on the IOM report. Clement McDonald and colleagues of the *Regenstrief Institute* of the *Indiana University Center for Aging Research* argue that the number of deaths attributed by the IOM report to "preventable adverse events" is exaggerated. In his rebuttal, however, Lucian Leape of the Harvard School of Public Health contends that the figures probably *underestimate* the problem.

Despite these questions, the IOM report itself is largely constructive rather than critical. The report emphasizes that the cause of most of these events is neither negligence nor carelessness but, rather, the result of the inevitability of human errors. *The theme is not that we must "do better" as individuals but rather that we must acknowledge our individual fallibility and implement systemic approaches to reducing and intercepting errors. As Leape puts it, "errors result from faulty systems not from faulty people."*[6] (emphasis added)

The problem with this argument is that it has created an unnecessary and dangerous *false dichotomy*.[7] Systems issues are vital to improving patient safety, but there are certainly many avoidable errors that are made at the individual level that are not systemic in their origin. Loaded terms such as "faulty people" drive an unnecessary wedge between what should be two symbiotic parts of a holistic solution.

To say that *some errors* are inevitable without saying *many are preventable* at the personal level by professionals with the right training is disingenuous. This should not be an either/or decision. It is not *either* the system that needs fixing *or* more personal error control – it is clearly both. Once again it appears we have hidden behind the white flag of "to err is human" and once again I will point out that when we make avoidable errors that result in the death or injury of others – **to err is inhuman**.

The healthcare example mirrors decisions across the spectrum of the business world. Systemic fixes are necessary, and the sooner the better. But they are also costly, difficult and systemic change management is time consuming. On the other hand, empowered accountability – training to understand and control personal error – is a relatively inexpensive and easy step that can be taken now to begin to reduce the cost and consequences of human error

---

6 Found at http://whsc.emory.edu/_pubs/momentum/2000fall/onpoint.html

7 A false dichotomy is an argument designed to force a decision between two choices that may not totally or accurately describe the situation at hand.

to gain near term traction and long term control. The people on the front lines with their hands on the controls – or in this case surgical instruments – are the last line of defense. They are also in the best position to do something about the challenge of human error **now**, while the systemic fixes are taking shape. But to do so, they must be rearmed with a new set of error control tools and be willing to take a more holistic approach to the challenge.

Storms Reshape the Landscape: How to Retool?

The recent economic hurricane is reshaping the landscape, not only for businesses large and small, but each and every one of us who earns a living working in the private sector. Never before in history have we seen sound decision making and error control as critical to success and continued livelihood from the sole proprietor to the largest corporate boardrooms.

When danger approaches it is natural for people to head for the safety of their comfort zones. In business, however, this can inhibit creative thinking and flexibility at the very moment you need it most. In David Halberstam's analytical book *The Reckoning*, written in 1986, he makes this point on change aversion clearly as he chronicles the decline of the American automobile industry in the face of the Japanese rise.

> ... the complacency and shortsightedness of American workers and their bosses, especially the automakers of Detroit, led to a decline of industrial know-how so critical that Asian carmakers, particularly the Japanese, have virtually taken over the market." Halberstam tells in panoramic detail a story that is alarming in its implications.[8]

"... the graveyards are full of generals who prepared to fight the last war instead of the next one."

There are two interesting pieces of Halberstam's analysis that are often missed. The first is that he blames both *the workers and their bosses* for shortsightedness. There is little doubt in Halberstam's mind that the costs and demands of American labor were instrumental in the U.S. automakers inability to adapt to the changing marketplace. The fact that Halberstam proved prophetic with regards to the perils of the auto industry should make his analysis of the risk of the future to the rest of the American economy that much more relevant for current and future workers and leaders in the U.S. and elsewhere.

---

8   *Publishers Weekly* book review, found at http://www.amazon.com/Reckoning-David-Halberstam

Immediately ahead lies a harsh scenario that will see America's standards of living fall appreciably and only sacrifices will restore our greatness. We must learn to retool ... or else.[9]

But what does it mean for an individual to *retool*? In the past, we have seen so-called *employee transition programs* that teach basic computer skills and other rudimentary information technology (IT) skills to displaced workers. These well meaning programs do little to develop any serious expertise. In point of fact, they are too little, too late. It is difficult to do much of substance when you are being tossed around in the surf of an economic and life changing hurricane simply trying to survive.

For both organizations and individuals, we must learn from the past, but preparation must be done <u>before</u> the next storm arrives. If you will forgive me for mixing metaphors, the graveyards are full of generals who prepared to fight the last war instead of the next one. Not all of us are as perceptive as David Halberstam, so how are we to know where and when the next storm is coming? That might be the wrong question.

> "Instead of trying to predict the future, perhaps what we really need to be doing is preparing ourselves to be more flexible, come what may."

Stretching Our Comfort Zones

Instead of trying to predict the future, perhaps what we really need to be doing is preparing ourselves to be more flexible, come what may. Regardless the direction or duration of the next storm, we can do two things to prepare. First, we can expand our comfort zones by stretching ourselves in what we are already doing well. Second, we can become experts in an area of great relevance to our future – no matter what it is.

Remember Mihaly Csikszenmihalyi, "Professor C" from Chapter 3? In his book, *Flow: The Psychology of Optimal Experience*, he describes a how nonlinear leaps in performance are often made by high achievers. Professor C says when we stretch ourselves in areas of existing competence we place ourselves in the "flow channel." Figure 11.2 illustrates this concept.

---

9 Ibid.

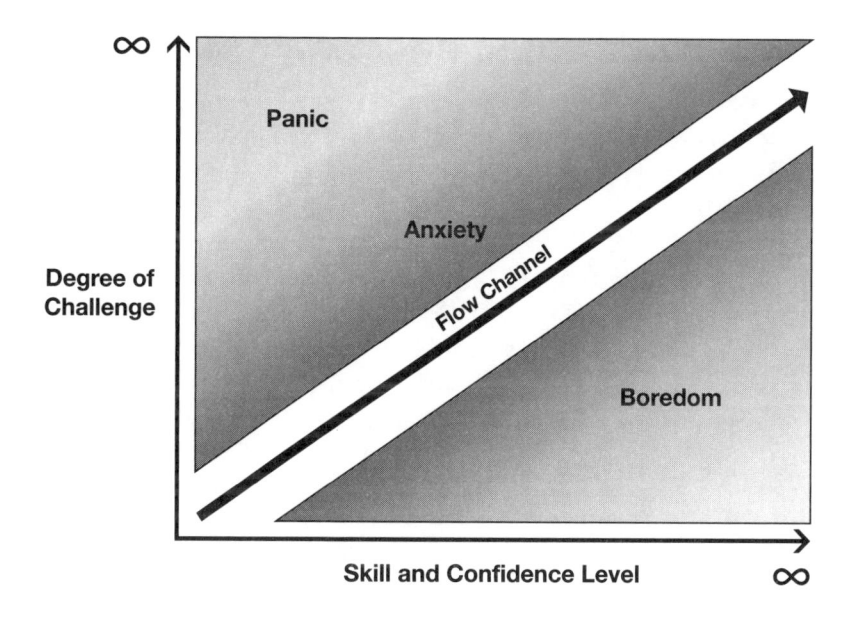

Figure 11.2
The Flow Channel[10]

By stretching – gradually adding load to our current competencies – we continue to improve while avoiding the performance robbing doppelgangers of boredom and panic. We must take care not to take on too much challenge for our competence level, lest we feel panic and anxiety and quit the process. At the other end of the spectrum, we may find ourselves overqualified, with too many skills and not enough challenge. Here we are in the personal and professional equivalent of a Lazy Boy recliner. Comfortable, but not a place to grow.

If we can use tools like the *flow channel* and the *Performance Evolution Ladder* (Chapter 3) and keep the balance right between the level of challenge and competence, we can be relatively sure we are preparing ourselves for the next big storm.

But what can we do from an individual perspective if our professional and economic future is shaped by external factors beyond our control? The first step is to get to the peak of your game in areas that will matter regardless of the setting or circumstances you find yourself in.

---

10 Csikszenmihalyi, Mihaly. *Flow: The Psychology of Optimal Experience*. 1988.

Professional Reliability: A Curriculum for a New Competency

The business case for reducing human error is pretty cut and dried. There is no longer much debate that error impacts our bottom line in far too many ways to risk maintaining the status quo. The operative question in fielding a new approach to human error is "how?" Over the past five years, a group of instructional system design (ISD) experts and subject matter experts (SME) have created a program of study to allow individuals and organizations to develop these competencies and keep them current. The curriculum (Figure 11.3) includes knowledge elements, applied techniques and a toolkit for immediate implementation. The program is interdisciplinary and builds sequentially to create an initial level of standardized competence as well as a growth based system for lifelong learning.

> "By stretching – gradually adding load to our current competencies – we continue to improve while avoiding the performance robbing doppelgangers of boredom and panic."

Equipped with new knowledge and tools against error and its consequences, the door is open to a new dimension of expertise. Thus empowered, you can more confidently step into a new job or life challenge with a greater expectation of success.

Becoming an Expert on You: Empowered Accountability as a Competitive Edge

There are no accidental experts. World class athletes have a mantra they use to move from a perception of adequacy to the next performance level. It goes like this: *Good – Better – Great – Best – How?* "I'm good, need to be better, want to be great, might someday be the best; how do I do it" I would like to add one more element to this five word formula for success – *how much?*

If we are going to convince ourselves to change our behavior and embark on a major self improvement effort, it is reasonable to want to know the return on investment (ROI) for our efforts. There is good and bad news here. The good news is that no learning or improvement is ever truly wasted. In fact, one of Professor C's major findings is that great leaps of performance are often influenced by external demands and can occur at <u>any time</u> you are in the flow channel. The bad news is that true expertise is a long time in coming, and this discourages the vast majority from ever making the attempt.

GLOBAL WAR ON ERROR

Knowledge
- Error Control Centers of Gravity
- Language of Error Control
- Error Producing Conditions
- Violation Producing Conditions
- Hazardous Attitudes
- Cognitive Bias
- Physiology of Error
- Intrapersonal Interfaces
- Blue Threat Proverbs
- Personal Trigger Events

Techniques
- Personal Countermeasures
- Personal SOP Development
- Preemptive Procedures
- Alternative Planning Strategies
- Trigger Decoupling
- Personal Error Tracking and Analysis (I-CAN)
- Situational Factors Analysis
- Habituation of Error Reduction Best Practices

Tools
- Error Pattern Survey
- Deep Dive Tool for Failure Analysis
- Self Audit Tool
- Personal Error Tracking Software
- Six Sigma Interface
- Executive Toolkit
- Blue Threat Fieldbook
- Electronic Community of Practice

Figure 11.3
Global War on Error® Empowered Accountability Program Curriculum

The 10,000 Hour Rule[11]

Maybe it is my cynical nature, but every time I see the cliché *"Success is a journey, not a destination,"* I read the unwritten subscript that says *"so if you'll never get there, why bother trying?"* There is a good bit of data to suggest that there is an end of the road to becoming an expert, but the road is a long one.

In Malcolm Gladwell's best seller *Outliers,* he explains *the 10,000 hour rule.* Evaluating those who have achieved world class expertise in everything from piano playing and chess to the Beatles and Bill Gates, researchers seem to have discovered that practice does indeed make perfect, or at least *expert.* If, as Gladwell suggests "ten thousand hours is the magic number of greatness,"

---

[11] *Outliers, The Story of Success*, Malcolm Gladwell. Chapter 2, The 10,000 Hour Rule.

what does that mean for those of us who can't find ten minutes to spare in our action packed lives, let alone 10,000 hours? We will deal with the time question in a moment, but the underlying questions are more important. What could you possibly study or do for 10,000 hours that would not be obsolete by the time you finished? Or a more sobering question. At this stage of your life, if you put 10,000 hours of effort into something, would you be too old to have it make any appreciable difference in your life?

> "... every time I see the cliché, *Success is a journey, not a destination*, I read the unwritten subscript that says *So if you'll never get there, why bother trying?*"

Let's first look at this from the vocational side. Assuming you work the standard 40 hour week and take a couple of week's vacation, you work about 2,000 hours per year. Ten thousand hours is five full years of 100% practice on whatever it is you are trying to become an expert in. Assuming you really can only dedicate 25% of your work on a single practice and you are dedicated to improving each and every day, we are looking at 20 years to become an expert at something under the 10,000 hour rule. Ouch.

If we look at trying to achieve the 10,000 hour goal in the time we have to spend on our hobbies or leisure activities the picture is even grimmer. Maybe in the next life, eh?

But what if the subject I was trying to become an expert on was *me*? What if, as a routine part of my daily life, I learned to see and analyze my performance day to day, hour by hour; not as an obsession, but as a routine life skill – a *discipline*? What if I could accumulate 10,000 expert building hours at work, at home, and at play? What would that buy me in terms of performance or competitive edge? How long would it take?

It turns out that most of us are awake and doing things for about 5,700 hours each year. Assuming that we learn to systematically review our daily performance and refine our performance awareness and analysis skills, it is reasonable to assume that in 3–5 years we would accumulate the requisite 10,000 hours of practicing *personal excellence*. Here is the cool thing. No matter where you go or what you are doing, you are right there doing it. All you need to do is pay attention.

The one common element in everything you will do in the future is **you**. Knowing that *blue threat* (internal) factors result in 80% of failures, applying the 10,000 hour rule to achieve expertise in personal excellence and empowered accountability seems reasonable, if only from a "save me from myself" point of view. But there's even a better reason to do it.

Most people never really get to know themselves, and that is a shame for both personal and professional reasons. Because we don't really know ourselves, we have a real problem with accurate self-assessment. Without a true picture of who we are, we lose confidence in ourselves or even worse, get unjustifiably over confident. When we fail, we blame others or the situation, further distorting our self image until self assessment becomes a completely unreliable mirror.

> "The one common element in everything you will do in the future is **you**."

However, by using the world as our classroom, and applying the tools to methodically *practice excellence as a life skill and not just a job skill*, we can get to know, love and be satisfied with who we are. We are then able to get an accurate reflection, and have justifiable and well earned confidence. Success and the economic security that comes with it will follow naturally in the wake of this type of expertise.

From a systemic perspective, this untapped potential raises the stakes. What would happen to our organizations if we could empower key personnel – or better yet, <u>all</u> personnel – with tools to systematically improve in the means we have described above?

Human Capital: Progress and Profit through People

At a conference a few years ago, I followed a famous human performance expert on stage and was faced with an uncomfortable moment. He had spent the previous 60 minutes telling the 1,500+ attendees that "all the easy things have been done" and in order to make any further inroads on profitability or safety, we "need to make significant investments to work the small margins we have not yet addressed." I tossed out my standard introduction and started my presentation by saying "With all due respect to our keynote speaker, I simply could not disagree more."

My point then – and now – is that we have not begun to leverage the full potential of people. I'm not talking about riding them harder or working them longer. I am talking about empowering them with new error control and opportunity seizing tools, providing a clear intent for them to drive improvement, and trusting them to do it. Empowered accountability and shared purpose will change the dynamics in the board room and on the assembly line or its equivalent. It has immediate applications for senior and middle management, program and project teams (especially those chasing competitive contracts), first line supervisors, IT professionals, human resources, industrial safety, quality and continuous improvement programs, marketing, sales and customer service.

How can one new concept or program impact all of these pieces of the puzzle? Heightened awareness seizes opportunities and reduces errors in all environments. By being able to see deeper into themselves and the situation, a new level of participatory excellence is not only possible, but practically guaranteed. Perhaps more than ever before in our history, people are making the difference between winning and losing.

Adaptive Intellect – Readiness and Every Level of Change and Challenge

To understand how empowered accountability is such a game changer in the business world, let's examine Figure 11.4, *Optimizing Performance Across the Spectrum*. On the left hand side of the figure your organization is operating in the "operations normal" mode. Assuming you have good procedures and well trained people, this is where you should be making money. It is the realm of *process, plans* and *procedure* and the keys to success *are contained in the work* in the form of solid plans, reliable checklists, procedures, supervision and quality control. Yet even here, danger lurks in the form of *apathy, boredom* and *routine noncompliance*. It is noteworthy to point out that many of the deadliest errors in history were made during "ops normal" conditions.

"It is noteworthy to point out that many of the deadliest errors in history were made during *ops normal* conditions."

What is generally recognized as the world's worst industrial disaster took place at a Union Carbide pesticide plant in the Bhopal, India in December 1984. At midnight on 3 December 1984, the plant released 42 tons of toxic *methyisocyanate* gas. Between 8,000–10,000 died within 72 hours, and it is estimated that 25,000 have since died from gas-related illness and health complications. The accident occurred during a routine cleaning of plumbing, when large amounts of water was allowed to enter a tank full of chemicals, causing a chain reaction and explosion. A mixture of poisonous gases flooded the city of Bhopal, causing great panic as people woke up with a burning sensation in their lungs. Thousands died immediately from the effects of the gas and many were trampled in the panic.[12]

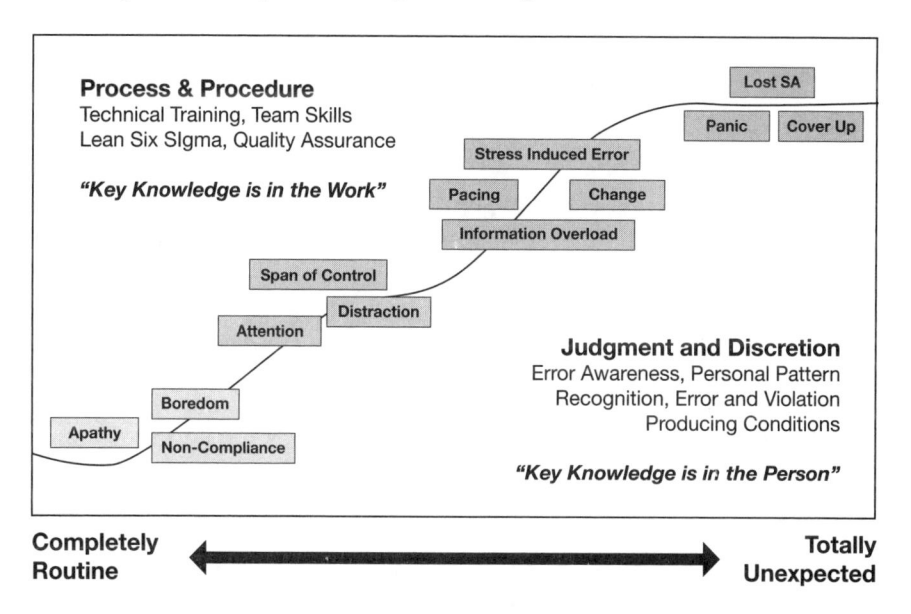

Figure 11.4
Empowered Accountability Across the Spectrum of Challenge

We see a completely different challenge at the far right of the chart. Here, our procedures and planning will no longer cover the novel situation. Perhaps a key supplier went out of business, you've had a major incident or accident, or financing fell through. Whatever it was that caused it, your standard operating procedures are not going to handle it. The key knowledge for success at this end of the spectrum must come from *within the minds of your people*. To use a football analogy, his is the realm of the broken field runner, but you don't get to choose who gets the ball. The enemies here are *lost situation awareness*, *panic*, and the urge to *cover up* the failure and place the blame somewhere else. Speaking of broken field running....

Apollo 13 was on its way to the moon when an explosion caused a loss of electrical power and failure of both oxygen tanks. The oxygen and

---

[12] http://www.bhopal.com/chrono.htm

battery in the Command Module were only designed to support the vehicle during the last hours of flight, so after consultation with experts and teammates back at *Mission Control* in Houston, they decided to use the Lunar Module as a "lifeboat" during the return trip to Earth. Despite great hardship caused by limited power, loss of cabin heat, and a shortage of water, the crew returned safely to Earth, and the mission has become the iconic tale of solid judgment and teamwork in do or die situations.

This figure also illustrates the insight that different types of errors tend to occur at different levels of challenge. We have already looked at the polar ends of the spectrum of challenge, but there are also lessons available in the middle. We see at the center left of the figure *that attention management, distraction* and *span of control* issues tend to arise as things first begin to change from the routine to the unexpected, as in the following example:

> Eastern Air Lines Flight 401 was a Lockheed L-1011 jet that crashed into the Everglades in December, 1972 causing 101 fatalities. The crash was a result of the flight crew's failure to monitor the flight instruments while trying to troubleshoot a nose gear indicator light. While all three crew members were working heads down on the indicator light, the autopilot tripped off and the aircraft slowly descended into the swamp. Subsequently, it was found that the landing gear was down and locked and it was just a malfunctioning light bulb.[13]

Further up the unexpectedness scale (center right), the challenges get a bit more severe. Process and procedures still are available, but often, *time pressure* makes it difficult to execute them. The pace of change induces high *stress* and *information overload* often contributes to *poor pacing* and bad decision making. Consider the following example:

> Off duty New York City Police Officer Omar Edwards was shocked to see his car being broken into, and immediately confronted Miguel Santiago who had just smashed the side window of his late model Nissan. After a brief struggle, Santiago broke away and Edwards pulled his gun and gave chase. At the same time, a 25th Precinct Anti-Crime team with a sergeant and two officers had just turned the corner and saw Santiago run in front of the unmarked car followed shortly by Officer Edwards, gun in hand and giving chase. One officer exited the car and yelled to Edwards, *"Police, stop and drop the gun. Drop the gun."* Officer Edwards turned,

---

[13] "The Crash Of Eastern Airlines Flight 401." http://eastern401.googlepages.com/home

with the gun still in his hand, toward the uniformed officer. Things were moving too fast, and before any more words were exchanged, the uniformed officer fired his Glock 9-millimeter six times. Medical personnel arrived moments later and rendered aid to Officer Edwards. In cutting off his outer garment they discovered he was wearing a Police Academy T-shirt. Checking further they discovered his police shield and ID in his front left pants pocket. Officer Edwards was transported to Harlem Hospital and was pronounced dead.[14]

According to the FBI, 43 police officers have been killed since 1987 by friendly fire, many in situations like the one above. David Klinger, a professor of criminology at the University of Missouri-St. Louis, formerly worked as a Los Angeles police officer and said threatened officers instinctively focus on the perceived threat and tune out other information that could be crucial to split-second decision making. "If an officer has this tunnel vision, and all he sees is the gun, he may not see the badge hanging on the detective's chest," Klinger said.[15]

> *"Adaptive intellect* is the ability to operate effectively across the spectrum of change and challenge."

Adaptive intellect is the ability to operate effectively across the spectrum of change and challenge. But to do this effectively, the organization and the individuals who work there must understand where they are on the challenge spectrum and also where the greatest error risks are at that point on the scale. In the example above, the police officer was faced with a dynamic high risk situation. His imperfect situational awareness, coupled with expectation bias led to a tragic conclusion.

Far more often, the risk lies at the routine end of the spectrum, where the challenges often boil down to understanding the difference between the terms *officially qualified* and *capable*. I highlighted an excellent example of this type of adaptive intellect in the blog post which follows.

The Freedom of a Locked Room
(*Commander's Intent*, Friday, December 19, 2008)

> I picked this short article up off the news wire and will use it to leverage a short discussion on compliance, judgment, and the difference between the terms *capable* and *qualified*. Here it is:

---

14 *A deadly encounter between two officers.* ABC Local News. Saturday, May 30, 2009. Found at http://abclocal.go.com/wabc/story?section=news/local&id=6837950

15 *Police rethink 'always on duty' policy.* Found at http://www.msnbc.msn.com/id/10228242/from/rs.3/

Pilot Tells Passengers 'I'm Not Qualified to Land Plane'

A pilot with more than 30 years experience was forced to turn his plane around – because he was not qualified to land in fog, an airline confirmed Thursday. Passengers on the 8:45 AM Flybe flight to Paris were just minutes away from landing at their destination when they were told they would have to go all the way back to Cardiff, England.

One passenger from Bristol missed a job interview in France because of the incident. Cassandra Grant explained: "Twenty minutes outside Paris, the Captain said, 'Unfortunately I'm not qualified to land the plane in Paris. They are asking for a level two qualification and I only have a level five. We'll have to fly back.'"

A spokeswoman for the airline said Flybe, a low-cost airline, backed the pilot's decision "100 percent." He had recently switched from flying a Bombardier Q300 to a Bombardier Q400 and has not completed the "requisite low-visibility training," she said. The dense fog covering Charles de Gaulle airport had not been there when the flight took off, she added. The plane was already three hours late due to bad weather in Wales. The pilot's situation is "quite unusual but probably not unheard of," according to the Civil Aviation Authority.

The obvious slant of this article – and the initial reaction from many readers – is *"What kind of pilot with 30 years of experience can't land in low visibility conditions?"* The key to answering this question lies in defining the difference between what an individual is *capable* of doing, and what he is formally *qualified* to do.

Capabilities Exceed Qualifications = Discipline and Compliance

There are many times when your capabilities will exceed your qualifications. I suspect this was likely the case with the airline Captain in this article. Although frustrating, this was a non-decision for the pilot. The decision was made for him by policy. Unfortunately, not everyone has the level of maturity or understanding to see the world though the simple but powerful lens of compliance.

Individuals who have this type of uncompromising personal and professional discipline operate with purpose and clarity – in the "freedom of a locked room." Absent an emergency situation, the rules make the decision for you, as well as protecting you from the second guessing of armchair quarterbacks operating at groundspeed zero. Compliance is the link between good policy and safe mission accomplishment. There is no need to ponder unauthorized options based on what your physical skill set might or might not be on any given day.

Qualifications Exceed Capabilities = Courage and Judgment

But there are also times when our qualifications exceed our capabilities – and this is a much more difficult test of professionalism. Let's assume for the moment that this Captain was qualified to fly to the lower visibility minimums, but was having difficulty flying a stabilized approach on this particular day due to any one of a hundred factors. Would he try to will the aircraft to the ground by continuing an unstabilized approach because his qualifications said he *should* be able to fly it – or execute a missed approach and proceed to an alternate based on his subjective evaluation of his limited abilities on this day?

Qualification levels are fixed sums – coldly objective, they are not affected by mission or peer pressures or the urgency of the moment. Or at least they shouldn't be. *Capabilities* on the other hand, are subjective, and by definition can be altered by different states of personal readiness (physiological or psychological) or internal or external pressures to perform. Accurately ascertaining our capability level in real time is true connoisseurship, and the decision to admit when personal proficiency is the limiting factor is one of the most distinguishing marks of a true pro.

"... the decision to admit when personal proficiency is the limiting factor is one of the most distinguishing marks of a true pro."

What kind of pilot tells his passengers he "can't land the plane?" Whether the decision is based on professional discipline, compliance or personal self-awareness, the answer is the same – a professional one. Well done, Captain.

This example shows how empowered accountability supports professional reliability through compliance, role modeling, and reinforcing standards. While it is difficult to put a firm ROI estimate on this type of positive intangible, had the pilot crashed following an act of willful noncompliance the error could have cost hundreds of millions of dollars in legal fees and settlements, quite likley enough to make a small airline like *Flybe* hang up its wings.

We conclude this chapter with a short list of applications for the *blue threat* empowered accountability approach.

A Few Intriguing Applications

As you have seen, the blue threat curriculum is about being human. Its educational components cross vocational lines and are applicable in literally every human endeavor where errors are currently made and therefore have an extremely wide base of applications. Some industries are in need of a new approach. Others could use the blue threat program to optimize and make further gains.

Here is a short list of current and potential applications at multiple levels. Some are already in experimental development. Others should be and could be in the near term.

Major Industries

- **Health Care and Patient Safety.** There is no question that the patient safety efforts are starting to come together. The blue threat programs provide immediate leverage at the individual level while system fixes are underway. Empowered accountability should become a cornerstone of the patient safety effort sponsored and required by organizations like the *Joint Commission*.

- **Military.** On and off-duty accidents and incidents are continuing to kill and injure our military men and women at an alarming and unnecessary rate. Current human factors training is a mixed bag of operational risk management (ORM), team training (CRM), and compliance, none of which address the core elements of personal error control through the uniqueness of each individual. The military technical training is some of the finest in the world. Their human factors training needs to come up to this standard if they are serious about protecting our soldiers, airman, sailors and marines.

  > "On and off-duty accidents and incidents are continuing to kill and injure our military men and women at an alarming and unnecessary rate."

- **Banking.** In the IDC white paper on the *costs of employee misunderstanding* referenced earlier, the banking industry was cited as the worst offender, losing more money to errors of this type than any other industry in the study. Bank staffs are typically centrally located and relatively easy to provide this type of training to. This could be a low cost, high impact program in this error prone environment.

- **Transportation (Maritime, Rail, Trucking, and Public Transportation).** Although aviation has been a leader in human performance training for nearly three decades, the rest of the transportation industry has lagged behind. The plethora of high visibility incidents and accidents across the spectrum of the transportation industry are indicative of deep seeded human error challenges. Rather than adopting and adapting revamped aviation programs, the blue threat curriculum offers an across the board cornerstone that can be tailored not only to the industry, but to the individual.

- **Hospitality Industry.** Hotel and restaurant employee errors are a major source of customer dissatisfaction. Customer satisfaction is closely tied to reducing simple errors made by staff.

- **Education.** From purely an instructional design perspective, the earlier we can teach people to identify and counter their own personal error patterns, the better off they will be as citizens and we will be as a society. Teachers should be offered this curriculum for their own purposes, and then evaluate how best to integrate and instruct it to future generations. As professional educators, they are in the best position to shape and deliver this curriculum for widespread impact.

> "... error control tools should be a mandatory part of every peace officer's initial and recurrent training."

- **Law Enforcement.** Law enforcement is one of the toughest jobs in any society, and one of the most underappreciated in terms of challenges and difficulties. Not only do they "serve and protect," they must do so within strict legal guidelines on the front lines of the battle against crime. For obvious reasons, error control tools should be a mandatory part of every peace officer's initial and recurrent training.

- **Firefighting (Wildland and Structural).** Much like law enforcement, volunteer and professional firefighters put their lives on the line every day in a rapidly changing, error intolerant environment. The blue threat curriculum should be mandatory for these selfless heroes.

- **Emergency Medical First Responders.** Emergency Medical Technicians (EMT) as well as their drivers and pilots operate in an incredibly high stress environment with lives on the line on nearly every call. The empowered accountability program elements should be a core component of a required human factors training program to protect themselves and the public they serve.

- **Software Development and IT Professionals.** Human error is the bane of the software and IT industry. IT professionals are highly trained technical experts with little or no background on human factors or error control. If there is one place to start to correct this challenge, it should be though heightened awareness of the individual error control process.

- **Amateur and Professional Sports: Coaching Staffs and Teams.** This is a most intriguing opportunity. Teams looking for a competitive edge should look very closely at a program that teaches and empowers high reliability under stress. Coaching staffs can be taught these skills to reduce interpersonal and intrapersonal errors in game preparation and management. Players aware of their own error tendencies can better manage them in real time.

  "Teams looking for a competitive edge should look very closely at a program that teaches and empowers high reliability under stress."

- **Criminal Recidivism Efforts.** In the United States, 68% of males and 58% of females are rearrested, and 53% and 39% respectively are re-incarcerated following release from prison "rehabilitation" programs.[16] Many end up back in trouble because they cannot break out of old patterns of behavior, a topic taught and supported in great detail within the *blue threat* curriculum.

- **Domestic Violence Programs.** The U.S. Department of Justice estimates that over 1.3 million people are victims of domestic violence in the U.S. every year. Domestic violence often results from individuals

---

16 Visher, Christy A. 2003. "Transitions From Prison To Community: Understanding Individual Pathways." The Urban Institute, Justice Policy Center, District of Columbia Washington, 20037

who cannot see and predict the triggers that will cause them to lose control. Protocols and procedures for "managing the moment" are key objectives in the empowered accountability programs and would seem to have cross over applicability in this environment.

- **Addiction Recovery.** Substance abuse remains a societal problem of immense consequence. Although there are many group programs (12 Step, etc.) that gain leverage on this challenge, many individuals cannot or will not participate effectively in the group setting. The empowered accountability approach gives traction for both thought and behavior at the individual level and may be a possible resource for these individuals as well as a complement for those successfully engaged in group based recovery programs.

It is often easier to integrate change inside an *existing* program. In addition to specific industries mentioned above, there are many opportunities to embed personal accountability education and training to improve already well functioning efforts. Here are a few high potential opportunities.

- **Character and Ethics Training.** This one is a no-brainer. Personal accountability is the core of these topics and the newly developed program materials are ready to go inside any existing program. Review Chapter 4 for the underpinnings of this requirement.

- **Just Culture Initiatives.** Any just culture effort that uses the terms *responsibility* and *accountability* but does not empower them through education, training and support is simply an oxymoron.

- **Safety Management Systems (SMS).** The entire blue threat program grew out of a gap analysis of current safety programs which discovered that individuals lacked the skill set to predict and prevent their own personal error patterns. Yet many SMS programs and standard setters still do not see the individual as a part of the system. This is a serious oversight that can be remedied by inclusion of personal error control programs as a required element in SMS programs.

> "Domestic violence often results from individuals who cannot see and predict the triggers that will cause them to lose control."

- **Program and Project Management Leader and Team Training.** More programs and project teams fail for interpersonal and intrapersonal reasons than any other. An entire buffet of new tools and skills are now available to help team managers and members to control error in the time constrained program or project environment.
- **Compliance.** As we discussed in Chapter 4, regulatory and procedural compliance is more complex than previously thought. By providing the pillars of empowered accountability to personnel at all levels, voluntary compliance and peer to peer accountability can dramatically improve existing programs.
- **Insurance Loss Control Programs.** Insurance companies are in the business of risk control and will directly benefit from human error control. Additionally, upon proven effectiveness, the industry can promote greater acceptance of the personal error control concept through reduced premiums.
- **Quality Programs** (e.g., six sigma, lean, achieving excellence initiatives). Current quality programs use the DMAIC (*define, measure, analyze, improve and control*) or similar process to drive systemic improvement. The personal I CAN™ (Identify, Categorize, Analyze and Neutralize) process using the *Blue Threat Report and Analysis Tool* (Appendix) takes *lean six sigma* to the next logical place, the personal errors that underpin defects and waste. A Blue Threat Certification for *six sigma* black belts is already developed.

> "A Blue Threat Certification for *six sigma* black belts is already developed."

- **Executive Leadership Development.** More high achievers derail themselves for personal reasons than any other. The self-awareness and self-control skills contained in the blue threat curriculum are keys to long term professional reliability.
- **Conflict Management.** Like domestic violence, conflict management requires an individual to know how to "manage the moment" through awareness of personal hot buttons and how to avoid emotional reactions in response to the words and actions of others.

- **Wellness Programs.** Physical, mental and emotional wellness are all supported throughout the empowered accountability curriculum in a wide variety of ways. Currently, there is nothing remotely like this in most existing wellness programs.

It's Really All About You

In additional to all of these potential organizational applications, the knowledge, tools, and techniques contained in the blue threat curriculum are all designed to be used at the personal level by individuals. Applications include:

- Continuous improvement (Kaizen)
- Fitness and wellness
- Weight control
- Relationship management
- Anger management
- Addiction recovery
- Emotional control
- Spiritual development

Final Words on the Business Side of Error Control

Error control is a competitive advantage for both organizations and individuals. As with all breakthroughs, the challenge will be integration of a new concept into existing paradigms.

Herb Brooks, the coach of the USA Hockey team that won the 1980 Olympic Gold Medal often referred to as the "Miracle on Ice" was criticized during the selection for the team for not picking the most well known amateurs for his squad. His response is enlightening. "I'm picking the right players, not necessarily the best players." He was building the *best team* which he knew was more about players that would complement and synergize with each other than it was about past goals scored or headlines.

Modern business leaders would do well utilizing the Herb Brooks' mindset to create a holistic solution to the human error challenge.

TWELVE

The Blue Threat Proverbs

*"Strength of numbers is the delight of the timid.
The valiant in spirit glory in fighting alone."*
– Mahatma Gandhi

Empowered accountability is the antidote against unnecessary suffering, lost lives, failed potential and mediocrity. The *Blue Threat Proverbs* (BTP) are designed as a collection of thought provoking ideas and insights into our eternal and most lethal foe – human error. They are designed to provide those who are ready to stretch their performance to new levels through new modes of self reflective thought and action.

Stated simply, when it comes to combating human error, the status quo is not good enough – not nearly good enough. As you have discovered in the pages preceding this chapter, every year, hundreds of thousands of innocent people die from avoidable human error, and that is just the tip of the iceberg of suffering caused by unnecessary and avoidable error.

The challenge of human error will never be remedied by any traditional education, training, quality or safety program that fails to address the differences between people. Error is a function not only of our situation, policies, procedures, and training, but of who we are as unique creations. Therefore, the fight against avoidable human error must take a new turn. There is an old military axiom that states that following a failed attack, the second assault on

> "The challenge of human error will never be remedied by any traditional education, training, quality or safety program that fails to address the differences between people."

a fortified enemy position should come from an entirely new direction. In the world of human performance, we have failed to apply this fundamental principle. We continue to invest vast resources to investigate incidents and accidents, and to hammer out new regulations, policies, team training and leadership programs – and the human error failure rate[1] remains relatively constant at 80%. It is time to try for a new vector of attack in the fight to protect our people, our families, our careers and our lives.

Human error challenges must be slowly untangled in a private battle within each of us. This is true for many reasons, but one stands out as nearly universal. In people who care about the perceptions of others – and don't we all – human error and personal weakness is secret and sacred ground, at least until the investigation team and lawyers sort out the accountability issues in the aftermath of a failed outcome.

People want to be successful, but often fall victim to errors they cannot see coming and do not know how to defend against. This is a correctable condition. Given the skill set to see and avoid error producing conditions, most people will act to improve, and in so doing improve the interests of those they represent, love, and protect.

Beyond personal satisfaction, serious concerns such as *profit, compliance, safety, employee retention, litigation risk, quality, and customer satisfaction* – all turn on the fulcrum of human error. Personal error limits our performance and puts at risk <u>everything</u> we value.

As you have learned in our discussions on empowered accountability, the blue threat concept is an extension of the *Global War on Error*©[2] and represents the internal threat we pose to our own performance through our lack of understanding to see and confront the internal threat. Read, reflect and internalize each of these proverbs, which are not intended as expert advice

---

1   A cross industry analysis of accidents and incidents tells a depressing story, that between 70–90% of failures result from human error.
2   The Global War on Error® is a registered trademark of Tony Kern, following a five year research program designed to develop personal error knowledge, skills and procedures for high risk, error intolerant operations.

from outsiders – but rather to provoke an internal dialogue on who you are and who you might become. Following each proverb are a few questions for reflection. Take the time to think about each of them.

"Human error challenges must be slowly untangled in a private battle within each of us." People are not grown in laboratories or manufactured by a sterile six-sigma process. We are **wildly unique** – formed by an incredible (and enjoyable) biological process and then molded by an even more complex set of environmental factors. But that does not mean we must remain baffling, incomprehensible creatures. We just need to learn to look a bit closer at who we are and why we do what we do. It is not rocket science, but it is science, and requires those who wish to improve to learn some new things. Here are a few of the principles to get us started on the journey.

1. Human error is not a victimless crime.

Everyone, it seems, loves to hide behind the famous quote that "to err is human." It is insightful that we seldom hear the second half of Cicero's quote that "to persevere in error is the act of a fool." More to the point, sometimes, **to err is inhuman**. If we were only putting ourselves at risk by our errors, it might be easier to give human error a free pass. But every year, hundreds of thousands die due to the errors of others. Moreover, advances in technology have reached the point where single errors or acts of noncompliance can kill or maim thousands, or wreak irreversible havoc on the environment. Examples include the nuclear meltdown at Chernobyl, the chemical accident in Bhopal, India or the devastating oil spill of the *Exxon Valdez* in Alaska.

Questions for personal reflection.

- Are you mugging your own performance? How are you a victim of your own errors?
- What do you lose – in terms of penalties or lost opportunities – as a result of those errors?
- Who else is at risk from your errors and what price might they pay?
- If you could better control your errors, how would work and life look for those around you without those losses?

2. Everybody's weird.

Every person on Earth has a distinct genetic code coupled with a unique upbringing that results in a personal performance fingerprint. Yet most organizational programs don't comprehend how to deal with this uniqueness, instead opting to (1) satisfy some minimum requirement, or (2) targeting "known problem areas" or (3) aiming for the middle ground in an audience of learners. The empowered accountability approach *teaches people to teach themselves*,™ tailoring life's lessons to the only environment that really matters – the one you are in. By comprehending and leveraging your own error and performance patterns, you not only stay true to yourself, but also find immediate relevance by tapping the power of self-discovered truths.

> "People want to be successful, but often fall victim to errors they cannot see coming and do not know how to defend against. This is a correctable condition."

Questions for personal reflection.

- What quirks might you have that others consider odd? Do you consider them odd – or just different?
- Can you see past differences in others to see them and their ideas objectively?
- Does your uniqueness clash with the real world on occasion? How can this work in your favor?

3. Life is a mission simulator.

Every day, life gives us free lessons on our drive to work, at home or in our daily interactions with our colleagues and family members. By learning how to mine data from our daily successes/errors, we can quickly improve in all areas of our personal and professional lives. Organizations large and small use mission simulators to train performance. Some of these devices so realistically mimic real life that airline simulators reduce actual flight training hours on a 1 for 1 ratio. Likewise, businesses spend millions of dollars to send executives through business case simulations at high end Ivy League schools. But why mimic real life when it is readily available to all of us for free?

Questions for personal reflection.
- What free lessons did life offer you this week?
- What could you do to "mine the data" from those lessons to learn and improve?
- How could you plan to learn from the lessons of tomorrow?

4. Experience is overrated.

One of the most common misconceptions in human performance is that experience is the best teacher. Sometimes, old age and grey hairs arrive all by themselves, unaccompanied by wisdom or even predictably sound judgment. A favorite quote states "experience is someone who has often gotten away with doing the wrong thing longer than you have." Of course, experience *can* be very powerful. High levels of experience coupled with a system for learning from that experience is how true experts are made. The problem is that we are never taught to mine our experience for lessons and bad habits are formed along with the good ones.

> "Sometimes, old age and grey hairs arrive all by themselves, unaccompanied by wisdom or even predictably sound judgment."

Questions for personal reflection.
- How do you view experience – as accumulated time or accumulated learning?
- What "wrong things" – negative habit patterns – have you been getting away with?
- How can you couple your daily experiences with a system of learning to build true expertise?

5. The time of reckoning is not of our choosing.

The world is a cruel teacher. She gives us pop quizzes without notice, and the penalties for failure can be death or worse – a lifetime of remorse and humiliation. Winston Churchill once said "There comes a time in every man's life when he is called upon to do something very special; something for which he and only he has the capabilities, has the skills, and has the necessary training. What a pity if the moment finds the man unprepared." The point here is simple – get *ready*, stay *ready*. When the test comes there will be no time to go back and catch up on weak areas.

Questions for personal reflection.
- What critical tests of competence could you face at any moment?
- Are you prepared? Are you ready? Would you stake your life on it?
- If not – how can you get ready, and stay ready?

6. Practice makes permanent.[3]

This truism has its origins in the martial arts – and points out the fallacy in the more common refrain of "practice makes perfect." Perfection through practice is <u>only</u> true if you are practicing the right thing in the right way, every time. Far more often, our lack of attention to detail and the demands of daily life encourage us to take short cuts or deviate from precise modes of thought and action. When these habit-forming actions occur without a bad outcome to highlight the error of our ways – we are rewarding failure and actually teaching ourselves sloppy performance lessons that may come back to bite us.

Questions for personal reflection.
- Are you building positive habits, or habits based on convenience?
- Do you do the right thing, the right way, every time?
- How do your habits reward failure and sloppy performance?

7. Habits are better than rules.

The key to understanding the creative and destructive power of *habit* is to comprehend the key point that *habits don't require choices*. The following three quotes hit key messages for improvement through *habit shaping* – building good habits as well as breaking bad ones. Rules have to be kept, not so a habit. "You don't have to keep a habit; it keeps you." Of course, this is a good thing only if it is a good habit. Millions are unnecessarily enslaved by negative habits such as alcoholism, drug addiction or some other self-destructive and self-programmed modes of thought and behavior. A second quote highlights the insidious nature of habits. "Habits are

> "Habits are tricky things. Their bonds are too weak to notice until they are too strong to break."

---

3   This is the first of many phrases I have drawn from others that populate the Blue Threat proverbs. Where I could find or remember the source, I cite the source. However, where I could not, I apologize in advance to the originator and beg the indulgence of the reader. All interpretations are mine alone unless otherwise noted.

tricky things. Their bonds are too weak to notice until they are too strong to break." Finally, "Habits are forces of nature, first you make them; and then they make you." Live accordingly.

Questions for personal reflection.
- What habits are you building and reinforcing in life and work?
- Which negative habits threaten to enslave you?
- Which of your habits have proven too strong to break in the past?
- If you could change negative habits, how would your work and life look?

8. The plain things are the main things.

Your everyday routine presents the most and best opportunities for both failure and improvement. There are several reasons for this. First, simple mathematics tells us that with greater frequency comes greater risk. Secondly, high frequency-low risk events allow more opportunities to fine tune your climb up the performance ladder. Finally, habits are formed more quickly in circumstances that can be practiced every day in the same way. So, if you want to be a world class performer, begin by seeking perfection in your daily drive to work, or basic administrative tasks – the rest will come much faster and easier when habits of excellence are established in the "plain things."

"… bad habits of thought are even more dangerous than bad habits of behavior – as they continuously block objective thinking and form an almost impenetrable barrier to reflective accountability."

Questions for personal reflection.
- What opportunities for improvement are available inside your everyday routine?
- What could you do better that might have a "spill over effect" into other areas of your life?
- How can you seek continuous improvement and practice positive habits in the "plain things" – every day?

9. It is hard to fight an enemy that has outposts in your head.[4]

This proverb completes the "habituation" lesson of *Blue Threat Proverbs* 6, 7 and 8. Humans are notoriously unreliable when it comes to judging our own level of responsibility for good and bad outcomes. This inability to objectively reflect on our role in a given outcome prohibits us from capturing valuable lessons that could immediately improve our performance. In this way, bad habits of thought are even more dangerous than bad habits of behavior – as they continuously block objective thinking and form an almost impenetrable barrier to reflective accountability. Learning to identify these negative thought patterns is not easy, but well worth the effort and will rapidly open vast new horizons of improvement.

Questions for personal reflection.

- What negative thought patterns are blocking your ability to think objectively about your performance?
- What mistakes are you making in judging your own responsibility for poor results?
- What opportunities do you have to identify and counter these thought patterns?

> "Between stimulus and response there is a space. In that space is our power to choose our response."
> – Viktor Frankl

10. Own the decision space between stimulus and response.

Holocaust survivor, author and psychiatrist Viktor Frankl tells us that "between stimulus and response there is a space. In that space is our power to choose our response. In our response lies our growth and our freedom." Far too often, our experiences, biases – and sometimes even our training – surrender this decision space and render us less able to manage our actions in response to certain triggers. This fatal flaw can lead to individual episodes of tragically poor judgment or lifetimes of slavery to unhealthy lifestyles.

Questions for personal reflection.

- In your work and life environments, is there adequate space between stimulus and response or do you act or react immediately like Pavlov's dogs to certain stimuli?

---

4 Sally Kempton, 1970's socialite and journalist who fought psychological challenges through yoga and meditation.

- What specific frustrations might trigger an immediate and regrettable response?
- When you surrender this decision space and say or do something without thinking, what might be the cost?

11. You can control the sail, but not the wind.

Locus of control refers to the extent to which individuals believe that they can control events that affect them. Individuals with a high internal locus of control believe that events result primarily from their own behavior and actions. Those with a high external locus of control believe that powerful others, fate, or chance primarily determine events. One of the most important aspects of personal performance control is knowing what is, and what is not, within our control. Trying to control what is not within our span of influence is a fool's errand. Even more disturbing are those who forfeit effort and responsibility for things that are well within their span of control – like most human error. Knowing the difference – makes all the difference.

"... learning how to do things right is not at all the same thing as learning how not to do them wrong."

Questions for personal reflection.

- Do you know anyone who is a chronic complainer about things beyond their control?
- Where am I trying to control things beyond my reach? What good/ill does this do for me or others?
- Where am I failing – or even failing to try – to control things within my span of influence?

12. Where instinct and intuition fail, intellect must venture.[5]

We are not born problem solvers. Humans must learn to successfully interact with the forces that surround us to succeed in the world. As we have seen in earlier *Blue Threat Proverbs*, without good habits and the diligence to apply them, our experience and intuition may well work against us. Absent innate abilities or intuitive cues, we must resort to the messy business of thinking our way though the challenge of self-improvement. To complicate

---

5   Modified from Jim Butcher, *Storm Front*, pg. 64

matters further, we now know that *learning how to do things right is not at all the same thing as learning how not to do them wrong.* As odd as this may sound, comprehending that our existing training does little to aid us in error control is the first critical step in accepting the need for new knowledge, skills and tactics against error.

Questions for personal reflection.

- To what extent are you relying on experience and intuition to solve your future problems?
- What problems, situations, or habits should you be thinking through to improve your work or life performance?
- What areas do you need to know more about to understand how to not do things wrong?

13. You are only as committed as you are convinced.

Far too often, we fall into the trap of trying to use a process, procedure, tool or technique we do not fully understand. There are many reasons for this, ranging from time pressure, to a streak of anti-intellectualism that runs deep through western culture. There are two serious problems with this. First, without comprehending how and why something is supposed to work, we are quick to abandon it at the first hint of a problem. Secondly, by not routinely asking the how and why questions, marketing trumps science, and we fall victim to the latest fad or slick advertising approach.

"... we often don't see ourselves as a point of origin of significant risk in our own lives...."

There is no truth like self-discovered truth, but the next best thing is to do your homework to convince yourself of the personal return on investment of any improvement tool or effort.

Questions for personal reflection.

- When have you adopted an improvement approach only to abandon it?
- Did you quit because it didn't work or you didn't give it the time, effort or understand enough to make it work?
- What do you need to understand about the blue threat approach to make it work for you?

14. The risk is not where you think it is.

There is a bit of Zen philosophy in this proverb. The first main point is that at the very moment you begin to recognize something as a risk, your awareness level of it as a hazard grows and therefore reduces the likelihood of it occurring or manifesting itself as a negative outcome. The second point is that we often don't see ourselves as a point of origin of significant risk in our own lives, in spite of the fact that over 80% of injury causing accidents and incidents are self-induced. This risk "blind spot" must be overcome if we are ever to truly manage risk from a personal perspective. In the immortal words of the cartoon character Pogo, "We have met the enemy – and he is us."

Questions for personal reflection.

- Where do you see your risks? In yourself, in the world, or both?
- How can you get line of sight on your own "risk blind spot"?
- Where in work and life are you your own worst enemy – the biggest obstacle to personal or professional success?

15. The fourth dimension is the first decision.

With apologies to Euclidean mathematics and orthogonal geometry, most people refer to *time* as the 4th dimension, and it is a key linchpin of performance. Life itself is sequencing priorities with one eye on the sand left in the hourglass. In each situation, three questions should be asked: (1) How much *time* do I have? (2) How much *time* might I need? And most importantly, (3) Can and should I alter that equation? The ability to creatively solve pacing problems is often directly correlated to our ability to ask and answer these questions. Far too often, we plunge into action without a good feel for the impact time will have on our performance, an error that only becomes apparent in the endgame. "Time is free, but it is priceless. Spend it wisely."[6]

"Make time to learn from success, and you will have more opportunities to do so."

Questions for personal reflection.

- Where does inept time management adversely affect my work and life?

---

[6] Harvey McKay

- Do I not allow enough time, understand how much time I need, or create the time I need to be successful?
- Am I simply being unrealistic in what I'm attempting to do in the time available?

16. Every post-game is a pre-game.

More improvement opportunities are lost in the immediate aftermath of successful events than in any other human endeavor. Simple questions such as *"Why did this plan work?"* or *"What could have been done better?"* routinely go unasked, and therefore the lessons they offer go undiscovered. Far too often, we assume success was the sole result of our personal or team actions, when the truth is more complex. Success, like failure is nearly always an interaction between human and situational factors. Unraveling success is enlightening and far more enjoyable than lessons learned from negative outcomes, or through incident or accident investigations. Make time to learn from success, and you will have more opportunities to do so.

"The ability to stay on task without losing either self- or situation awareness is the mark of an expert...."

Questions for personal reflection.

- What would you learn from conducting an "after action review" of each success by asking:
    - What worked?
    - What didn't work?
    - What will you do differently next time?
    - How can you make the time and effort to really understand what is driving success?

17. You can analyze the past, but you must design the future.[7]

Smart people use data and evidence to help make good decisions in life. Regrettably, some won't take the time or make the effort. Many others are stuck at the other end of the data driven scale in a continuous state of "analysis paralysis," looking for a map of the future they will never find there. Everyone knows you cannot drive safely looking only in the rear view mir-

---

7   Edward Debono

ror. Combining reliable insights of the past with a personal vision of the future merges the best of both worlds. In the words of the famous French author and pilot Antoine Saint-Exupery, "as for the future, your task is not to foresee it, but to enable it."

Questions for personal reflection.

- Name three things you have learned from past mistakes.
- How have these lessons shaped your present life?
- How will you use today to shape tomorrow?

18. Grow or die.

Everything in nature is dynamic – advancing or retreating, growing or dying. We are no different, which makes it odd that so many of us stop growing once we achieve some early or mid-life goal. We resist new ideas and change and eventually develop a stubborn anti-learning streak, which in turn leads to bitterness, frustration and error. Choose to grow. Embrace the new, test it against your experience, turn back the clock.

> "This crucial point – the apex of the improvement effort where gains become apparent – is where permanent change becomes a serious reality."

Questions for personal reflection.

- Have you hit cruise control and stopped growing?
- Are you automatically resistant to change and new ideas?
- How can you convert new ideas and change opportunities into personal growth and development?
- What would work and life look like if you embraced a philosophy of lifelong learning and improvement?

19. Lost self awareness precedes lost situation awareness.

Our ability to monitor and steer our own attention is one of the most important and elusive tools of personal performance control. Our goal should be to develop an ongoing and balanced internal and external scan, mindful of both our ever-changing environment and the state and direction of our attention. The ability to stay on task without losing either self- or situation awareness is the mark of an expert and a skill that must be consciously developed to the point of habit. When you lose track of what you are thinking about and why, it will not be long until you lose track of everything else and become one with the tumbleweed – out of touch, out of control and blowing in the wind.

Questions for personal reflection.

- How good are you at maintaining awareness of your internal dialogue and other distractions competing for your attention?
- Can you stay on task or do you seek distractions to relieve boredom, frustration, complexity and difficult tasks?
- When was the last time you lost full awareness of your mindset or situation and what was the result?

20. Never trust a dead villain.

Every Hollywood thriller movie script contains a "dead villain leaps back to life" scene, where the hero or someone in his/her care is nearly killed because they failed to finish the bad guy off. In the blue threat world, life mimics art. Broken bad habits – like unwanted fat cells – never really die. They lie patiently dormant waiting for the hero to become complacent and look the other way. Failure to keep an active check on performance challenges we have successfully engaged often results in relapse into error, lost advantage and frustration. Use the blue threat tools to drive a stake through the heart of performance-robbing habits – then stay vigilant.

Questions for personal reflection.

- Which of your bad habits won't stay dead and buried?
- How and why do they keep rising from the grave to haunt you?
- How can you "drive a stake" and rid yourself of these error-producing habits forever?

21. Strange things happen near the boundaries.[8]

This *Blue Threat Proverb* is taken directly from author James Gleick's excellent book *Chaos: Making a new Science*, and cautions us to maintain a watchful posture when we approach "boundaries" in our personal and professional lives. So what exactly is a boundary? Mr. Webster's dictionary gives us two hints: (1) *A separation, natural or artificial, which marks the division of two contiguous properties;* or (2) *the line or plane indicating the limit or*

---

8   Gleick, *Chaos: Making a new Science*

extent of something. From these definitions, two guidelines emerge. First, carefully manage "border crossings" interactions outside your normal personal or professional lines of communication. Secondly, monitor personal warning signals as you approach your own physical or mental limits and give them the respect they deserve.

Questions for personal reflection.

- What are the "boundaries" in my work and life? Are they clear lines or "grey zones?"
- What are the critical personal and professional border crossings where I interact and communicate?
- How can I anticipate the warning signals of physical or mental limits near these boundaries?

22. At the Church of the Blue Threat, every day is Sunday.

Life provides no breaks in the flow of circumstances or events that produce human error; or from the opportunities to reap the potential lessons and rewards from them. Personal performance improvement is an "all the time thing" where we receive in accordance with what we are willing to put in. The second aspect of this religious metaphor is *up front sacrifice* – always a tough sell in the modern world. There is an old fisherman's saying that "you have to lose a fly to catch a trout." Translation: You must first invest something to gain the reward, but the reward is worth the investment.

"There is truly only one expert on you."

Questions for personal reflection.

- What percentage of my life's time and effort do I currently invest in improving my work and life?
- How often have I missed opportunities to grow by failing to make the "up-front sacrifice" of time and effort?
- When I look at what I want to achieve – do I have a clear idea of what I'm prepared to do and give-up – to get it?

23. Self improvement defies gravity.

There comes a point in every improvement effort where we begin to see the results of our efforts. From that point forward, what was once an uphill climb – laborious effort for no apparent gain – becomes worth the time and effort, and eventually effortless and nearly automatic behavior. Indy race car driver Danica Patrick explains; "I really had this obsession to keep getting better. I got hooked on the improvement, and the gains that can be made, and the satisfaction that comes from it." This crucial point – the apex of the improvement effort where gains become apparent – is where permanent change becomes a serious reality. Manage this correctly, and you will achieve the "normalization of excellence" where further improvement fuels itself.

Questions for personal reflection.

- If you made improvement an "all the time thing" how would work and life be different?
- In your current improvement efforts, what will be the first signs of improvement and when will you see them?
- When they emerge, how can you anchor the change to make the improvement permanent?

"You can't swing a dead cat these days without hitting someone who will tell you how flawed we are as a species."

24. Beware the guru.

Human performance gurus often fall victim to their own specialization bias – and sometimes lead millions down the same potentially flawed path. These so-called experts have often spent their life climbing up the academic hierarchy, or written a bestselling book on a particular topic – and they tend to view the world exclusively through that lens. This can lead to a false model being applied in your life – one that may, or may not, make sense for you or work for you. Duke professor Henry Petroski writes, "things work because they work in a particular configuration, at a particular scale, and in a particular culture."[9] One size does not fit all, no matter how smart or famous the guru is. Read and learn from these specialists, but remember that they do not know you or your unique circumstances. There is truly only one expert on you. Trust yourself – but only after you really get to know yourself. Remember the Zen wisdom; "Do not seek to walk the path of the Masters. Rather, seek what they sought."

Questions for personal reflection.

- Have you ever adopted an improvement program that turned out to be a one-size-fits-all approach that didn't fit?

---

9   Harvard Business Review, October 2004, "Look first to Failure" p. 18–20.

- How can you adopt and adapt the blue threat program to meet your unique individual circumstances?
- If you become your own guru – how might your self-esteem and self perception change?

25. Harness the Merlin Effect[10]

Merlin was the wizard to King Arthur. Merlin's imperative wasn't to make himself the world's greatest wizard; it was to make Arthur the best king. Ironically, as you seek to make others better, you don't slow your own improvement efforts – you actually accelerate them. *It has long been known that the best way to learn is to teach*, so as you apply the blue threat tools to eliminate your errors and pursue precision, strive to lift those around you by your example and your support. As Gandhi said, be the change you want to see in the world. Conquer error. Improve performance. Lead the way.

"... it is not someone else's duty to make us better...."

Questions for personal reflection.

- Who are you currently mentoring – either formally or informally?
- Who was your role model?
- Who's role model are you?

26. You can't uneducate someone who has learned to read.[11]

This quote from civil rights activist Caesar Chavez drives home the point that while static knowledge may at some point become obsolete, the process for getting it is **permanent** and can never be taken from you. In the same way that learning to read opens a door that can never be closed, learning this discipline of thought to pull the lessons of improvement from our day to day experiences provides one with the never ending fountain of personal improvement knowledge and opportunities. Instead of a glassful of information, you gain access to the spring from which it flows.

Questions for personal reflection.

- Do you currently have the ability to "read" the nuances of your day to day activities?

---

10 With many thanks to Dale Condit, who taught me the *Merlin Effect* metaphor in a world class Program Management training course at the USAF Academy in 1998.
11 Caesar Chavez quote: "You can not uneducate a person who has learned to read."

- How many free improvement lessons are you letting flow by because you haven't yet learned how to pull them out of your life experience?
- Since learning to read, when was the last time you learned a new way to extract information from the world?

27. Fear not the depths.

Bad things happen all the time. Some give up. Some endure. And some see these emotional moments as the opportunity to make real change in themselves. In *The Road Less Travelled*, author M. Scott Peck says, "the truth is that our finest moments are most likely to occur when we are feeling deeply uncomfortable, unhappy, or unfulfilled. For it is only in such moments, propelled by our discomfort, that we are likely to step out of our ruts and start searching for different ways or truer answers." Armed with an opportunity to change and a new process for doing so, each moment of failure and pain become launching pads for a stronger and better you. But only if you have the understanding of how to recognize the moment and the skill set to leverage it.

> "Broken bad habits – like unwanted fat cells – never really die."

Questions for personal reflection.

- What was the last painful event or personal failure you experienced?
- Did you merely endure it – or use it to make a difference in your life or the world?
- Do you get beaten down by the world, or do you use misfortune to gain wisdom and slingshot you to higher levels of understanding and performance?

28. Socrates was right.

Man, know thyself, is inscribed into the temple wall at Delphi and is attributed to at least six ancient Greek philosophers. As the most famous, Socrates usually gets the credit. When it comes to improving performance and controlling error at any level, these words are the key to the kingdom. Controlling human performance occurs at the level of the individual, but impacts teams, projects, programs and entire organizations. Any effort to control the risk of human error must begin by providing the tools and motivation for individuals to first, comprehend their own thoughts and behaviors, and then take action to improve. As the first and last line of defense against human error, the individual is the obvious and necessary starting point.

Questions for personal reflection.

- Are you still a mystery to yourself?
- How much do you understand about why you think, act and react as you do?
- Do you know enough right now to anticipate and prevent life and career threatening errors before they cause harm at work or other areas of your life?

29. "Only human" is the ultimate oxymoron.

You can't swing a dead cat these days without hitting someone who will tell you how flawed we are as a species. This victim mindset is debilitating, destructive and deceiving. Within the realm of known science, humans represent the pinnacle of creation. We are the creators of language, builders of bridges, curers of diseases. We have unlocked the mysteries of the human genome and walked on the moon.

"become true *Blue Threat Ninjas*, capable of seeing and deflecting errors that used to take us by surprise as a matter of routine."

As individuals and as a collective, we have power and potential beyond comprehension. The solutions to nearly all of our problems lie within our immediate grasp. Don't buy into the "flawed human" mindset as an excuse for mediocrity. "Only human" is not only the ultimate oxymoron, it is an insult to our Creator.

Questions for personal reflection.

- Do you think human error is inevitable or avoidable?
- Is the acceptance of human error just a cop out, excusing ourselves from the time, effort and work of controlling errors and improving our performance?
- How can you escape the mediocrity mindset that says: *We've done all we can. What more can we do?*
- How much *avoidable* error is acceptable for you to remain competent, your business viable or your lifestyle safe?

30. If it is to be, it is up to me.

Ten words, twenty letters, one life changing idea – *responsibility*.

Performance control is far more about personal responsibility than it is about organizational fixes. Robert H. Jackson, former Supreme Court Justice and the chief prosecutor of the surviving Nazi leaders at Nuremberg, Germany said it best. "It is not the function of government to keep the citizen from falling into error; it is the function of the citizen to keep the government from falling into error." Likewise, it is not someone else's duty to make us better, it is *our* duty – first to ourselves – and then to the organization, teams, peers and family we live and work with.

Life is a self-service buffet. Take charge, belly up and dig in.

Questions for personal reflection.

- Have you ever felt like it's someone else's job to improve your performance?
- Have you waited for your boss, colleagues or organization to deliver the fix that will lift your game?
- If you took full responsibility for your own growth and improvement, how different would work and life look?

A Few Final Words

We get one life. Why so many choose to waste it through apathy or neglect is a mystery to me. The materials inside these covers represent my best effort to provide traction for the average man or woman to take life by the horns and create a more positive future. Some will buy this book and never read it. Others will browse it and put it on the shelf with the rest of their self improvement literature. But a few of you will engage, and it is those of you I wish to hear from to create a community of positive thinkers and doers, all dedicated to making this one life count. If we pass these stories and lessons learned on, we are creating our own Merlin Effect, empowering others to improve as well.

Begin Where You Are and Commit to the Effort

The German writer Johann Wolfgang von Goethe recognized the fast food mentality of human performance long before the first set of Golden Arches went up, when he wrote in the early 1800's "Everybody wants to be somebody; but nobody wants to grow." Don't let this be you.

You are now on the launching pad. The countdown to new levels of performance began when you picked up this book. Assuming you have read and somewhat internalized the lessons in the previous chapters, you are strapped in and ready for liftoff. Begin your journey by trying to visualize what perfection might look like in all aspects of your life, then detect and repair your personal flaws as they reveal themselves through the process.

This last lesson is for those of us to take the time to master the elements of self-defined excellence and continuous improvement contained in this book; who become true **Blue Threat Ninjas**, capable of seeing and deflecting errors that used to take us by surprise as a matter of routine. It is called the *Parable of the Black Belt*.[12]

> A young martial artist kneeling before the Master Sensei in a ceremony to receive a hard-earned black belt. After years of relentless training, the student has finally reached a pinnacle of achievement in the discipline.
>
> "Before granting the belt, you must pass one more test," says the Sensei.
>
> "I am ready," responds the student, expecting perhaps one final round of sparring.
>
> "You must answer the essential question: What is the true meaning of the black belt?"
>
> "The end of my journey," says the student. "A well-deserved reward for all my hard work."
>
> The Sensei waits for more. Clearly, he is not satisfied. Finally, the Sensei speaks.
>
> "You are not yet ready for the black belt. Return in one year."
>
> A year later, the student kneels again in front of the Sensei.
>
> "What is the true meaning of the black belt?" asks the Sensei.
>
> "A symbol of distinction and the highest achievement in our art," says the student.
>
> The Sensei says nothing for many minutes, waiting. Clearly, he is not satisfied. Finally, he speaks.
>
> "You are still not ready for the black belt. Return in one year."
>
> A year later, the student kneels once again in front of the Sensei. And again the Sensei asks: "What is the true meaning of the black belt?"

---

12 Found at www.bankofideas.com.au/Stories/fables.html#BlackBelt

"The black belt represents the beginning – the start of a never-ending journey of discipline, work, and the pursuit of an ever-higher standard," says the student.

"Yes. You are now ready to receive the black belt and begin your work."

Please keep in touch and contact me with your insights and success stories at tony@convergentperformance.com

To conquer oneself is the best and noblest victory; to be vanquished by one's own nature is the worst and most ignoble defeat.
– Plato

Appendix

Blue Threat Report and Analysis Tool (BRAT™)
- Sample Event and/or Error Report
- Blank Event and/or Error Report
- Tally Sheet

APPENDIX 237

Blue Threat Report and Analysis Tool (BRAT)™
EVENT AND/OR ERROR REPORT

EXAMPLE

Date/Time *18 July 2006 1830 EST* **Ref. #** *06-126*

☐ Error Avoided/Opportunity Achieved

Error Category
☑ Defective Outcome ☐ Waste/Inefficiency ☐ Missed Opportunity

Background—What was going on?
Mowing the yard after work —tired and thirsty but had to get it done for weekend BBQ. Mower had bad battery so I didn't want to shut it off and was running low on gas. I had the hose and a power cord running across the back yard.

Action taken?
I decided to raise the mower deck and drive over the top of them (laziness) rather than pick them up.

Consequence/Potential Consequence?
Mower blade sucked up both the hose and electrical cord. I felt the jolt and bailed off as I shut off the mower. Circuit breaker worked as advertised and tripped the power. Out $40 for new hose and extension cord. Could have been worse.

Risk Assessment Guide

Probability of Recurrence	Potential Severity
A—Very likely to occur routinely	1—Death, serious injury, or failed mission
B—Probably will occur at short intervals	2—Minor injury, damage to mission
C—May occur but infrequently	3—Lower quality, time or resource waste
D—Unlikely to occur again	4—Minimal threat, inconvenience

Probability of Recurrence   A (B) C D
Potential Severity   (1) 2 3 4

Immediate Follow-up Actions (if required)
Four BIG red flags—pressing, fatigue, thirsty and in a hurry. The only good thing is that I'm the only one that knows.

Error Producing Conditions
☐ Physiology/Fatigue
☐ High Risk-Low Frequency Event
☑ Time Pressure
☐ Low Signal to Noise Ratio
☐ Normalization of Deviance
☑ One-Way Decision Gate
☐ Information Overload
☐ Poor Communication
☑ Faulty Risk Perception
☐ Inadequate Standards
☐ Previous Error
☐ Distraction
☐ Broken Habit Pattern

Violation Producing Conditions
☐ Mission Expectations
☐ Power + Ego
☐ Unlikely Detection
☑ Poor Planning
☐ Leadership Gap
☐ Poor Role Models/Copycat
☐ Unique/Special Event

Hazardous Attitudes
☐ Anti-Authority
☑ Impulsiveness
☐ Invulnerable/Bulletproof
☐ Too Competitive/Macho
☐ Resignation
☑ Pressing Too Far
☐ Vanity/Ego Protection
☐ Emotional Jetlag
☐ Along for the Ride
☐ Procrastination/Delayed Decision

Mental Bias
☐ Expectation Bias
☐ Confirmation Bias
☐ Specialty Bias
☐ Framing Error
☐ Fundamental Attribution Error
☐ Other _____

Group Dynamics Traps
☐ Strength of the First Idea
☐ Excessive Deference/Halo Effect
☐ Groupthink
☐ Lack of Assertiveness

Situational Factors
Time
Location
Team members
Type of event
Other

Blue Threat Report and Analysis Tool (BRAT)™
EVENT AND/OR ERROR REPORT

Date/Time _____   **Ref. #** _____
☐ Error Avoided/Opportunity Achieved

Error Category
☐ Defective Outcome   ☐ Waste/Inefficiency   ☐ Missed Opportunity

Background—What was going on?
_____
_____
_____
_____

Action taken?
_____
_____
_____
_____

Consequence/Potential Consequence?
_____
_____
_____
_____

Risk Assessment Guide

Probability of Recurrence	Potential Severity
A—Very likely to occur routinely	1—Death, serious injury, or failed mission
B—Probably will occur at short intervals	2—Minor injury, damage to mission
C—May occur but infrequently	3—Lower quality, time or resource waste
D—Unlikely to occur again	4—Minimal threat, inconvenience

Probability of Recurrence   A B C D
Potential Severity   1 2 3 4

Immediate Follow-up Actions (if required)
_____
_____

Error Producing Conditions
☐ Physiology/Fatigue
☐ High Risk-Low Frequency Event
☐ Time Pressure
☐ Low Signal to Noise Ratio
☐ Normalization of Deviance
☐ One-Way Decision Gate
☐ Information Overload
☐ Poor Communication
☐ Faulty Risk Perception
☐ Inadequate Standards
☐ Previous Error
☐ Distraction
☐ Broken Habit Pattern

Violation Producing Conditions
☐ Mission Expectations
☐ Power + Ego
☐ Unlikely Detection
☐ Poor Planning
☐ Leadership Gap
☐ Poor Role Models/Copycat
☐ Unique/Special Event

Hazardous Attitudes
☐ Anti-Authority
☐ Impulsiveness
☐ Invulnerable/Bulletproof
☐ Too Competitive/Macho
☐ Resignation
☐ Pressing Too Far
☐ Vanity/Ego Protection
☐ Emotional Jetlag
☐ Along for the Ride
☐ Procrastination/Delayed Decision

Mental Bias
☐ Expectation Bias
☐ Confirmation Bias
☐ Specialty Bias
☐ Framing Error
☐ Fundamental Attribution Error
☐ Other _____

Group Dynamics Traps
☐ Strength of the First Idea
☐ Excessive Deference/Halo Effect
☐ Groupthink
☐ Lack of Assertiveness

Situational Factors
Time
Location
Team members
Type of event
Other

BRAT™ Tally Sheet: Error Frequency and Severity Estimate [Dates ────────]

Error Category	Frequency	Avg. Severity	Notes
Defective Outcome	1-2-3-4-5-6-7-8-9-10-11-12-13-14-15	1-2-3-4	
Waste/Inefficiency	1-2-3-4-5-6-7-8-9-10-11-12-13-14-15	1-2-3-4	
Missed Opportunity	1-2-3-4-5-6-7-8-9-10-11-12-13-14-15	1-2-3-4	

Error Producing Conditions (EPCs)	Frequency	Avg. Severity	Notes
Physiology/Fatigue	1-2-3-4-5-6-7-8-9-10-11-12-13-14-15	1-2-3-4	
High Risk-Low Frequency Event	1-2-3-4-5-6-7-8-9-10-11-12-13-14-15	1-2-3-4	
Time Pressure	1-2-3-4-5-6-7-8-9-10-11-12-13-14-15	1-2-3-4	
Low Signal to Noise Ratio	1-2-3-4-5-6-7-8-9-10-11-12-13-14-15	1-2-3-4	
Normalization of Deviance	1-2-3-4-5-6-7-8-9-10-11-12-13-14-15	1-2-3-4	
One-Way Decision Gate	1-2-3-4-5-6-7-8-9-10-11-12-13-14-15	1-2-3-4	
Information Overload	1-2-3-4-5-6-7-8-9-10-11-12-13-14-15	1-2-3-4	
Poor Communication	1-2-3-4-5-6-7-8-9-10-11-12-13-14-15	1-2-3-4	
Faulty Risk Perception	1-2-3-4-5-6-7-8-9-10-11-12-13-14-15	1-2-3-4	
Inadequate Standards	1-2-3-4-5-6-7-8-9-10-11-12-13-14-15	1-2-3-4	
Previous Error	1-2-3-4-5-6-7-8-9-10-11-12-13-14-15	1-2-3-4	
Distraction	1-2-3-4-5-6-7-8-9-10-11-12-13-14-15	1-2-3-4	
Broken Habit Pattern	1-2-3-4-5-6-7-8-9-10-11-12-13-14-15	1-2-3-4	

Violation Producing Conditions (VPCs)	Frequency	Avg. Severity	Notes
Mission Expectations	1-2-3-4-5-6-7-8-9-10-11-12-13-14-15	1-2-3-4	
Power + Ego	1-2-3-4-5-6-7-8-9-10-11-12-13-14-15	1-2-3-4	
Unlikely Detection	1-2-3-4-5-6-7-8-9-10-11-12-13-14-15	1-2-3-4	
Poor Planning	1-2-3-4-5-6-7-8-9-10-11-12-13-14-15	1-2-3-4	
Leadership Gap	1-2-3-4-5-6-7-8-9-10-11-12-13-14-15	1-2-3-4	
Poor Role Models/Copycat	1-2-3-4-5-6-7-8-9-10-11-12-13-14-15	1-2-3-4	
Unique/Special Event	1-2-3-4-5-6-7-8-9-10-11-12-13-14-15	1-2-3-4	

Hazardous Attitudes	Frequency	Avg. Severity	Notes
Anti-Authority	1-2-3-4-5-6-7-8-9-10-11-12-13-14-15	1-2-3-4	
Impulsiveness	1-2-3-4-5-6-7-8-9-10-11-12-13-14-15	1-2-3-4	
Invulnerable/Bulletproof	1-2-3-4-5-6-7-8-9-10-11-12-13-14-15	1-2-3-4	
Too Competitive/Macho	1-2-3-4-5-6-7-8-9-10-11-12-13-14-15	1-2-3-4	
Resignation	1-2-3-4-5-6-7-8-9-10-11-12-13-14-15	1-2-3-4	
Pressing Too Far	1-2-3-4-5-6-7-8-9-10-11-12-13-14-15	1-2-3-4	
Vanity/Ego Protection	1-2-3-4-5-6-7-8-9-10-11-12-13-14-15	1-2-3-4	
Emotional Jetlag	1-2-3-4-5-6-7-8-9-10-11-12-13-14-15	1-2-3-4	
Along for the Ride	1-2-3-4-5-6-7-8-9-10-11-12-13-14-15	1-2-3-4	
Procrastination/Delayed Decision	1-2-3-4-5-6-7-8-9-10-11-12-13-14-15	1-2-3-4	

Mental Bias	Frequency	Avg. Severity	Notes
Expectation Bias	1-2-3-4-5-6-7-8-9-10-11-12-13-14-15	1-2-3-4	
Confirmation Bias	1-2-3-4-5-6-7-8-9-10-11-12-13-14-15	1-2-3-4	
Specialty Bias	1-2-3-4-5-6-7-8-9-10-11-12-13-14-15	1-2-3-4	
Framing Error	1-2-3-4-5-6-7-8-9-10-11-12-13-14-15	1-2-3-4	
Fundamental Attribution Error	1-2-3-4-5-6-7-8-9-10-11-12-13-14-15	1-2-3-4	
Other _____	1-2-3-4-5-6-7-8-9-10-11-12-13-14-15	1-2-3-4	

Group Dynamics Traps	Frequency	Avg. Severity	Notes
Strength of the First Idea	1-2-3-4-5-6-7-8-9-10-11-12-13-14-15	1-2-3-4	
Excessive Deference/Halo Effect	1-2-3-4-5-6-7-8-9-10-11-12-13-14-15	1-2-3-4	
Groupthink	1-2-3-4-5-6-7-8-9-10-11-12-13-14-15	1-2-3-4	
Lack of Assertiveness	1-2-3-4-5-6-7-8-9-10-11-12-13-14-15	1-2-3-4	

Situational Factors
Time
Location
Team members
Type of event
Other

Glossary

Alternative Planning Strategies. Tools to counter internal or external error producing conditions allowing individuals to preplan approaches to avoid the error or minimize its consequences

Blue Threat. The internal threat that human error poses to personal, program or organizational missions

Blue Threat Field Book. A companion to this book for field implementation of the empowered accountability concept and blue threat tools

Blue Threat Software Suite. Software to track and analyze personal error patterns

Blue Threat Proverbs. A collection of short axioms that outline the key elements of the empowered accountability approach

Blue Threat Report and Analysis Tool (BRAT). Reporting tool (hardcopy and software versions) used to identify and analyze personal or organization blue threats

Cognitive Bias. An individual's tendency to make errors in judgment based on mental filters and preconceptions that have developed over a lifetime. Leads to distortion in the way we perceive reality

Crushing Grip of Mediocrity. The area of the performance ladder where individuals and organizations find themselves getting the job done, but with no resources, plan or process to improve

Decisive Point. A key condition, event, critical system, or function that allows an individual to gain a marked advantage over an obstacle or adversary. In blue threat terminology, this often involves a key leverage point against an *error control center of gravity*

Deep Dive Tool for Failure Analysis. A tool that uses blue threat elements to uncover personal and organization error casual factors in the aftermath of a failure

Daffodil Principal. Based on a magnificent and huge garden of daffodils in Running Springs, California planted and tended by one woman over 40 years, it means slow steady progress over time yields big results

Exit Strategy SOP (Standard Operating Procedure). A procedure designed as a "last chance" opportunity to prevent a negative outcome. Examples include missed approach procedures for pilots or a final read through of an important email before hitting the "send" button

Empowered Accountability. A learned set of skills that enable an individual to take greater control of personal error and seize more opportunities through a deeper view into their personal performance and situational factors

Error Control Center of Gravity. A point of maximum leverage against error, usually identified through personal error tracking and analysis

Error Producing Conditions. A set of specific conditions that are known to raise the probability of error

Global War on Error® (GWOE). A campaign against human error that uses a military science approach to combat human error at individual, organizational and systemic levels

Hazardous Attitudes. A set of known mindsets that have been proven as frequent causal factors in accidents and incidents in high risk industries

Human Alchemy. The concept of using flawed performance as motivational and informational leverage to improve; turning human performance "lead into gold"

I CAN™ (Identify, Categorize, Analyze, and Neutralize). The four step process used to discover personal error patterns in support of continuous improvement and error control

Intrapersonal Interfaces. These are the points where we consciously conduct option analysis and interact with our conflicting desires

NIFITI™ Technique – *Name it – Frame it – Tame it*. A tool that allows an individual to specify what the error challenge is, how it might impact their situation and tools to avoid the error or its negative consequence

Normalization of Deviance. A long term phenomenon in which individuals or teams repeatedly accept a lower standard of performance until that lower standard becomes the "norm"

Normalization of Excellence. The inverse of the *Normalization of Deviance*, where habit patterns of continuous improvement are developed leading to high levels of performance with less effort

One Way Decision Gate. A decision from which there is no way to reverse the intended action; examples include firing a gun or jumping out of an airplane

Personal Error Pattern (PEP). An individual fingerprint of the types of errors made by a single person; discovered through the systematic I CAN™ process

Personal Error Tracking. The daily process of real time awareness and recording of personal errors leading to the development of a personal error pattern

Personal Operating Procedure (POP). A tool used to prevent and mitigate known error challenges in response to a personal error pattern or error control center of gravity. Usually a multi-step procedure that is refined over time to get the desired impact

Personal Error Triggers (PET). Fine discriminations of internal and situational factors that activate errors; PET's are typically identified through error tracking and can be predicted and neutralized with heightened self awareness and practice

Performance Evolution Ladder. A tool used to provide fine discriminations in levels of personal and/or organizational performance

Red Threat. External factors that pose a threat to any course of action

Six Sigma Interface. Blue Threat tools that are designed to integrate with existing quality and continuous improvement programs

Sudden Loss of Judgment (SLOJ). A self explanatory term that is often caused by common specific and identifiable factors that can be seen in advance

Violation Producing Conditions. Common known causes of noncompliance

Selected Bibliography and Resources

Andersson, B. E., & Nilsson, S. G. "Studies in the reliability and validity of the critical incident technique." Journal of Applied Psychology 48 (6), (1964): 398–403.

Angell, Auflick, Austria, Kochhar, Tijerina, Biever, Diptiman, Hogsett, and Kiger. "Driver Workload Metrics Project: Task 2 Final Report." National Highway Traffic Safety Administration, Nov. 2006. Research Report.

Arnstein, F. "Catalogue of human error." British Journal of Anesthesia (1997): 645–656.

Barber, Safdar, and Franklin. "Can human error theory explain non-adherence?" Pharmacy World and Science (2005): 300–304.

Besnard, Greathead, and Baxter. "When mental models go wrong. Co-occurrences in dynamic, critical systems." International Journal of Human-Computer Studies (2004): 117–128.

Blank, Musch, and Pohl. "Hindsight Bias: On Being Wise After the Event." Social Cognition (2007): 1–9.

Bond, Verheyden, Wingrove, and Curran. "Angry cognitive bias, trait aggression, and impulsivity in substance users." Psychopharmacology (2004): 331–339.

Brennan, Gawande, Thomas, and Studdert. "Accidental Deaths, Saved Lives, and Improved Quality." The New England Journal of Medicine (Sept. 2005): 1405–1409.

Chedekel, Lisa. "Iraq Vet Drivers Gamble Lives." Leatherneck Aug. 2006. <http://www.Leatherneck.com>.

Collins, James C. Good to Great: Why some companies make the leap . . . and others don't. HarperCollins, 2001.

Crandal, Klein, and Hoffman. Working Minds: A Practitioner's Guide to Cognitive Task Analysis. The MIT Press, 2006.

Croskerry, Pat. "Cognitive Forcing Strategies in Clinical Decisionmaking." Annals of Emergency Medicine (Jan. 2003): 110–120.

Csikszentmihalyi, Mihalyi, and Isabella Selega Csikszentmihalyi. Optimal Experience: Psychological Studies of Flow in Consciousness. Cambridge University Press, 1988.

Csizkszentmihalyi, Mihaly. Flow: The Psychology of Optimal Experience. Harper Perennial, 1990.

Damasio, Antonio R. Descartes' Error. Quill, 1994.

Dekker, Sidney. "Doctors Are More Dangerous Than Gun Owners: A Rejoinder to Error Counting." Human Factors (April 2007): 177–184.

Dekker, Sidney. "Illusions of Explanation: A Critical Essay on Error Classification." The International Journal of Aviation Psychology (2003): 95–106.

Dekker, Sidney. The Field Guide to Understanding Human Error. Ashgate Publishing, 2006.

Diehl, Alan E., Silent Knights: Blowing the Whistle on Military Accidents and Their Cover Ups. Brassey's Inc., 2002.

Dismukes, Berman, and Loukopoulos. The Limits of Expertise: Rethinking Pilot Error and the Causes of Airline Accidents. Ashgate Pub Co, 2007.

Dörner, Dietrich. The Logic of Failure: Recognizing and Avoiding Error in Complex Situations. Perseus Books. 1996.

Elias, Marilyn. "Calls detour drivers' brains." USA TODAY Aug. 2006: 5D.

Endsley, Mica R. "Situation Awareness and Human Error: Designing to Support Human Performance." Proceedings of the High Consequence Systems Surety Conference. 1999.

Ericsson, Charness, Feltovich, and Hoffman. The Cambridge Handbook of Expertise and Expert Performance. Cambridge University Press, 2006.

Ericsson, Prietula, and Cokely. "The Making of an Expert." Harvard Business Review (July–Aug. 2007): 115–121.

Fallat, Mary E., and John W. Overton. "Air medical transport safety." Bulletin of the American College of Surgeons (May 2007): 19–23.

Gawande, Atul. Better: A Surgeon's Notes on Performance. Metropolitan Books. 2007.

Gladwell, Malcolm. Outliers: The Story of Success. Little, Brown and Company. 2008.

Goh, Wiegmann. "An Investigation of the factors that contribute to pilots' decisions to continue visual flight rules flight into adverse weather." Proceedings of the 45th Annual Meeting of Human Factors and Ergonomics Society. 2001.

Gohm, Baumann, and Sniezek. "Personality in Extreme Situations." Journal of Research in Personality (Sept. 2001): 388–399.

Gonzales, Laurence. Deep Survival: Who Lives, Who Dies and Why. Norton, 2003.

Goodman, Barker, and Monk. "A Bibliography of Research Related to the Use of Wireless Communications Devices from Vehicles." National Highway Traffic Safety Administration, Feb. 2005. Research Report.

Green, Marc, and John Senders. "Human Error in Road Accidents." VisualExperts.com 2004. <http://VisualExpert.com>.

Green, R. "The psychology of human error." European Journal of Anaesthesiology 16:3 (1999): 148–155.

Greene, T. William. "Legislating Self-Risking Behaviors." Criminal Justice Policy Review (March 2007): 95–110.

Groopman, Jerome. How Doctors Think. Houghton Mifflin. 2007.

Halberstam, David. The Reckoning. Morrow. 1986.

Hallinan, Joseph T., Why We Make Mistakes: How We Look Without Seeing, Forget Things in Seconds, and Are All Pretty Sure We Are Way above Average. Broadway Books. 2009.

Helmreich, Robert L., and Jan M. Davies. "Culture, Threat, and Error: Lessons from Aviation." Canadian Journal of Anesthesia (2004): R1–R4.

Hobbs, Alan and Ann Williamson. "Associations between Errors and Contributing Factors in Aircraft Maintenance." Human Factors (Summer 2003): 186–201.

Holroyd, C. B. and Coles Michael G.H. "The Neural Basis of Human Error Processing: Reinforcement Learning, Dopamine, and the Error-Related Negativity." Psychological Review (2002): 679–709.

Huntsman, Jon. Winners Never Cheat: Even in Difficult Times. Wharton School Publishing. 2009.

Iani, Christina, and Christopher Wickens. "Factors Affecting Task Management in Aviation." Proceedings of the 48th Annual Meeting of the Human Factors and Ergonomics Society. 2004.

Inglis, Sutten, and McRandle. "Human Factors Analysis of Australian Aviation Accidents and Comparison with the United States." Australian Transport Safety Bureau, Jan. 2007.

Javaux, Denis. "Human Error, Safety, and Systems Development in Aviation." Reliability Engineering and System Safety (2002): 115–119.

Johnson, C. "Representing the impact of time on human error and systems failure." Interacting with Computers (1998): 53–86.

Kahneman D, Slovic P, Tversky A. Judgment Under Uncertainty: Heuristics and Biases. Cambridge, UK: Cambridge University Press, 1982.

Kern, Anthony T. A Historical Analysis of U.S. Air Force Tactical Aircrew Error in Operations Desert Shield/Storm. Thesis. Fort Leavenworth, Kansas, 1995.

Kern, Tony. Flight Discipline. New York: McGraw-Hill, 1996

Klein, Gary. Intuition at Work: Why Developing Your Gut Instincts Will Make You Better at What You Do. Currency, 2002.

Klein, Gary. Sources of Power: How People Make Decisions. The MIT Press, 1999.

Klein, Orasanu, and Calderwood. Decision Making in Action: Models and Methods (Cognition and Literacy). Ablex Publishing, 1993.

Kumar, Umesh, and H. Malik. "Analysis of Fatal Human Error Aircraft in IAF." International Journal of Agile Systems and Management (2003): 30–36.

Lagadec, P., Phelps, J., Preventing Chaos in a Crisis: Strategies for Prevention, Control and Damage Limitation. McGraw Hill. 1991.

Langens, Thomas A. "Regulatory Focus and Illusions of Control." Personality and Social Psychology Bulletin (Feb. 2007): 226–237.

Leape, Lucian L. "A systems analysis approach to medical error." Journal of Evaluation in Clinical Practice (1997): 213–222.

Leduc, Patricia A., Clarence E. Rash, and Sharon D. Manning. "Human Factors in UAV Accidents." Special Operations Technology (Dec. 2005) Online.

Loewenstein, O'Donaghue, and Rabin. "Projection Bias in Predicting Future Utility." March 2000: 1–52.

Mann, Zhao, Stoduto, Adlaf, Smat, and Donovan. "Road Rage and Collision Involvement." American Journal of Health Behavior (2007): 384–391.

Masson, M. and Y. Koning. "How to Manage Human Error in Aviation Maintenance? The Example of a JAR 66-HF Education and Training Programme." Cognition, Technology & Work (2001): 189–204.

Maurino, D.E., Reason, J., Johnston, N., & Lee, R.B. Beyond Aviation Human Factors. Aldershot: Avebury Aviation, 1995.

McClarley, Wickens, Goh, and Horrey. "A Computational Model of Attention/Situation Awareness." Proceedings of the 46th Annual Meeting of Human Factors and Ergonomics Society. 2002.

McDonough, W., Braungart, M., Cradle to Cradle: Remaking the Way We Make Things. North Point Press. 2002.

Narumi, Miyazawa, Miyata, Suzuki, Kohsaka, and Kosugi. "Analysis of human error in nursing care." Accident Analysis and Prevention (March 1999): 625–629.

Nickerson, Raymond S. "Confirmation Bias: A Ubiquitous Phenomenon in Many Guises." Review of General Psychology (1998): 175–220.

Pinker, Steven. How the Mind Works. Norton. 1997.

Peters, George A., and Barbara J. Peters. Human Error: Causes and Control. CRC, 2006.

Rauderberg, Matthias. "Why and What Can We Learn From Human Errors?" Advances in Applied Ergonomics, 827–830.

Reason, James. "Human Error: Models and Management." British Medical Journal 320 (2000): 768–70.

Reason, James. Human Error. New York: Cambridge University Press, 1990.

Reason, James. Managing the Risks of Organizational Accidents. Ashgate. 1997.

Reinhart, Richard O. Fit to Fly: A Pilot's Guide to Health & Safety. TAB Books, 1993.

Ross, Phillip E. "The Expert Mind." Scientific American (Aug. 2006): 64–71.

Saurin, Formoso, and Cambraia. "Analysis of a safety planning and control model from the human error perspective." Engineering, Construction, and Architectural Management (2005): 283–298.

Senders, JW, Moray NP. Human Error: Cause, Prediction, and Reduction. Hillsdale, NJ: Lawrence Erlbaum Associates, 1991.

Senge, Peter M. The Fifth Discipline: The Art and Science of The Learning Organization. Currency Doubleday. 1990.

Shappell, Scott A., and Douglas A. Wiegmann. "The Human Factors Analysis and Classification System – HFACS" Feb. 2000.

Simpson, Peter, and Mark Wiggins. "Attitudes Toward Unsafe Acts in a Sample of Australian General Aviation Pilots." The International Journal of Aviation Psychology (1999): 337–350.

Strauch, B. Investigating Human Error: Incidents, Accidents, and Complex Systems. Ashgate Pub Ltd, 2004.

Taleb, Nicholas Nassim. The Black Swan: The Impact of the Highly Improbable. Random House. 2007.

Tucker, Anita L., and Amy C. Edmondson. "Why Hospitals Don't Learn from Failures: Organizational and Psychological Dynamics that Inhibit System Change." California Management Review (2003): 55–72.

United States Air Force, Operational Risk Management, Handbook.

Vaughan, D. "Autonomy, interdependence, and social control: NASA and the Space Shuttle Challenger." Administrative Science Quarterly 35 (1990): 225–257.

Vaughan, Diane. "The Dark Side of Organizations: Mistake, Misconduct, and Disaster." The Annual Review of Sociology (1999): 271–305.

vonThaden, Terry L. "Information Behavior Among Commercial Aviation CFIT Accident Flightcrews." 12th International Symposium on Aviation Psychology. 2003.

Waddle, Scott. The Right Thing. Integrity Publishers. 2002

Weathers, Beck. "Left for Dead: My Journey Home from Everests." Villard Publishers. 2000.

Weick, Karl E., and Sutcliffe, Kathleen M., Managing the Unexpected: Assuring High Performance in an Age of Complexity. Jossey Bass. 2001.

Wenner, Caren A., and Colin G. Drury. "Analyzing Human Error in Aircraft Ground Damage Incidents." International Journal of Industrial Ergonomics (2000): 177–199.

Wiegmann, Zhang, von Thaden, Sharma, and Mitchell. "A Synthesis of Safety Culture and Safety Climate Research." Technical Report, Aviation Research Lab Institute of Aviation (June 2002): 1–20.

Williams, J. "The Human Error Assessment and Reduction Technique (HEART)." Federal Aviation Administration (FAA) Human Factors Workbench. <http://www.faa.gov>.

Wylie, Shultz, Miller, Mitler, and Mackie. "Commercial Motor Vehicle Driver Fatigue and Alertness Study: Technical Summary." Transportation Development Centre, Nov. 1996.

Zhang, Patel, Johnson, and Shortliffe. "A Cognitive Taxonomy of Medical Errors." Journal of Biomedical Informatics (2004): 193–204.

Index

A

Accurate xi, 40, 44, 48, 49, 152, 193, 201
Aim small, miss small 50
Alchemy 42, 51
Alistair Begg 175, 176
Anger management 3, 18
Anti-authority 141, 142
Attention steering 138
Attention to detail 92
Avoidable errors xi, 3, 14, 43, 194

B

Baby boomer 9
Behavioral science 4, 43
Blue Threat Field Book 7
Blue Threat Report and Analysis Tool (BRAT)™ 113
Borrowed time 185, 186
Brown rules 87
Bud Holland 142

C

Cal Ripken, Jr. 45
Centers of gravity 31, 32, 37, 112, 119
Christopher McCandless 147
Cognitive dissonance 115
Cognitive forcing strategy 119

Cognitive psychology 27
Ccomplexity theory 35
Compliance through enforcement 7, 71
Confirmation bias 155
Corrosive narcissism 75
Crushing grip of mediocrity 58

D

Data smog 132, 187
David 176–177
Decision space 87–88, 90, 221, 222
Defenses in depth 25
Deja moo 2
Differentiation 42
Diligence 92, 222
Discipline xi, 2, 6, 18, 22–23, 80, 82, 87–88, 91–92, 114, 126, 128, 147, 149, 171, 200, 206–207
Disease model 24
Distraction 136, 174
Dynamic energy 29

E

Edgar Cayce 95
Edward de Bono 95–96
Effectiveness 48, 54, 82, 121, 131, 212
Ego & power 80
Empowered accountability vii, ix, 1, 2, 4, 8, 19, 31, 44, 46, 51, 58, 60, 112, 161, 163, 170, 176, 188, 194, 201–202, 207–208, 210–213, 215, 217, 240
Entropic energy 29
Error producing conditions 8, 14, 100, 111, 117, 119, 122–124, 139–140, 215
Exit strategy SOPs 131
Expectation bias 152–153
Expert's curse 152–153
External locus of control 24, 222

F

Failure 7, 14, 30, 51–52, 57, 59, 77, 83, 91, 151, 187–188, 203–204, 215, 218–220, 225, 241

Fatigue 24, 52, 125–126, 181
Fatigue/physiological degrade 125
Faulty risk perception 134
Flow 9, 43, 88, 137, 156, 196–198
Framing error 158
Fundamental attribution error 157

G

Global War on Error® 31, 32, 199, 215
Godly sorrow 168–169
Goliath 175
Gordon Graham 23
Guru 2, 230

H

Habit patterns 18, 24, 46, 128, 138, 218
Halo effect 102–103, 153
Hazardous attitudes 8, 117, 139–141, 151, 159
Human error x, 1, 4–5, 7–9, 13–15, 17–21, 23, 26–27, 30–40, 42, 44, 50, 65, 109, 111–113, 121–125, 134–135, 180–181, 184–185, 188, 190–195, 198, 209, 212–216, 222, 228, 231–232
Human improvement 4
Human reliability assessment 124, 125

I

I CAN™ 7, 46, 112, 117, 151, 212
Impulsiveness 141–143
Inadequate standards 135
Information overload 132
Integration 42–43, 213
Invulnerability 144

J

Jack Ward Thomas 5
Jesus 164, 168, 174
Jonathan Edwards 172
Jon Huntsman 73
Jon Krakauer 148
Josephson Institute of Ethics 74

L

Laurence Gonzales 148
Leadership gap 83
Lean Six Sigma 54
Locus of control 24, 29, 222
Low signal to noise ratio 128, 132

M

Mark Dykeman 142
Memory flags 138
Merlin Effect 230
Metanoia 169
Mihaly Csikszenmihalyi 42, 196
Military science 31–32, 35
Mission expectation 80
Motivation 2, 9, 23, 28, 141, 231
Myth of compliance 7

N

Need to be right (confirmation) bias 155
Neuroscience 27, 35
Niccolo Machiavelli 177
Nietzsche 94, 107
NIFITI™ technique 123, 139
Normalization of deviance 15, 80, 85, 129, 144
Normalization of excellence 24, 44, 114, 229
Normalized excellence 58–59

O

One-way decision gates 131
Over competitiveness 141
Oversized ego/vanity 148

P

Perfection 51, 54–58, 60, 139, 220
Performance Evolution Ladder™ 48
Perseverance 45
Personal and organizational failure zone 57
Personal error patterns 20, 112

Personal operating procedures (POPs) 112, 121
Person model 25
Poor communications/information transfer 133
Poor planning 82
Poor role models 83
Precise 19, 49–50, 65, 133, 219
Predictable is preventable 23, 139
Pressing too far 147–148
Procrastination 2, 82, 137, 141, 149–150
Professional bias 154
Psychology of achievement 27

R

Recognition primed decision making 128
Red rules 87
Red threat x, 34–35
Resignation 146
Rob Hall 146

S

Satan 174
Self awareness 2, 6, 29, 40, 170, 184, 226, 242
Self discovery 6
Serious setback 51
Sleeping prophet 95
Source credibility bias 154–155
Specialization bias 229
Specialty bias 154
Sports psychology 35
Substance abuse 3
Systems model 24, 26

T

Tawbah 169
The Daffodil Garden 66
Threat assessment x, 31–33
Time pressure 24, 86, 101, 123–124, 126–128, 134, 143, 150, 204, 223
Timothy Treadwell 144
To err is human x, 5, 13, 22, 25, 35, 194, 216
To err is inhuman 22, 194, 216

Too competitive/macho 145
Total mental fatigue factor 125–126
Total quality management 65
Trigger event 17, 111, 138

U

Uncommon sense x, 39
Unique event 84
Unlikely detection 81
U.S. Department of Justice 78–79, 210
U.S. Forest Service 5, 78, 257

V

Violation producing conditions 79, 85, 87, 130, 242

W

William McDonough 41

Z

Zero tolerance policies 89

About the Author

Dr. Tony Kern is the CEO of *Convergent Performance*; a veteran owned small business formed and dedicated to reducing human error in high risk environments. Tony is one of the world's leading authorities on human performance and the author of five books on the subject, including *Redefining Airmanship, Flight Discipline,* and *Darker Shades of Blue: The Rogue Pilot.* Dr. Kern is an internationally recognized expert in the field of applied human factors and performance improvement, and has lectured on the subjects around the globe for nearly two decades. Tony has deep operational roots as a Command Pilot and Flight Examiner in the B-1B bomber, as well as service as the Chair of the Air Force Human Factors Steering Group and Director and Professor of Military History at the USAF Academy. Upon retirement from the Air Force in June of 2000, Dr. Kern served as the National Aviation Director for the U.S. Forest Service, where he directed the largest non-military government aviation program in the world in support of federal wildland fire suppression. He has appeared frequently on talk radio and TV, including segments on the Discovery Channel, NBC Nightly News and *48 Hours with Dan Rather.* Dr. Kern has received multiple awards for his work, including the USAF Academy *McDermott Award for Research Excellence* (1999), Flight Safety Foundation *Distinguished Service Award* (2003) for Aviation Leadership and the Aviation Week and Space Technology *Laurel Award* (2002) for Outstanding Achievement in Government and Military Aviation. Tony holds Masters Degrees in Public Administration and Military History as well as the Doctorate in Higher Education, specializing in human factors training design. He enjoys outdoor sports of all kinds and lives with his wife Shari in Monument, Colorado.